Ask the Rabbi

The Who, What, When, Where, Why, and How of Being Jewish

Rabbi Ron Isaacs

AN ARTHUR KURZWEIL BOOK

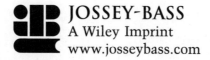

JOSSEY-BASS
A Wiley Imprint
www.josseybass.com

Published by Jossey-Bass
A Wiley Imprint
989 Market Street, San Francisco, CA 94103-1741   www.josseybass.com

Jossey-Bass books and products are available through most bookstores. To contact Jossey-Bass directly call our Customer Care Department within the U.S. at 800-956-7739, outside the U.S. at 317-572-3986 or fax 317-572-4002.

Jossey-Bass also publishes its books in a variety of electronic formats. Some content that appears in print may not be available in electronic books.

The reader should be aware that websites mentioned or referenced may have changed or disappeared since this was written.

Library of Congress Cataloging-in-Publication Data

Isaacs, Ronald H.
  Ask the rabbi : the who, what, when, where, why, and how of being Jewish / Ron Isaacs.
       p. cm.
"An Arthur Kurzweil book."
Includes bibliographical references and index.
  ISBN 0-7879-6784-X (alk. paper)
  1. Judaism. I. Title.
  BM562.I83 2003
  296—dc21   2003008143

Printed in the United States of America
FIRST EDITION
HB Printing   10 9 8 7 6 5 4 3 2 1

Contents

Chapter 1   God   1

Theology   1

Chapter 3   Bible   32

Chapter 10   Sex   96

Chapter 11   Death and Dying   102

Chapter 15
Jewish Denominations   128

Chapter 20   *What Others Think of the Jews*   167

Chapter 21   *Jews and Christians*   174

Chapter 25   Holy Objects   202

The Torah   202

Mezuzah   206

Chapter 30   Kabbalah   221

Chapter 31   Classic Jewish Books   224

Chapter 32   Jewish Renewal   231

Foreword

I'll bet that nearly every Jew remembers the first time she or he was called upon as a child to ask the "Four Questions" at the Seder table. Asking questions is what Judaism is all about, and most Jewish children (and adults too) have lots of them—questions about God, prayer, holidays, customs and traditions, Jewish history, Israel, Jews around the world, etc., etc., etc. So the question is: where can we go to get all those questions answered? Well, there is an answer to that one.

Rabbi Ron Isaacs, a congregational rabbi and well-known author, has written *Ask the Rabbi*. In it he poses and answers hundreds of questions asked by his students over the past decade. They're questions that you and your children have probably asked at one time or another—and some you may never have thought of. The questions range from some of the most profound and searching that our tradition has to deal with to ones that express a healthy curiosity about the small details that make Jewish life so interesting and so varied. The answers are brief, honest, informative, often entertaining, and sometimes quite personal. They're filled with facts and also with wisdom. If you've ever wanted a resource to turn to when your children ask you questions about Judaism or if you've got a whole bunch of leftover questions from your own childhood, *Ask the Rabbi* will fill the bill beautifully. It's like having your own personal—and knowledgeable—rabbi available on call and without the long sermons! This is a book you'll value and enjoy.

I dedicate this book to
all of my professors at the Jewish Theological Seminary,
who taught me that there is no more rewarding profession
than that of being a rabbi and teacher

Introduction

Everyone asks questions. For Jews, asking questions is a national pastime. Even our holiest books are filled with questions. The great sages of Jewish tradition ask every conceivable question about every conceivable topic.

Children love to ask questions. I know, because since 1975 I have been fortunate to serve as the rabbi of Temple Sholom, a synagogue in central New Jersey.

One of my passions is to teach, and for the past twenty-eight years I have been fielding the many questions of my Hebrew school and Hebrew High School students in a session we call "Ask the Rabbi." Students of all ages continuously invite me into their classes and are encouraged to ask me questions on a variety of Jewish topics. In addition, an Ask the Rabbi box is available at all times in the Hebrew school, into which students can place their questions. I have collected hundreds of questions over the years. The questions in this volume are the best or the most interesting ones that have been asked of me over these past three decades.

Nothing would make me happier than to know that your reading this book encourages and challenges you to study further and do your own research about my responses to the questions. I am old enough now, and wise enough, I hope, to realize that I don't have all the answers, and to realize that the responses in this book may serve only to inspire you to seek further and come up with your own answers. We know that with some of these questions, it's really a matter of interpretation; as the old joke goes, with two Jews you could easily have three or four opinions.

The medieval sage Solomon ibn Gabirol once taught, "The finest quality of the human being is asking questions." I could not agree more with his statement. So continue to ask questions, and enjoy studying and exploring the wonderful religion that we call Judaism. This has always been the way of the Jewish people.

I am grateful to the families of Temple Sholom for allowing me the privilege of being their rabbi. Over the years they have asked me numerous questions on a variety of subjects. Their questions and queries have served as the motivation for writing this book. My appreciation goes to my editor, Alan Rinzler, who invited me to develop this volume. His keen editorial skills, clear vision, and knowledge of publishing are reflected in its pages. I also want to thank Seth Schwartz (editorial assistant), Andrea Flint (production editor), and Paula Goldstein (director, creative services) for their help and assistance in enhancing this book. Lastly, my sincere gratitude goes to my good friend Arthur Kurzweil. His many suggestions and insights have also helped to shape this book and better structure its questions and answers.

Chapter 1

❧ ❧

God

❧ **Theology** ❧

How was God born?

I don't know.

How's that for the very first answer to the very first question in this book?

The only honest answer is that no one really knows. Jewish tradition teaches that God always was, always is, and always will be. One of the basic Jewish beliefs about God is that God wasn't ever born, having no mother and father. God was and is the mother and father of all that is created. God is the only one that was here before there was a before.

One of the prayers that best sums up the belief that God was always there is the well-known *Adon Olam,* which we often sing at the end of morning prayer services. We say *"hu haya, hu hoveh, hu yihiyeh"* (God was, is, and will always be). This means that God had no beginning or birth because God has always existed. To me, it's very comforting that God has always existed and will continue to exist forever. That's why the Adon Olam prayer ends with the comforting thought that when I go to sleep at night, knowing all I know about God, I have nothing to fear.

Is it possible to prove God's existence?

No, I do not believe that the existence of God can ever be proven. For some people, belief in God is no problem at all. I cannot remember a time when I did not believe in God. However, for some, having faith in God's existence is easier said than done.

People don't generally become believers because of a convincing argument. Yet the quest for an argument to prove the existence of God is natural enough. Medieval philosophers in particular spent a considerable amount of time on the problems concerning the existence and nature of God.

A number of classical proofs for the existence of God have been presented by theologians and philosophers. I first learned of them in one of my undergraduate Jewish philosophy courses at the Jewish Theological Seminary of America. Here are several:

1. *Creation implies a Creator.* Experience teaches us that everything in existence has a creator. It is reasonable to assume that the universe did not make itself either. Thus the mere existence of the universe implies a creator, and that creator is God.

2. *The primary cause.* Just as every effect has a cause, every cause is itself the effect of some prior cause. If everything in nature is the effect of some cause, we must look for some initial cause outside of nature. The first uncaused cause is the Ultimate Cause of the chain of events that proceed from it. This first supernatural cause is God.

3. *Prime mover.* A physical body does not move until it is set into motion by some outside force. The universe consists of physical bodies in constant motion. What force is responsible for having started, and maintaining, them in motion? That force was the Prime Mover, God, who alone possesses the power to move and make move without a preceding natural cause.

4. *Ultimate designer.* Probably the most popular of all arguments, and one that has always seemed most compelling to me, is the argument from design. The argument runs something like this. Suppose you have never seen a watch and that you find one lying

on the sand. All you can see in it is a mechanical structure exhibiting an intricate adaptation of parts to one another. You are likely to infer from this that it was constructed by an intelligent being who designed this mutual adaptation in order to accomplish a certain end. This (so runs the argument) is just what we encounter in the universe: order and design. This Ultimate Designer is God.

5. *Moral argument.* There is a good, and there is a better, but there is no such thing as perfect (that is, best) in earthly experience. Without the existence of a best, the concept of a good and better is imperfect. Therefore the Perfect must lie beyond the earthly experience. This Perfect is God.

For me, the beauty and design of this magnificent world is proof positive that there is a God. When I see the sun rise every morning or a beautiful sunset at night, when I see a rainbow in the sky or shooting stars on an August summer's night, I become ever more convinced that this Ultimate Designer is none other than God.

Why does God have so many names in the Bible and the prayer book?

One way to begin thinking about the many names of God is to realize that each of us also has many names.

Perhaps you have a nickname used by your close friends or family. My nickname is "Reeve," given to me by my grandmother, who with her Eastern European accent turned my Hebrew name *Reuven* into *Reeven*, which then was shortened to Reeve. The nickname, usually a term of endearment, reflects a special relationship you have with the user of the nickname. Almost everyone in Toronto, Canada (my birthplace), who knows me well calls me Reeve, never Ron. Some of our Hebrew High School students who feel especially close to me also call me Reeve.

Giving God several names serves a similar purpose. The nature of your conception of God plays a role in your relationship with God and the words you use to address God. The Bible uses many terms for

God: Father *(Av)*, Shepherd *(Ro'eh)*, King *(Melech)*, Judge *(Shofet)*, Holy One *(Kadosh)*, Warrior *(Ish Milchama)*, Righteous One *(Tzaddik)*, and others. The prayer book also uses a variety of names for God: Rock of Israel *(Tzur Yisrael)*, the Place *(Hamakom)*, God of Abraham *(Elohay Avraham)*, King of Kings *(Melech Malchay Hamelachim)*, Creator *(Boray)*, Healer *(Rofay)*, the Good One *(HaTov)*, Lover of Israel *(Ohev Yisrael)*, and the Merciful One *(HaRachaman)*.

Each of these names for God is intended to reveal some aspect or characteristic of God that the others do not. For example, Father and Shepherd might make you think of the qualities of tenderness or mercy, while God of Abraham might remind you of the special relationship that God had with Abraham, the father of our people.

Although each name reflects a quality, God is not limited to any one particular quality, or to the sum of them together. Different words are used to describe God simply because the human mind needs some kind of description, and everyday language must be used for that purpose.

So, what's your favorite name for God? Personally, I like *Hamakom* (the Place).

Why do people write *G-d* for God in some books?

Jewish tradition relates that one particular name of God, consisting of the four Hebrew letters *yod, heh, vav, heh,* was revealed to Moses at the burning bush. Its exact pronunciation was passed on to his brother Aaron and kept a secret among the kohanim, the Jewish priesthood, so that the Israelites would not use God's name irreverently. The only time the High Priest actually pronounced the real name of God was on the Day of Atonement, Yom Kippur, during the confession of sins. When the *kohen* uttered the holy name, his voice was lost in the singing of the other priests so that the Israelites would not hear the secret pronunciation.

Outside of the ancient sanctuary the term *Adonai* (often translated as "Lord") was used to connote God's name. Whenever the original four Hebrew letters *(yod, heh, vav, heh)* are found in the Bible, or when God's name is invoked in prayer, it is pronounced Adonai. But even this name of God is confined to use during sacred events. In conversation, the name *HaShem*, meaning "the Name," is often used to protect God's name even further from improper use.

Jewish law has always tried to protect the way in which people use the name of God, always fearing the possibility of God's name falling into a bad mouth. The rabbinic sages prescribed a variety of injunctions concerning the pronunciation and writing of God's name. For example, if written, the name of God should not be erased and can only be discarded through ritual burial, similar to that of sacred texts and ritual items.

It has become a custom to extend our reverence for the various names of God to include nontraditional names, for example, the word we use in English, God (G-d). But regulations in Jewish law concerning how to treat written and printed materials with God's name on it apply, in most Orthodox communities, only to the names of God in Hebrew.

What does it mean to say that Jews are the chosen people? Does God *really* have a favorite people?

Chosenness does not mean that the Jews have been singled out for special favors. Far from it. Chosenness means being selected to carry out the special duties of being God's servant. Our task is to be a holy people, and our mission is to remind the world that God demands righteousness and justice. We are partners with God, and our mission as a member of the Chosen People is helping and working with God to bring about a more just and peaceful world. Being chosen means joining God and doing it together.

The idea that the Jewish people were selected by God to carry out some special purpose is prominent throughout the Bible and in other Jewish teachings. According to a story in the Bible, in the Book of Exodus, God chose Israel to be a special people when God led them out of Egypt and gave them the Torah on Mount Sinai. God said, "You will be My own treasure from all peoples" (Exodus 19:5).

In a later passage in the Book of Deuteronomy (chapter 7), God tells the Israelites that He chose them because "they were the fewest in number and that God loved them."

Some twenty-six hundred years ago, the Prophet Isaiah expanded upon the idea of the Jews as chosen ones by saying: "I have given you as a covenant to the people. For a light to the nations, to open the eyes of the blind" (Isaiah 42:6–7). This verse is quite significant. It means that the Jewish people, according to Isaiah, were assigned the special mission of improving the world and teaching other peoples to see the light. So Jews must understand that being chosen is not a privilege about which to boast, but rather a responsibility and a task to be undertaken. It requires contributing to the betterment of the world, which ultimately means increased responsibilities and hardship.

Can you be Jewish and doubt the existence of God?

God has an opinion about this question.

According to the Jerusalem Talmud (Hagigah 1:7), God says, "better that the children of Israel abandon Me but follow My laws." Thus, according to the rabbis, one can be a good Jew while doubting the existence of God. One should incorporate Judaism's ideals into daily living by studying and practicing Judaism even when one has doubts about God's existence, because Jewish practice and study have spiritual and moral benefits in and of themselves.

The basic Jewish view on this question, and one that my own experience has confirmed, is that once you begin to study and live Judaism, you will come to the conclusion that God is the ultimate source of morality and of life. The Talmud put it this way: "Whereas one may begin to practice Judaism for non-divine reasons, one eventually will become convinced that it represents God's will" (Talmud, Pesachim 50).

When I first came to Temple Sholom, I had a Hebrew High School student who very much doubted God's existence. He therefore had trouble praying and didn't even want to sign his confirmation certificate, which talked about his affirming his faith in God and the Jewish people. A couple of years ago, I met up with this student again when he came back from Texas to visit his parents. Curious to know about his life and the importance of Judaism in it, I proceeded to ask him whether he belonged to a synagogue. He answered by saying: "I love my synagogue. I enjoy working with my kids on their Hebrew school homework, and by the way, I am the president of my congregation. And yes, my God beliefs have changed as well!"

Why do we call God *He* when we also say that God has no gender?

All efforts to describe God are considered to be failures. God is imageless, without body or form.

If we think of God as a male every time we use a word like *He* or *Lord* or *King*, we are making a mistake. In fact, we are taught that God is beyond anything conceivable. Thus God is neither male nor female.

As our society grows more egalitarian and inclusive, a new sensitivity has emerged to the God language we have always used, with its excessive dependence on masculine imagery. As a result, many of the new prayer book translations have attempted to eliminate masculine-sounding names for God, replacing them with gender-neutral language. For example, instead of translating the Hebrew words *Avinu Malkenu* as "Our Father our King," prayer books often substitute "Our Parent our Sovereign One."

Other, more feminist prayer books have substituted "She" for God. One popular feminine metaphor for God in kabbalistic literature is the "Shechinah," a feminine word always associated with God's nearness either to the people of Israel or to the individual Jew. This "mystical motherly" aspect of God is especially present with Israel in times of tragedy, and it even follows the people into exile.

Why would God have made a world with so much suffering?

Although the Jewish people have perhaps suffered more than any other, I do not for a moment believe that God intentionally bestowed the suffering upon us. Very often it is people who cause others to suffer. A life-threatening illness can also cause one to suffer, but I do not believe that the illness is the will of God.

Jewish tradition throughout the centuries has sought to capture the meaning of suffering and explain pain. The book of the Bible that deals extensively with this topic is Job, which records the spiritual agony of a man who has tried to harmonize his experience with his belief in an all-powerful and all-wise God. One of the lessons of the book is that a person's sufferings are a test of fidelity. No person is ever able to probe the depths of the divine omniscience that governs the world.

The more important issue for me is what people can do for one another when suffering occurs. Here, Judaism does tell us how to act, for no matter what we think about suffering, Judaism expects us to care for its victims—to comfort mourners, help heal the sick, feed the hungry, clothe the naked, house the homeless, defend the oppressed, liberate the enslaved, find a cure for life-threatening disease, and root out the causes of suffering from nature.

Our rabbis held that it is not in our power to understand suffering, particularly the suffering of righteous people. Some experiences and events that we cannot explain must simply be accepted with faith in the ultimate wisdom of God's will and our trust in the goodness of people and of God's creation.

I have faith in God's justice, in the worthwhileness of life and in the goodness of humanity. I hope that you too will never lose that faith, and when you see suffering do your God-given part to help alleviate it by putting out your hand and helping people in need.

❧ Experiencing God ❧

What's the best place to find God?

The Kotzker Rebbe, a great hasidic master, once asked someone "Where is God?" The person responded, "Everywhere!"

"No," said the Kotzker Rebbe. "God is where He is let in."

One of the difficulties with finding God is that God is invisible. It is quite difficult to try to find something you cannot see. Of course, there are many things that we cannot see but we can find or feel. If we are outside on a windy day, we can easily feel the wind on our face and hair.

For me, the best place to go find and feel God's presence is out of doors. I love nature, and as a youngster I would love to take walks in the forest, especially in the fall when the colorful leaves were dropping to the ground. I would often collect the leaves, press them, and put them in a book, trying to label them as I went along. It was in the forest where I felt close to God. I think it was a combination of the beauty of the trees and the quietude of the place.

A couple of months before my Bar Mitzvah, my parents sent me to a sleep-away camp some 150 miles north of Toronto, Canada, my birthplace. This special place, called Camp Ramah, had beauty beyond belief. It was also a Hebrew-speaking camp, with Hebrew classes and prayer services throughout the week. I went there for many summers, but I shall never forget an experience I had the first summer while sitting with my fellow campers at an outdoor Kabbalat Shabbat service on a Friday evening at dusk. All of the campers and staff were required to wear white, and we were sitting outside on log benches, facing a beautiful lake with white birch trees all around. As we rose to recite the Aleynu prayer toward the end of services, the sun shone through the treetops and made the white clothing of all of the participants glisten. The birch trees sparkled too, and I felt my body shudder, looked up at the magnificent sky, and experienced God's Presence like never before. It's been forty-two years since that experience, and I still remember it as though it happened only yesterday.

Have you ever heard God's voice? Why doesn't God talk to people anymore?

I began to hear God's voice in a number of ways when I worked on my listening skills. I can offer you a couple of suggestions. The next time you take an outdoor walk and find yourself in a relaxed mood, listen carefully to the sounds all around you. If you do, I believe you will hear God's voice. When you next have occasion to attend a prayer service, take the opportunity to ponder the words of one particular prayer. I believe that if we fine-tune our listening skills, at prayer services and in other places, we will be better equipped to hear God's voice.

In the Bible, God frequently speaks to people. What is even more significant is that God speaks to people before people speak to God.

For example, "And God spoke to Moses saying . . ." almost invariably initiates the many dialogues between God and Moses. Adam, Eve, Noah, Abraham, and all the Jewish prophets spoke to God. I am often asked, If God spoke, *literally*, in Bible times, then why doesn't God speak to us today in the same compelling way?

Because God is God, God's speech must be unlike human speech. Many of the great prophets, sages, and poets of Israel saw and heard God everywhere. Psalm 29 refers many times to God's voice having the capability of breaking cedar trees, hewing out flames of fire, and stripping forests bare. They heard God in the winds, the rushing waters, and the driving rain. They heard God in the laughter and weeping of the human heart, the whispered pledge of lovers, and the quiet song of the burning bush. Amazingly, all six hundred thousand of our people, even the little ones, were said to have heard God's voice as they stood at the foot of Mount Sinai.

A final truth test of what we interpret as the voice of God is whether it leads us to the fulfillment of God's mitzvot, the many obligations that God has given us. Every time you perform and fulfill a God-given mitzvah, there is no question in my mind that you have heard God.

Has God ever answered one of your prayers? When was the first time?

I remember that when I was eleven years old I had difficulty one night going to bed. My brother, Mendy, who was sleeping in another bed across from me, had a severe throat infection. He was coughing incessantly and seemed to be in a great deal of discomfort. I can remember putting my head under the covers and praying to God to help soothe my brother's throat and stop his coughing. Not too much time passed, and to my great surprise the coughing stopped, and both he and I were able to have a relaxing night's sleep.

The next morning, when he awakened he told me how much better he was feeling and how well he slept at night. I couldn't help smiling, but I never did tell him about the prayer I said on his behalf. It still amazes me how vividly I remember this incident. As a child, it certainly helped me become a believer in the power of prayer.

Do I know for sure that my prayer really had an impact on my brother that night? Certainly not. But I do know that this event, and my memory of it, has been a part of my lifelong effort to build a relationship with God. As has been said by many, God always answers our prayers; sometimes He says no.

The next group of questions explores the subject of prayer in more depth.

Chapter 2

❧ ☙

Prayer

❧ Reasons to Pray ☙

Why do people pray?

Prayer is a natural part of a person's religious expression.

In Jewish tradition, prayer has always occupied a position of importance. The Bible records the personal and often spontaneous prayers of the great men and women in the early history of the people of Israel. Prayer has always been our attempt to establish a conversation with God and express our feelings, reactions, and needs.

The Greek word that translates into "to pray" means "to wish," and the French word means "to beg." The English word means "to ask earnestly." The Hebrew word *l'hitpallel*, usually translated as "to pray," is derived from a word meaning "to judge" or "assess." For Jews, prayer is a way of relating to us, to our fellow human beings, and to God. Prayer gives us an opportunity for reflection and self-examination, to consider who we are and what we should become.

Does God answer our prayers? It often seems otherwise.

Since God created the world and everything in it, I believe that God is truly concerned about every one of its creatures. Many people who pray to God asking for something specific are disappointed when God does not answer them to their satisfaction. People who have faith and pray regularly have told me that their prayers have helped them physically, psychologically, and spiritually. For example, I had a student in my class who took her driving test and failed it in two successive tries. She came to me somewhat dejected, asking for some advice. I told her to pray to God for the courage and determination to relax while next taking her test, and for new confidence as well. The next time she took the test, she passed with flying colors.

A woman in a state of bad health asked me for some prayers to say before her next operation. I gave her several of my favorite healing prayers, and she emerged from her surgery with new confidence and renewed determination.

Praying makes me increasingly susceptible to God's influence. Whenever I pray, I feel closer to God and am no longer alone.

❧ Worship Services ❧

Why are Jewish prayer services so long and boring?

There are many prayers in the liturgy of a Jewish service, especially on Saturday morning, which also has the Torah service. As a Conservative rabbi who conserves tradition, I lead a service that is going to be lengthy, simply because there are so many prayers we are required to say. I must tell you, though, that just because services take over three hours on Shabbat morning they need not be boring. We have many children in our Temple who come to services every week because they like to pray and enjoy the prayers, and they do not find them boring.

There are many goals in praying, but the main one is to draw close to God and communicate with God. I like to think of praying as a form of meditation. Focusing and concentrating are essential to its practice.

Here is some advice that I have given to people in our Temple to assist them in their quest for finding spirituality in the synagogue and making the prayers come alive and be more meaningful:

- Before entering the synagogue, briefly pause to arouse your awe and love for God, and the respect for the sanctuary. Look at the beauty and the holiness of the place, and begin to appreciate it.
- When taking a seat, people have told me that they find it best to sit fairly close to where the cantor or prayer leader is, so that you can hear well and participate more fully. Try sitting in or close to the same location each time, for then you truly get "comfortable" with your special place.
- Try to select a seat away from people you know to be "big talkers."
- Try to the best of your ability to avoid casual conversation, particularly during the service and the Torah reading.
- If you are wearing a tallit, try wrapping it fully around your head as you put it on, briefly meditating on being close to God. Then sit down, and with your eyes closed calm yourself and put yourself in a peaceful mood. Preparation for prayer is a key to real praying. The Kotzker Rebbe once said that the time spent in sharpening the ax is as important as the time spent in chopping the tree.
- Bring a book of Bible commentary or a prayer book with commentary that you can read and peruse during services. A Bible commentary is of particular use during the Torah reading service.
- During the service, don't be afraid to close your eyes. It helps you block out distraction and further concentrate on the prayers.
- Follow the prayers in the English translation, and you will begin to learn what some of the Hebrew words mean.
- During every prayer service, add some of your own private and personal prayers and thoughts.
- Try chanting and swaying during the prayer service. This helps you enter into the prayers.

Like anything else in life that is done well, praying requires preparation and practice. The more you attend and familiarize yourself with the prayers and the service, the better you become.

Why do so many people pray in Hebrew when they don't understand what it means?

Although Hebrew is the preferred language for Jewish prayer, as I will explain in a moment prayers need not be said in Hebrew. Jewish law decrees that one may pray in any language that one understands. A folk tale illustrates the spirit of this ruling:

> A boy from a small town where there were hardly any Jews and no synagogue accompanied his father into town to do some shopping. While there, they entered a synagogue. The boy had never been in a synagogue before and was very impressed as he watched the congregants praying. He also wanted to pray but did not know how. His father had once taught him the letters of the Hebrew alphabet, but that was it. So a thought came to him. The boy began to recite the Hebrew alphabet over and over again. Then he said: "O God, You know what it is that I want to say. You put the letters together so that they make the correct words."

That too was a Jewish prayer!

The Mishnah refers to the Hebrew language as *leshon ha-kodesh,* the holy tongue, to distinguish it from other secular languages. Hebrew is God's language, the language of the Torah. It was the Hebrew language in which the prophets expressed their lofty ideas and our ancestors breathed forth their sufferings and joys. One cannot understand the people of Israel without understanding Hebrew, the spoken language of today's Israelis.

Today and in bygone years, Hebrew has been the preferred language of prayer, even if many people do not understand what the words mean. There are numerous reasons for encouraging the use of Hebrew in services. A relatively uniform Hebrew service helps preserve and maintain the unity of the Jewish people throughout the world. Not only does it bind every Jew to the Holy Land but it enables a Jew to feel at home in synagogues around the word, even in a country where fellow Jews speak another language and one is otherwise unable to communicate with them. A few years ago, I attended an

Italian Sephardic synagogue in Jerusalem and was amazed how at home I felt with the Hebrew that I recognized in their service.

If one does not understand the Hebrew, it is best to use a prayer book with a translation. I remember as a youngster referring to the English translation while singing the prayers. Eventually I began to familiarize myself with certain Hebrew words and their meanings, which helped me better understand the Hebrew words as well as the general meaning of each prayer.

When my rabbi gives a sermon, it's usually about politics, not religion. Why is that?

I remember hearing a joke about a congregant who attended services each week. He was critical of his rabbi and said: "Rabbi, every week you either talk about the Sabbath, keeping Kosher, praying, or God. When, Rabbi, are you going to talk about Judaism?"

I've been told that there are lots of rabbis who talk about politics and things other than Judaism. Your rabbi likely enjoys politics and finds that through politics he can present to his congregants many engaging and contemporary topics. If you listen more carefully to your rabbi, my guess is that you are likely to find him connecting various political issues and concerns with Jewish values and thinking. Occasionally, I too, talk to the congregation about a particular issue or politician who is running for local or national office. (I am most likely to want to do this during an election year.) Usually when I do, though, I try to present some Jewish angle to my talk, in keeping with my goal as a rabbi to be a teacher of Jewish tradition.

❧ Communal Versus Private Prayer ❧

Can I pray alone, or do I have to go to synagogue to be with other Jews?

When I was a teenager, I was not able to attend daily morning services at my synagogue because I could not have gotten to school on time. So I decided each morning to put on my tallit and tefillin and say the morning prayers in my home. The sages advised that if one couldn't pray in a synagogue, at least one should pray at the same time others are praying. In that way we identify with the group. I think this is sound advice.

According to most rabbinic opinion, communal prayer is of greater significance than private prayer. Our sages have taught that God listens more readily to the prayers of a congregation than to those of an individual. Though an individual is permitted to pray alone if unable to participate with a group, the preferred situation has always been group prayer. There is an extra dimension to prayer recited by the community. Having other people around us when we pray reminds us that we must never be selfish when saying our prayers, but include others as well in our thoughts. Community prayer is also our way of strengthening the ties of the individual with the Jewish community. It is not accidental that the most important of our formal prayers are all given in the first person plural. We pray to *our God* and we ask that God's blessing be *upon us.*

What is a minyan, and where does the idea for a minyan at prayer services come from?

Rabbi Nachman of Bratslav said, "Nine righteous people do not make a minyan, but one common person, joining them, completes the minyan."

The number (*minyan*) of ten adult Jews is the minimum required for congregational worship, public Torah reading, recitation of the *kedusha*, and the kaddish prayers. The number ten, required for the minyan, is said to have been derived from the Book of Numbers 14:27, where the ten spies (exclusive of Joshua and Caleb) are referred to in the verse as an *edah*, the Hebrew word for congregation. It has traditionally been deduced that a congregation for prayer must consist of at least ten male adults.

Today the Reform, Conservative, and Reconstructionist branches of Judaism also include adult women in their count for a minyan.

Waiting for the tenth person can often be quite a chore. In our synagogue, when we realized that we were going to be short of people for the minyan, a person would begin to call Jewish homes that were close by the synagogue, telling them of our shortage of people and asking them whether they could come down as soon as possible. People, when home, are happy to come and assist.

A West coast synagogue was known to have a blue light outside on the synagogue marquis. When short a minyan, a member of the ritual committee would turn on the blue light. Jewish passersby who saw the light knew that it was a sign that they were needed.

❧ Enhancing the Prayer Service ❧

What should I do if I can't keep up with the service?

My advice to you is to take your time and not race through the prayer book. It's better to skip parts of the service and say the rest with full concentration than to try to pray all of the prayers in a confused state of mind. Do not be overly concerned with where the minyan is, so as not to disrupt the meditative mood that you are trying to establish. Always remember that prayer is service of the heart, and heartfelt prayers that are said with feeling are those most likely to find their way to God.

The cantor in the synagogue where I serve as rabbi loves to sing lively melodies. Because he is fluent in Hebrew and gets so excited about singing and leading prayers, he tends to move at a very quick pace. Quite a few in the congregation have difficulty keeping up with the Hebrew.

I remember one of my seminary teachers, the late Abraham Joshua Heschel, telling our class that to pray is to take hold of a word. I believe what he meant by his statement is that we must all find a time to concentrate on a particular prayer passage, and that it is quite all right to do this without worrying too much as to where the minyan or the rest of the congregation is in its prayers. For example, while the cantor is chanting two Psalms back to back, you might say and concentrate on just one of them. The mitzvah is to pray and connect with God, not necessarily to be on the same page as everyone else. Finally, remember that there is also nothing wrong with praying in English. God understands English too!

Our rabbis taught that whether a person prays little or much, the main thing is if his or her heart is directed to God. One of the most famous folk tales concerns a little boy who didn't know how to pray in Hebrew. The only thing he knew was how to play the flute, and that's what he did at prayer services. God was impressed that the melody the little boy created was from the heart, and his prayers rose up to the heavens and were accepted. The other worshippers were known to simply rush through their prayers without proper feeling, and the words of their prayers fell to the ground, never to be heard by God.

When I pray, what should I do if I can't read Hebrew or can read a little and only partially understand what I am saying?

Increasing your knowledge of Hebrew furthers your ability to pray, but the main thing is not to let your lack of Hebrew prevent you from having a spiritual experience.

Some people pray in Hebrew but always make it a habit of looking over to the English to see what it means. If you find that glancing back and forth prevents you from focusing on the prayers and concentrating, then try reciting some of the prayers in English.

The other thing you may wish to do is spend some time identifying the key Hebrew words in each prayer, which helps in identifying its basic theme and meaning. For example, in the prayer *Ahavat Olam* (Everlasting Love), the Hebrew word *ahavah*, meaning "love," appears a number of times and in various forms in the prayer, indicating that the prayer's main theme is both our love for God and God's love for us.

One last thing: while singing the prayers in Hebrew, try to focus your mind on God, and let the singing of the prayer carry your soul.

If I want to say only a few prayers, which are the most important?

All prayers are important, and each has its own specific purpose. However, I'd like to single out three prayers that I believe are definitely significant.

The first is the prayer known as the *Shema*. The first line is the most well known: "Hear O Israel, Adonai is our God, Adonai is One." This prayer comes closest to being Judaism's credo. It sums up Judaism's belief in monotheism, and its rejection of all idols. The Shema is literally confession of the Jewish faith. It proclaims God as one and reminds us of our obligation to love God with all of our heart and soul. It is customary to recite the Shema both in the morning and as a bedtime prayer before going to sleep at night.

For two thousand years, the Shema has been the verse with which many Jewish martyrs have gone to their death. Jews who are more fortunate to meet with a peaceful end also try to die with the Shema on their lips.

The second core prayer is the *Amidah* (which means "standing"); it is recited three times a day. The rabbis have called this prayer *Hatefillah*, meaning the prayer *par excellence*. The Amidah is recited standing and without interruption; it consists of three main thoughts: the glory of God, our hope for personal and group well-being, and our thankfulness for God's blessings. Jewish law dictates that the Amidah be recited with one's feet together while standing—the manner in which talmudic tradition assumes angels stand.

Finally, concluding every worship service is the *Aleynu* prayer. There is in it a place in which worshippers bend their knee and bow; it includes the universal prayer for the day when all people will be united under the Kingdom of God and will proclaim God's oneness. According to an old tradition, Joshua, the successor to Moses, composed the Aleynu at the time he entered the Promised Land. It is generally held, however, that the prayer was first introduced by Rav, founder of the Sura academy some seventeen hundred years ago.

For many children in our own Hebrew school, the favorite prayer is Adon Olam. They love the many melodies to which it is sung, and it doesn't hurt either that it comes at the end of services!

Is it OK according to Judaism to meditate?

Absolutely.

In fact, meditation is a traditional activity in the Jewish religion. One of the first times we read about meditation in the Bible is in the Book of Genesis. There, Isaac is said to have gone out into a field to meditate (Genesis 24:63). In this passage, the rabbis understood the word meditate to mean "to pray," and on the basis of that verse they attributed the afternoon *Mincha* services Jews recite each day to our patriarch Isaac.

You might be surprised to learn that Judaism produced an important system of meditation. Furthermore, since Judaism is an Eastern religion that migrated to the West, its meditative practices may well be those most relevant to westerners. There is considerable evidence that the Jewish mystical masters had dialogue with the Sufi masters and were also aware of the schools of India.

Jews are by nature a spiritual people, and many Jews today are actively seeking spiritual meaning in life, often on a mystical level. Today, many American Jews have become involved in Eastern religions; a large percentage practice disciplines such as Transcendental Meditation. Until Jews become aware of the spiritual richness of their own tradition, they will continue to search for greener pastures elsewhere.

Meditation has been a part of Jewish prayer and life for the longest time. In the Talmud, we read that the early *Hasidim* would spend an hour before prayer in meditation, to direct the mind to God.

Meditation has often been defined as thinking in a controlled manner, deciding exactly how one wishes to direct the mind for a period of time, and then doing it. Jewish meditation uses images, words, and symbols that come from Jewish tradition. The meditations themselves, and the teachings that go along with them, reflect Jewish understanding. I have used meditative techniques at Shabbat services with our congregants, and each week in our teenage Hebrew High evening service we do a meditation with our students. It is one of the highlights of their entire evening.

People are often surprised to hear the term *Jewish meditation*. They have been taught that Judaism is an "in-the-world" religion rather than one that can lead to spiritual transformation. Thus, from an early age many Jews have been given the impression that any technique possibly leading to a spiritual experience is not Jewish and therefore ought to be avoided.

Not too long ago, books on meditation paid little attention to Judaism. Most of those books emphasized Eastern practices, and in some instances Christian meditation, but Jewish meditation was for all intents and purposes ignored.

Now, there are many books on Jewish meditation to help you learn the art. One of my favorites is *Discovering Jewish Meditation: Instruction and Guidance for Learning an Ancient Spiritual Practice,* written by Nan Fink Gefen and published by Jewish Lights. This book clearly helps guide the Jewish meditation that perhaps you have been searching for.

❧ Blessings ❧

I've heard there is a Jewish blessing for everything. Is this true?

Yes, there are blessings that have been formulated for practically every experience of daily life—arising from sleep, dressing, eating, drinking—and for the usual happenings, such as escaping from danger, recovering from illness, or seeing something wondrous in nature. There is even a blessing to recite when losing a loved one, which proclaims God the True Judge.

The genius of the blessing formula is the opportunity for the worshipper to establish a close relationship with God by speaking directly to God. Rabbi Meir, a second-century scholar, stated that it is the duty of every Jew to recite one hundred blessings daily! This seems like a lot of blessings, but Jews who recite the three daily services and the other appropriate blessings throughout their day offer to God more than the requirement.

In reciting blessings, a person acknowledges his or her dependence on God for all things. There are many special blessings for a variety of situations and occasions. Here are some that I find interesting, and unusual too:

- *Upon seeing blossoms for the first time*: Praised are You, Adonai our God, Ruler of the universe, who has withheld nothing from His world and who has created beautiful creatures and trees for people to enjoy. (We use this one with our family at our first Passover Seder each year. Before the meal we go outside, look for a new blossom or flower, and recite the blessing together.)
- *Upon seeing six hundred thousand or more Jews together*: Praised are You, Adonai our God, Ruler of the Universe, knower of secrets. (I said this one for the first time when I marched with hundreds of thousands of Jews in the early 1980s at a Soviet Jewry rally. We marched down Fifth Avenue in downtown Manhattan.)
- *Upon hearing good news*: Praised are You, Adonai our God, Ruler of the universe, who is good and does good. (This is the perfect blessing upon receiving a good report card or getting a clean bill of health after a doctor's annual physical.)
- *Upon seeing the ocean*: Praised are You, Adonai our God, Ruler of the universe, who has made the great sea. (I say this one each year when we go on a family vacation to Cape May, New Jersey, located along shores of the Atlantic Ocean.)
- *Upon seeing a rainbow*: Praised are You, Adonai our God, Ruler of the Universe, who remembers His covenant, is faithful to it, and keeps His promise. (I love seeing a rainbow. To me, it is one of the most beautiful natural wonders of nature. At camp a few years ago, I was working as a staff member. During the evening meal, it began to rain very heavily for about twenty minutes. When the rain stopped, a double rainbow appeared in the sky. I was the first to notice it and proceeded to tell the camp director. The entire camp, all six hundred of us, left the dining room and went outside to view it, and together we recited the rainbow blessing. It was a group experience I will never forget!)

What are some unusual prayers in Jewish tradition?

Over the centuries, a number of specialized and unusual prayers have been written and offered by people in a variety of situations. Here are several of them that might surprise you.

- *Blessing of the sun.* The rabbis taught that a person who sees the sun at its turning point, the moon in its power, the planets in their orbits, or the signs of the zodiac in their order should recite "Blessed are You Who makes the work of Creation." The opportunity to say this blessing only occurs once every twenty-eight years. Essentially the blessing of the sun (known in Hebrew as *Birkat Hachamah*) is a prayer of praise to God. The sun is blessed in thanksgiving for its being created and set into motion in the firmament on the fourth day of creation. According to Jewish tradition, the blessing is said after the Shacharit morning service, when the sun is about ninety degrees above the eastern horizon, on the first Wednesday of the month of Nisan. The last time we blessed the sun was on March 18, 1981. I hope you will put on your calendar the next time we are going to say it: April 7, 2009.

- *Blessing the moon.* The moon blessing originated in the time of the Second Temple. It can be recited from the third evening after the appearance of the new moon until the fifteenth of the lunar month. The blessing is recited because in Jewish tradition the moon is seen as the symbol of both the renewal of nature and Israel's renewal and redemption. The moon must be clearly visible and not obscured by clouds. Last year on a Friday evening after Shabbat services, I invited my entire congregation to go outside with me and recite the blessing. Here it is:

  > Blessed are You, Adonai our God, Sovereign of the universe, whose word created the heavens, whose breath created all they contain. God set statutes and seasons for them, that they should not deviate from their assigned task. Happily they do the will of their Creator, Whose work is truth. God said to the moon that it should renew itself, a crown of glory for those who were borne from the womb, who are destined to be renewed and to extol their Creator for the name of God's glorious sovereignty. Blessed are You, Adonai, who renews the months.

- *Blessing upon seeing a friend after a lapse of twelve months.* Friendship was highly valued in Talmudic times, and friends saw each other with great frequency. If a friend had not seen his or her friend for a year, it was a likely sign that he had died. This fact prompted the creation of this blessing: Blessed be God who revives the dead.

- *Prayer for eating chametz.* During the Passover of 1944, there was no *matzah* at the Bergen-Belsen concentration camp. The rabbis would not permit the inmates to endanger their lives by fasting, and they decreed that it was permissible for them to eat bread, provided this prayer was recited before meals:

> *Avinu Shebashamayim* (our Father in heaven), it is evident and known to you that it is our desire to do Your will and to celebrate the Passover Festival by eating matzah and by observing the prohibition of leavened food. But our heart is pained that the enslavement prevents us, and we are in danger of our lives. We are, therefore, prepared and ready to fulfill Your commandment: "And you shall live by my commandments, and not die by them." We pray to You that You may keep us alive and preserve us and redeem us hastily so that we may observe Your laws and do Your will and serve You with a perfect heart. Amen.

- *Prayer for the journey.* According to a Talmudic statement (Berachot 29b), one should offer a prayer before starting a journey. It is called *Tefillat HaDerech*, or prayer for the journey:

> May it be Your Desire, Adonai our God and God of our ancestors, to guide us in safety, and to bring us to our destination in life, happiness and peace. Deliver us from every enemy and danger on the journey. Let us obtain favor, kindness and love from You and from all the people we meet. Hear our supplication, for You are our God, who hears prayer. Praised are You, Adonai, who hears prayer.

The first time I ever said this prayer was when I took a trip to Israel. On El Al, Israel's national airline, the attendants passed out the prayer on a small card to every passenger. Since then, I always carry the prayer card in my wallet. In our own Hebrew High School, we have instituted the custom of giving every student who gets a driver's license a Lucite key chain with the prayer for the journey on it. We have a special ceremony for each new driver in our small chapel in which we remind the student body of the importance of safe driving. After the prayer is read aloud, we all sing *siman tov u'mazal tov* along with spirited clapping.

- *God's prayer.* In Talmudic times, Rabbi Yochanan once wondered what God prays. Here is God's prayer as quoted in the talmudic tractate of Berachot 7a:

> Rabbi Zutra says in the name of Rav that God prays as follows: "May it be My will that My mercy overcome My anger, and My loving qualities override My strict traits; that I treat My children with the quality of mercy and that I always deal with them beyond the letter of the law."

A friend of mine once told me that some Jewish people say a prayer after going to the bathroom. Is this true?

Yes, there is a custom to say the prayer known as *Asher Yatzar* after going to the bathroom. The idea is to remind us that even something as routine as going to the bathroom ought to be considered wondrous, since without being able to do so we simply could not survive.

The ancient Asher Yatzar appears early on in the daily prayer book. The prayer praises God for creating the wondrous mechanism of the body and for preserving our health and our lives. For many who choose to recite it, it is a constant reminder that our body belongs to God and is on loan to us for the duration of our days. Because of this, we must do everything in our power to take care of ourselves. This includes eating food that is good for us, and even exercising.

❦ Prayer Movements ❧

Why do some Jews sway when they pray?

The custom of swaying (called *shuckling* in Yiddish) while praying is an old one. There are some who sway slightly while they pray; others do so with great exaggerated and rapid movement of the body.

One notices swaying most often among those standing in prayer, but some worshipers sway even when they are seated. Swaying during prayer is primarily a matter of habit, and the result of early training. One explanation for the swaying custom is that it symbolizes a verse in Psalms: "all my limbs shall declare, O God, who is like unto You" (Psalm 35:10). When one sways to and fro, it is as though the entire body is caught up in prayer.

Judah HaLevi, a twelfth-century philosopher, suggests a totally different reason for swaying. He said that when books were rare, it was the practice for people studying the Torah to gather about in a circle to read from the same volume. Each would take a turn to bend down to read a passage, resulting in a continual bending and sitting up. Those who observed such groups tended to copy the practice, which then became habit that was later transferred to prayer.

For some people, swaying is an aid to concentration in their prayer. Personally, I enjoy swaying, particularly when I am singing a lively prayer with the rest of the congregation. It helps my concentration and adds to my personal devotion.

Why is there so much standing and sitting down in the synagogue service?

To those who do not regularly attend synagogue services, the congregation looks like the crowd at a football game, with people constantly popping up and down. Not knowing when to stand and when to sit sometimes causes one to feel uncomfortable.

The formal posture for prayer is the standing position. As the synagogue service grew longer, it became difficult for congregants to stand for a long period of time, so only the more important prayers were recited while standing. The rabbi, cantor, or prayer leader generally motions the congregation as to when to stand and when to sit.

Standing in prayer before God is a mark of respect, and the prayers for which we are required by Jewish tradition to stand are those that have special significance: the Amidah, Hallel Psalms of Praise, the Morning Blessings, the Prayer for the New Month, the Aleynu, and the special memorial prayers called Yizkor.

It is also proper to stand when the prayer leader says the Barechu, when the Ark is open, and when the Torah is in motion and being carried to or from the Ark. In traditional congregations, it is customary for everyone to stand when the Kaddish is said, either by the prayer leader or by the mourners. Finally, in some Conservative and Reform congregations, the Shema is considered so important that congregants rise out of respect when it is recited.

When in doubt, the best practice is to follow the general conduct of the congregation.

Why is kneeling rarely seen at prayer services?

Bowing and kneeling were an integral part of the ceremonies and rituals in the Jerusalem Temple. In the Book of Nehemiah, we are told that after Ezra blessed God, the people bowed their heads and fell down before God with their faces to the ground. The Talmud (Berachot 36a) says of Rabbi Akiba that when he prayed privately he would begin in one corner of the room, and as a result of his kneeling he would end up in the opposite corner of the room.

When Christianity adopted kneeling as a prayer posture, the Rabbi prohibited it in Jewish worship. The only exception was on Yom Kippur. During the Avodah service, when an account of the ancient Temple service was read, the cantor kneeled and prostrated himself, as did the *Kohen Gadol*, the Jewish High Priest, when he officiated back in Temple times. For congregants, this is one of the highlights of the entire Yom Kippur service.

Why do some Jews close their eyes during certain prayers?

To deepen concentration and block out distraction while reciting certain prayers, some people close their eyes and cover them with the palm of one hand. There are still others who wear prayer shawls to cover their heads with their tallitot, to keep out all potential distraction. One is quite likely to see people close their eyes during the Shema, because of its great importance. If you've never tried closing your eyes at some point during the prayer service, give it a try. You will be amazed as to how you can increase your level of concentration.

☙ Ten Commandments ☙

Why isn't reciting the Ten Commandments part of the prayer service?

Since the Ten Commandments are one of the most significant elements in the Bible, it is somewhat surprising that they have not been incorporated into the Jewish worship service. According to a Talmudic statement (Berachot 12a), the Ten Commandments were recited in the Jerusalem Temple as part of the daily liturgy, before the Shema prayer. On account of the heretics, however, who asserted that only the Ten Commandments were divinely ordained, the custom of reciting them was abolished.

Today the Ten Commandments are often included as an additional supplementary reading in Reform, Conservative, Orthodox, and Reconstructionist prayer books. Perhaps this uncertain status of including them as a supplementary reading arose from the fear of it being considered that the Ten Commandments were the sole essence of Judaism and other commandments could be discarded.

If you want to be sure to hear the Ten Commandments being read at services, make certain to attend services on the festival of Shavuot. In addition, the Ten Commandments are also read as part of the Torah reading of the portion called *Yitro* (found in chapter twenty of the Book of Exodus), usually occurring in midwinter. Be prepared to rise when they are being recited too.

It looks as if Christians count the Ten Commandments differently from Jews. Is that true? Why?

Here is the Jewish division of the Ten Commandments:

1. I am the Lord Your God, who brought you out of the land of Egypt.
2. You shall have no other gods beside me. You shall not bow down to idols or serve them.
3. You shall not use the name of the Lord your God to take a false oath.

4. Observe the Sabbath day, to keep it holy.
5. Honor your father and your mother.
6. You shall not murder.
7. You shall not commit adultery.
8. You shall not steal.
9. You shall not bear false witness against your neighbor.
10. You shall not covet your neighbor's house, nor his wife, his man and maidservant, his ox, donkey, nor anything that is your neighbor's.

Roman Catholics and Lutheran theologians endorse a different system of numbering, while the Episcopal, Eastern Orthodox, and majority of Protestant denominations accept yet another designation.

The difference centers upon two of the commandments, the first and the last. Roman Catholics and Lutherans list their first commandment as "You shall have no other gods before me. You shall not make yourself a graven image."

The rest of the Christian Church divides this into two parts, making the first part commandment number one and the second, about graven images, commandment number two. Designating a separate command regarding graven images was done by leaders of the Reformed movement following the German Reformation, who wished to strike out against the alleged evils of statues—aids to worship commonly used by Roman Catholics.

To make the final number of the commandments total ten, Catholics and Lutherans separate the commandment regarding coveting into two. The ninth commandment becomes "You shall not covet your neighbor's house" and "You shall not covet your neighbor's wife, or his manservant, or his maidservant" as the tenth. The other denominations choose to combine these two sentences into one commandment.

❦ Prayer Responses ❧

What does *amen* mean?

Rabbi Hanina of the Talmud taught that the Hebrew letters making up the word *amen* stand for the three Hebrew words *El Melech Ne'eman*, meaning "God is the Faithful King."

The Hebrew word *amen* has entered almost every language in the world and is today one of the most universally known words. It is also one of the most ancient, originating in the Torah as a response of affirmation. In Deuteronomy 27:16–26, we find a series of pronouncements by the Levites to which the people responded, "Amen."

When a person says "amen," this indicates his or her endorsement of the words just heard and affirms belief in the truth of what has been said. It acknowledges one's identification with the prayer or the blessing, as though one has said it.

According to Jewish law, any person who hears another person recite a blessing is required to respond with "amen" upon its conclusion. This ruling was especially significant before printed prayer books came into widespread use. Since most people were unable to pray by heart, they could fulfill their prayer obligation by listening to the prayers said by the Prayer Leader and answering, "Amen." Even after prayer books became commonplace and most people were able to recite the prayers for themselves, the congregation's response of "amen" remained a meaningful part of the worship service.

Chapter 3

❧ ❧

Bible

❧ Authorship ❧

Who wrote the Torah?

Since the Torah's other name is the Five Books of Moses, many traditional Jews believe that Moses wrote the words of the Torah, with God speaking the words to Moses. By the time the Talmud was completed in the year 500 C.E., some of the rabbis were beginning to question certain biblical passages. For instance, the Book of Deuteronomy describes the death of Moses. This fact makes it difficult to believe that Moses wrote the Torah, and several rabbis said that Joshua, not Moses, composed the last portion of the Book of Deuteronomy.

A Frenchman named Jean Astruc, who found that various Bible passages employed different names for God, made a most fascinating discovery in the eighteenth century. Astruc found that, when he separated the passages containing each name, he had two parallel accounts of certain biblical stories. Astruc's discovery earned him a place in history as the father of scientific study of the Bible. Instead of viewing the Torah in the traditional sense, as a collection of writings produced by God through Moses, Astruc and later Bible scholars began to study it as material written by many people over a long period of time.

I believe that Astruc was right: the Bible is the product of numerous people over a long period of time, with Moses certainly being one of the contributors. The material was gathered and edited over a span of many centuries. That's why at times we find varying or contradictory statements in the Torah. Despite all of this, the Torah is a unified work, on the basis of common agreement shared by all its authors about God's important role in the life of the Israelite people.

What's the difference between the Old Testament and the New Testament?

The Old Testament is what Christians call the Hebrew Bible, which in Jewish terminology is known by the word *Tanach*, an acronym for the three categories of books that make up the Hebrew Bible: *Torah*, *Nevi'im* (*Prophets*), and *Ketuvim* (*Writings*). There are a total of thirty-nine books in the Tanach.

The New Testament is the second part of the Christian Bible. Christians believe that it records a "new covenant" or "new testament" that fulfills and completes God's old covenant with the Hebrews, described in the Old Testament. The New Testament is a collection of twenty-seven writings gathered into a single book about one-fourth as large as the Hebrew Bible. They contain information about the life and teachings of Jesus, the development of early Christianity, and the faith and regulations of the newly formed religion.

Some Jews believe that to refer to a New Testament is to give credence to the Christian idea that the New Testament is the fulfillment of the promises and teachings of the Hebrew Bible. In fact, Jews often refrain from the use of the words Old Testament because it implies a New Testament.

How can people believe that God gave some laws to a man named Moses on a mountain thousands of years ago? It sounds like a religious myth, not something that really happened.

In Jewish tradition, Moses is considered the greatest prophet who ever lived. The Bible tells us that as the Israelites camped below, Moses ascended Mount Sinai and received the word of God. We call the act of God revealing words to people the act of revelation.

With regard to revelation, the most commonly asked questions are: What really happened at Mount Sinai? How do we know for sure that it was God speaking to Moses, and not just something that Moses imagined? Even if God did in fact speak, how can we be sure that the Israelites understood it correctly? Even if God revealed words and laws at Mount Sinai, surely human beings throughout the generations have copied and transmitted what we said, so how can we be certain that the words we have today were God's exact words? These are all excellent questions, and it's necessary to deal with them if we are going to understand the authority behind Jewish law.

The branches of Judaism have differing beliefs when it comes to Moses and what happened on Mount Sinai. Let's summarize the predominant views in the major branches.

Orthodox Jews generally believe that God revealed His will at Mount Sinai in written and oral forms. The oral form was later written down in what is today called the Talmud, consisting of the application and interpretation of the law by rabbis who were divinely inspired. Exactly how this communication between God and the people of Israel occurred is a mystery. But for the Orthodox, it remains fact that the Torah was revealed by God using words directed to the people. Thus God spoke words and the people directly received God's communication.

In Conservative Judaism, the nature of God's communication has been understood in various ways. For some, God communicated with mortals both at Sinai and in the era of the prophets. Human beings wrote down these revelations, and thus the writings included in the Bible are of diverse origins. Another Conservative position posits that human beings (Moses one of them) who were divinely inspired with a specific message wrote the Torah at various places and times.

Reconstructionists generally believe that human beings wrote the Torah, claiming no divinity for the product. The Reform position also maintains that the Torah is God's will as written by human beings. They believe that as time goes on, people are better able to understand God's will.

The bottom line is that we do not know, nor can anyone ever really know, exactly what Moses or the people at Sinai actually heard, saw, or felt. Many of the words used in the Bible's descriptions of revelation are figurative. The Bible speaks of fire, smoke, the voice of a horn, thunder, and lightning to give us some idea as to what it was like to hear God's voice. In the end, though, they could only refer to having experienced the greatness of the presence of God.

✺ Famous Bible People ✺

How old were Adam and Eve when they were born?

First of all, Adam and Eve were not born; they were created by God. Adam was made out of the earth and God breathed life into him. Eve, as you may recall, came from Adam's rib.

If you read the story in the Book of Genesis, nowhere does it specify their ages. We must assume that Adam and Eve were young, but certainly not infants, when they were created. They were able to speak in full sentences. We also know that they had to be young adults because God placed both of them in the Garden of Eden and asked and expected them to care for it. God could have created a maintenance-free world but decided that it would be better for us to take responsibility for the world we live in, so he made Adam and Eve work for their food.

If Eve gave birth to Cain and Abel, where did all the other people in the Bible come from?

If you read the Bible carefully, you will see that a wife of Cain is mentioned, but not by name. There must have been some other women born to Adam and Eve, not mentioned in the Bible, who were sisters to Cain and Abel. As a matter of fact, there are Jewish legends that tell us that both Cain and Abel had twin sisters, and each was expected to marry his own twin. However, Cain fell in love with Abel's sister, causing jealousy among the brothers. In any event, Cain killed Abel, so he was unable to have children. Cain however, must have married one of his sisters. Later in the Bible, in the Book of Leviticus, we are told that a marriage between a brother and sister is no longer allowed.

Why did God pick Abraham to be the father of the Jewish people?

The Bible never tells us. All we learn is that Abraham hears a voice telling him to leave his parents and country and go to a new land. Abraham obeys without asking even a single question. He clearly was a man of great faith.

There are many interesting Jewish legends about Abraham and how he convinced others to believe in one God, when everyone in his day believed in many gods. One of my favorites is the popular legend telling us that his father Terach owned an idol store in Mesopotamia:

> One day Abraham was asked to mind the store, and Abraham simply could not believe that these strange looking idols could actually be gods. After all, his father Terach was a man, and how could a man make God?
>
> Suddenly a man entered the store and was in tears. He had business problems and needed to buy a special idol to help him change his fortune. Abraham sold him, and many other people who came into the store, many different kinds of idols. But in his heart, Abraham realized that the idols could not help anyone, because his father had made them with his own hands.
>
> Now very angry, he picked up a stick and began to smash all the idols in the store into small little bits. Finally, Abraham took the stick and placed it in the hands of the only remaining idol in the store.
>
> The next day his father Terach returned from his trip and went into his store. He could not believe his eyes—all the idols were smashed to bits. Turning to Abraham, he asked him what had happened. Abraham responded by telling his father that one by one the idols argued with each other, and in fighting broke each other into little pieces.
>
> Terach then responded by saying to his son: "That's impossible! I made these idols out of clay with my own hands."
>
> "That's true," answered Abraham. "Humans cannot make the true God." Seemingly convinced, his father left the store and his business forever. Soon thereafter, Abraham began convincing other

people that there was only one God in the world. Eventually Abraham became known as the first Hebrew and the father of the Jewish people.

By the way, Abraham is mentioned seventy-two times in the New Testament.

How large was Noah's ark?

The ark was made of wood. According to a fellow in my congregation who owns a lumberyard, it would have taken forty thousand tons of lumber to build the ark.

In the Book of Genesis, Noah's ark is described as being three hundred cubits in length. One cubit is roughly eighteen inches (in ancient times, it was based on the average distance between the tip of the elbow and the tip of the middle finger; it was used like an ancient yardstick), which means that the ark was 450 feet, or one and a half times longer than a football field. The width was fifty cubits (80 feet), and the height was thirty cubits (45 feet).

The ark rested on Mount Ararat (which is in Turkey) after the flooding stopped. There are some archaeologists who claim that they have found some wood remnants dating back more than five thousand years, which they say might be part of Noah's ark. Nobody knows for sure, and probably no one ever will.

What are angels, and do you believe in them?

A few years ago I taught a course on Jewish angelology. We went around the room on the first day of class, and each person had a personal angel story of his own to tell, which convinced them of the existence of angels.

According to a recent poll, more than 75 percent of the American teenage population believes in angels. These winged wonders of the Bible are more popular than ever, turning up in newspapers, toy departments, comic books, and angel stores. In the Bible, there are more than three hundred references to angels. They appear in many forms, sometimes as humans and sometimes in other shapes. Some have wings, some have animal faces, some spew fire, some sing to God. Some angels can speak, sit, stand, walk, wear clothes, ride horses, and even descend from heaven on a ladder.

The angels in the Bible are primarily God's messengers, doing only what God orders them to do. For example, when Abraham is about to put a knife to the throat of his beloved son Isaac, an angel of God stops him. Angels also appear in the prayer book. The opening prayer of the Friday night service, *Shalom Aleichem,* welcomes God's angels.

Yes, I am happy to say that I do believe in angels. Although I've never seen one, I've felt them around me at certain times in my life. A few years ago, as I was driving on a slick road, my car slid past a stop sign into a busy intersection during rush hour. My heart began to pound, anticipating a bad car crash. To my amazement, I emerged unscathed and unhurt. I immediately pulled over to the side of the road and thanked God for the guardian angels that helped pull me through a difficult situation.

Who do you think was the greatest prophet to have ever lived?

There are many excellent and immortal prophets in the Jewish tradition. Ezekiel was the first major prophet to have had a vision of God's throne in heaven. In the first chapter of Ezekiel, he has an incredible vision of the Divine Throne-Chariot, a strange and mysterious apparition whose main feature was its ability to be drawn by four-faced living creatures.

Jeremiah the Prophet, a contemporary of Ezekiel's, is considered the most self-revealing. No prophet told so much about himself as he did, revealing an array of emotions that allows the reader to feel his poignant sorrow toward an Israelite people that went astray.

As a young child, I fell in love with the prophet Jonah. The intrigue of this book is Jonah's attempt to escape from the Divine command by sailing from the Land of Israel. After his wonderful deliverance from drowning by being sheltered in the body of a whale, he was obedient to a second commission from God. Jonah went to Nineveh and there proclaimed that it would be destroyed in forty days. God spared the city after all the people of Nineveh repented.

It is ironic that Jonah, a prophet who attempts to flee from his Divine mission, is the only prophet to be successful in changing the ways of a people, who are spared from destruction.

The prophet who is most intriguing to me is Moses. According to the great rabbis, and even the Bible itself, Moses was considered the greatest of all of the prophets. The Bible describes him as the only prophet able to see God "face to face." I interpret this to mean that Moses got God's attention whenever he chose to do so. Moses certainly went through numerous challenges and saw firsthand many of God's divine wonders, including the splitting of the Red Sea and the formulation of the Ten Commandments. I still continue to be perplexed about why God did not allow him to enter into the Promised Land, given all that he did for the Jewish people. But that's a discussion for another time.

✢ Biblical Miracles ✢

How was it possible for Jonah to live for three days in the whale?

No one will ever know for certain what happened to Jonah. Perhaps it was all a dream or a vision. We do know, however, that the story has been read (and will likely continue to be) as the *haftarah* on the afternoon of Yom Kippur. Its message is that God will always listen to and forgive those who sincerely repent. Of course, it's impossible to try to run away from God!

The Book of Jonah is one of the great stories in the Bible. As a child, I too was always intrigued with how a person could stay in a whale for three days and survive. Since the story was in the Bible and because there are so many wondrous and miraculous occurrences, I never for a moment doubted this possibility as well.

As I got older and began to study the Bible as an adult, I learned that there were many people who saw a great deal of symbolism in the story and did not take it literally. For example, several commentators have viewed the episode of the whale swallowing Jonah as the captivity that swallowed up Israel, represented by Jonah. Israel's deliverance from exile has been linked to being disgorged alive from the mouth of the whale. Like Jonah, Israel flees from the duty God has laid upon him, and like the people of Israel he exhibits an ill will to believe that God would desire to save a non-Israelite people from destruction.

Did God really turn Mrs. Lot into a pillar of salt?

The Bible tells us that Sodom and Gomorrah were two cities filled with evil people. When God decided to destroy the cities, Abraham protested and asked whether God would consider saving them if he could find fifty righteous people. When Abraham was unable to find even ten, he walked away, and God proceeded with the destruction. When Lot's wife looked back to see the rain of brimstone and fire befall the people, the Bible says that she became a pillar of salt.

I have always had every reason to doubt this story. But I must tell you another story. A few years ago I visited Israel with members of my congregation. We went to an area near the Dead Sea. The Dead Sea is the lowest point on the face of the earth, and the sea is ten times saltier than even the Atlantic or Pacific Oceans. In fact, there is so much salt that nothing lives in the Dead Sea, and if you gently lie in the water, you automatically float. Toward the end of our day at the Dead Sea, our guide took us to a nearby hill, and there for the first time he told us that this is where some people believe Lot's wife became a pillar of salt. I could hardly believe my eyes; there, encrusted in a small hill, was the likeness of the figure of a woman. Our guide said: "There she is: Mrs. Lot." I since have learned that many other guides have pointed out to their tour group the likeness of a woman in this same spot. Perhaps one day you too will visit this place, see for yourself, and then decide what you think. I know that on that day many members in our touring group became believers!

❦ Biblical Disappearances ❧

Do we know what happened to the Ten Lost Tribes?

There is no reliable historical information on the fate of the Ten Tribes, but many legends have arisen about them. In the Middle Ages, when Jews lived under Christian or Muslim rule, stories spread about a vast kingdom beyond the legendary river Sambatyon, inhabited by the Ten Lost Tribes. Some rabbinic authorities today claim that the Ethiopian Jews are descended from the tribe of Dan.

Throughout the centuries, the Jewish world has been periodically excited by reports of the discovery of the so-called Ten Lost Tribes in various regions. Eldad Ha-Dani, a late-ninth-century traveler, reported finding them in the mountains of Africa. Benjamin of Tudela, in the twelfth century, heard of them in Central Asia. David Reuveni claimed to be the brother of one of their rulers in some region of Arabia, while Manasseh ben Israel reported that he found them in South America. The fact of the matter is that no Jews have been able to trace their ancestry accurately to any of the tribes, with the exception of Judah and Levi.

It appears that most of the descendants of the Ten Tribes were integrated into the societies in which they were exiled.

What is the reason for animal sacrifice in the Bible?

The Hebrew word for sacrifice, *korban*, literally means to "bring near" or "to approach"; it occurs more than eighty times in the Bible, especially in the books of Leviticus and Numbers. A sacrifice was a means by which people in biblical times approached God, to feel nearer. About 25 percent of all of the Torah's laws deal with sacrifice.

Throughout the ancient world, human beings connected with their gods in part through sacrifice. Altars abounded and received gifts of all manner of animals, and in some cases human beings as well. It is therefore not surprising that the narratives of the Hebrew Bible, including the Torah itself, are full of instances in which an altar is built as a vehicle of sacrifice and communication.

The medieval philosopher Maimonides believed that animal sacrifices were created to wean people from the ancient practice of human sacrifice. His reasoning may have been based on Abraham's substitution of a ram in lieu of sacrificing his son Isaac.

The first sacrifices recorded in the Bible were in Genesis 4:4 by Cain, who offered the fruit of the soil; and Abel, who offered the choicest of the firstborn of his flock.

Although libation of wine and meal offerings played a prominent role in some of the biblical ritual sacrifices, the most important
sacrifices were animals. The sacrificial animal had to be wholly un-
blemished, domesticated, and the property of the person making the
sacrifice.

A sacrifice called *olah* ("going up") used bulls, sheep, goats, and
birds in its ritual. A continuous burnt offering was made twice daily,
consisting of two male lambs that were sacrificed, one in the morning and one in the evening.

The sin offering, called the *chattat*, was another type of animal
sacrifice. It was suited to the rank and circumstance of the person
who offered it. The High Priest would bring a young bull, while a
commoner would bring a female goat or lamb.

Rites of purification called for lesser sin offerings. For instance,
lambs or birds were offered after childbirth or contracting leprosy.

Peace offerings, called *shelamim*, were the basic offerings of all
communal sacrifices. Any domesticated animal was permitted for use
as a peace offering, which always concluded with some type of communal meal. The peace offering was specified only for celebration of
Shavuot, the ritual for completion of the Nazirite vow, and installa-
tion of the priests. National events that called for a peace offering included successful completion of a military campaign, the end of a
famine, and the praising of a candidate for the kingship.

The most famous Bible sacrifice was the one on Passover known
as the Paschal lamb. It commemorated God's deliverance of the
Jews from Egyptian bondage. A Jew would bring a lamb to the Jerusalem Temple and give it to a priest, who would in turn sprinkle its
blood on the altar and burn the entrails and fat. The remainder
would be given back to the person who donated the lamb. The animal would be taken back to the donor's family, who would eat the
lamb, along with matzah, bitter herbs, and other foods. The roasted
shankbone that Jews have on their Passover Seder plate is a reminder
of the Paschal lamb sacrifice.

During Temple times, animal sacrifices were offered within the
Temple itself. Priests and Levites took turns officiating at the sacrifices. The destruction of the Temple by the Romans in 70 C.E. ef-

fectively ended sacrifice as a form of Jewish worship. The rabbis, led by Yochanan ben Zakkai, ruled that study, prayer, and performance of good deeds were acceptable substitutes for sacrifice.

The Conservative and Orthodox branches of Judaism continue to refer to the Temple's sacrifices in their worship services. Reform Judaism has dropped the Musaf additional service, with its many references to sacrifices, believing that it is no longer relevant to the modern Jew. The Orthodox prayer book reiterates its belief that the Temple will one day again be built, along with a return to sacrifice. The Conservative movement has changed all references to sacrifice in the Musaf service into the past tense, expressing no desire to have it reinstated.

Chapter 4

❧ ❧

Jewish Holidays

❧ **Time and the Calendar** ❧

Why do all Jewish holidays begin at night?

It does seem strange that celebration of all Jewish holidays begins in the evening. According to Jewish law, the holiday actually begins at sundown, at which time candles are lit and a blessing is said to usher it in.

The custom of beginning a holiday at sunset is based on the story of Creation as depicted in Genesis: "It was evening, it was morning, the first day." The evening came first! Thus, each new day begins with the sunset of the one before, so that the Sabbath is ushered in as the sun sets on Friday. If the Festival of Purim falls on March 15th, the celebration actually begins on the evening of the 14th.

Why do Jewish holidays fall at different times each year?

In a little more than a thousand years from now, Hanukkah is going to arrive very late in the year. In fact, in the year 3031 of the Gregorian calendar (the one used in the Western world, including the United States, of course) Hanukkah will arrive so late that there will be no festival of Hanukkah. Most interestingly, in the following year, 3032, there will be two Hanukkahs, one beginning in January and a second Hanukkah late that year in December.

In our time, you might hear people saying: "The High Holidays are early this year," or "the High Holidays are so late this year." Yes, it is a fact that sometimes Rosh Hashanah falls in early September, and in other years it can be as late as October. I like to think of the Jewish holidays always falling at the same time, at least according to the Hebrew calendar. Rosh Hashanah every year is on the first of the Hebrew month of Tishri.

The reason Jewish holidays fall at changing times on the secular calendar is because of the difference between the Gregorian calendar, used by most of the Western world, and the Hebrew calendar. The Hebrew or Jewish calendar is based on a lunar year, running 354 or 355 days, rather than the solar year of the Gregorian calendar, which runs 365 or 366 days in a leap year. For this reason, Jewish holidays, which always fall on the same date of the Hebrew calendar, come out on varying dates of the Gregorian calendar every year. Seven times in nineteen years (about once every three years), an entire additional month is added to the Jewish calendar for a leap year. This is in order to keep the Jewish holidays, which continue to slip later in time relative to the Gregorian calendar, synchronized with their proper seasons. Because of the cleverness of the Hebrew calendar (invented by Hillel almost two thousand years ago), the fall holiday of Sukkot will always come in the autumn months, and Passover in its proper time in the spring.

❧ Shabbat ☙

Why is our Sabbath on Saturday and the Christian Sabbath on Sunday?

For the Jewish people, the Sabbath begins on Friday night and extends through Saturday until nightfall, when three stars emerge in the sky. For Christians, Sunday is their Sabbath. Historically, the Early Church recognized Sunday as the day of worship because it was on a Sunday that Jesus rose from the dead. Since the resurrection of Jesus is the focal point of the Christian faith and the confirmation of all that Jesus taught, the first Christians gathered to celebrate this event on the first day of the week (Acts 20:7), which is Sunday.

Undoubtedly, another important reason early Christians worshiped on Sunday was to distinguish themselves from the Jewish community to which many of them belonged before their conversion.

Today, with the exception of the Seventh Day Adventists, Christians hold Sunday as their day for public worship. Seventh Day Adventists believe that God's command "Remember the Sabbath day to keep it holy" referred to the seventh day of the week, since it was on the seventh day that God rested at the end of creating the world. They believe, too, that the Early Church was in error when it started a tradition of conducting worship on a day other than that set aside by God.

Why aren't we supposed to drive on Shabbat?

I think the biblical idea of asking people to stay at or near their home on the Sabbath is an attempt to mold the Sabbath day into one of serenity and spirituality, when even animals were allowed to rest as well.

Prohibiting travel on the Sabbath was a vital contribution to preparing the day for its mission to sanctify life. The basis of the prohibition is the verse in Exodus 16:29 "Let everyone remain where he is: let no one leave his place on the seventh day." This law was originally directed at the gatherers of manna, the heavenly food that fell in the wilderness. Travel on the Sabbath in Bible times, by riding on an animal, was also forbidden for the reason of seeking to avoid involvement in incidental labor, such as possibly cutting down a twig to prod the animal on its way.

When automobiles were invented in the twentieth century and when suburbs sprang forth outside of cities, many Jewish people began to find it difficult even to reach a synagogue on the Sabbath, unless they traveled in a car. When one analyzes the nature of travel in a car, one must conclude that it involves both an element of physical exertion as well as the possibility of a mechanical failure that could lead to further anxiety. Furthermore, actual fire is created in the engine of the car when starting it, and lighting fire is one of the Sabbath's prohibitions.

In the Conservative movement there is a Law Committee, which makes rulings for its own constituents. Under today's conditions, many people live so far away from their synagogues that unless they ride, they cannot attend them. For some of these people, attendance at services is their only contact with religious life and practically their only awareness of the sanctity of the Sabbath. For this reason, the Conservative movement's Law Committee ruled that the positive value involved in participation in public worship on the Sabbath outweighs the negative value of refraining from riding in an automobile. Thus, only for purposes of getting to the closest synagogue and then returning home, if one lives too far away to walk, is one allowed to ride in an automobile. For most Reform and Reconstructionist Jews, there is no official ban on use of the automobile on the Sabbath. For Orthodox Jews, the ban remains, but they are likely to want to locate close enough to a synagogue so they do not have to drive there.

As a twelve year old, I was always driven to and from my synagogue, which was more than two miles away. On Saturday afternoon, it was our family's tradition to drive to my grandmother's house, where my brother and I would visit and spend the afternoon. As I began to seriously contemplate a possible career in the rabbinate, I thought I should begin looking at additional mitzvot to perform that I was not currently performing. The summer before my thirteenth birthday, my parents sent me to the Hebrew-speaking Camp Ramah for eight weeks. There, for the first time in my life, I spent a summer where an entire community observed the Sabbath in all of its glory and sanctity. At camp, there was no need to drive a car at all.

Returning home after the summer, I made a vow that I would no longer drive to prayer services on the Sabbath. Thus began my custom of walking to synagogue with my family. Not using a car on the Sabbath also meant my not going to movies, or to the shopping mall. It meant that I could fulfill the Bible's precept of staying around the house and being with my family and friends who came over to visit us.

This was the official beginning of my journey toward great Jewish observance. It made all the difference in the world!

Why aren't we supposed to use money on Shabbat?

The Sabbath is the only holy day mentioned in the Ten Commandments. We are told to observe the Sabbath by keeping it holy and refraining from work. *Melacha*, the Hebrew word for "work" that is used in the Bible, generally applies to work that involves creation, production, or transformation of an object.

The Sabbath is a time for spiritual refreshment, and for a break in the monotonous routine of daily labor. It is a reminder that the need for making a living must not blind us to the need for living. Since money is used in business transactions, it is not allowed to be used on Shabbat. By refraining from using money, one is not tempted to go shopping or go to the movies. This allows time for prayer, festive eating, and sharing moments at home with one's family and friends.

Why aren't we supposed to watch TV on Shabbat? I thought Shabbat is a day to rest and enjoy oneself. I enjoy resting by watching TV.

Although Shabbat is a day of rest, it is not a day to do whatever one wants to enjoy oneself. Shabbat is a unique experience; its atmosphere and meaning are derived from the many positive commandments as well as prohibitions described in Jewish holy books.

One of the work prohibitions on Shabbat is kindling fire. One is not allowed to light fire on the Sabbath, and using electrical instruments and appliances, such as a television, has been deemed by some rabbinic authorities as synonymous with using fire.

There are other reasons for opting not to watch TV on Shabbat. Rabbi Joseph Telushkin and Dennis Prager have suggested in their book *Eight Questions People Ask About Judaism* that Shabbat and television have antithetical purposes. Whereas the purpose of television is to entertain and enable people to kill time, Shabbat's purpose is to teach people how to use and sanctify time. Even though people are known to watch television for more than five hours each day, keeping the television off on one day of the week liberates a person from dependence on it. Telushkin and Prager say it best when they write that "the Shabbat is a natural day, no artificial additives are permitted. Therefore, no television!"

❦ Fast Days ❧

Why do Jews fast on certain days?

Fasting has three main purposes in the Jewish faith: self-denial, mourning, and petitioning God. In addition to the Fast of Yom Kippur, several public fasts are observed by traditional Jews. Probably the most important of them is the Fast of the Ninth of Av, or in Hebrew *Tisha B'Av*, which occurs in July or August each year. This fast commemorates the destruction of both of the Temples in Jerusalem. The period of fasting is usually twenty-four hours, from sunset of one day to sunset of the next.

The Fast of Gedaliah, or *Tzom Gedaliah*, is another of the fast days on the Jewish calendar. It falls on the third day of Tishri, the day following the second day of Rosh Hashanah. Gedaliah, a Jewish official appointed by the Babylonian King Nebuchadnezzar to govern the Jews, was assassinated on the third day of Tishri. Mourning him as a hero, traditional Jews begin fasting at sunrise on the third day of Tishri and end their fast when the stars appear in the evening.

The Fast of the Tenth of Tevet (*Asarah B'Tevet*) occurs in the month after Hanukkah. It too is observed as a fast in commemoration of the beginning of the siege of Jerusalem in 588 B.C.E. The Temple was destroyed two years later, and a day of national mourning and fasting was proclaimed. As with other minor fasts, the fast begins at dawn and ends with the appearance of evening stars.

The day before Purim, there is a fast called the Fast of Esther. This fast day, occurring on the thirteenth of Adar, was fixed in the eighth century. Called *Ta'anit Esther* in Hebrew, this fast is observed in commemoration of the three days' fast undertaken by the Jews of Persia at the request of Queen Esther prior to her pleading the cause of her people before King Ahasuerus.

Several additional private fasts are observed by traditional Jews. For instance, some brides and grooms choose to fast on the day of their wedding while repenting for their past misdeeds and acknowledging a new beginning. On the eve of Passover, firstborn sons fast in memory of the deliverance of the Israelite firstborn, who were not stricken in Egypt by the tenth plague. Individual fasting was also customary as an act of piety during a crisis or as an exhibition of sorrow or prayer during a period of suffering. Finally, a person who dropped a Torah scroll was obliged to fast. In certain places, those who saw the Torah fall were also obligated to fast. So you want to be especially careful when you are given the honor to lift or carry a Torah scroll!

Why do we still fast to commemorate events that happened a few thousand years ago?

The various fast days throughout the Jewish year were instituted for a variety of purposes: to express repentance for one's misdeeds, to seek special requests, or to mourn a tragic event.

The fast of the Ninth Day of Av, the most solemn day of the calendar, commemorates the destruction of both Jerusalem Temples. To commemorate the destruction, the rabbis declared not only a fast but a three-week preparation before the fast as well. Beginning on the seventeenth of Tammuz, weddings are avoided until after the Ninth of Av. So are haircuts, buying or wearing new clothes, and musical celebrations. A general atmosphere of somberness and self-examination is encouraged.

Nine days before the Fast of Av, the atmosphere of mourning deepens. Meat and wine disappear from the table. Washing and bathing are forbidden, except when it is directly a matter of health.

Beginning at sundown on the ninth of Av, we do not eat or drink at all. We do not wear leather or anoint our skin with oils or perfumes; nor is lovemaking permissible. We even go far beyond these prohibitions, which are the same as those for the more joyful Fast of Yom Kippur. We adhere to the traditional mourning customs. We study only sad and painful passages. The Book of Lamentations is chanted in a mournful tone in the evening to candlelight, while we are seated on the floor, a traditional mourning custom. The Torah Ark is draped in black.

The next morning we gather again. We do not wear tallit or tefillin. The words of the worship service are neither sung nor chanted, because the mood is too mournful.

The intention of all of these customs is to attempt to re-create the experience of having lost the most precious religious institution of the Jewish people, the holy Jerusalem Temple. It is a day of national mourning, and all Jewish people who commemorate the Ninth of Av relive the horror of the event by means of these experiential customs and rituals.

For me, commemoration of this fast over the years has been one of the most powerful and moving experiences in my entire life. It was especially moving during many years at summer camp, when I was part of a much larger summer community of observant campers and counselors. On the Ninth of Av, hundreds of kids and adults (dressed in dark clothing and wearing no leather) joined together in one large room, lit by candles, to chant the haunting book of Lamentations.

Since the reestablishment of the state of Israel, some people maintain that the Fast of the Ninth of Av and the other fasts connected with the destruction of Jerusalem have lost their meaning and should be discontinued. Some even claim that with the establishment of the Jewish state we should actually observe the fast days as festivals.

Opponents of this view insist that the fast must still be observed, since the redemption of Israel is far from complete. For me, the events commemorated by the Fast of Av can never be undone, and it is necessary to remember them forever, both to establish continuity with our past and as a constant stimulus for repentance and good deeds. For many Jews who observe the day, it also helps to remind them of the long record of sacrifice and suffering of past generations, and thus prevent the cultural degeneracy that would follow from ignoring the achievements of Jews in exile.

❦ High Holy Days ❧

Why do rabbis and cantors wear white on the High Holy Days?

The color white is symbolic of humility and purity of thought in Jewish tradition. Centuries ago, when the Kohen Gadol (High Priest) entered the Holy of Holies on Yom Kippur, he wore white garments instead of his usual gold vestments.

Wearing a white robe, known as a *kittel*, is a custom that not only rabbis and cantors follow; members of the congregation do so too. We have a congregant, a Kohen, who wears a kittel every year on the High Holy Days. In the haftarah, which is read on Rosh Hashanah, there is this verse: "Though your sins be as scarlet, they shall be as white as snow." This has been interpreted to mean that one can cleanse oneself of sin, if one truly repents.

The custom of using white spread over time, and today it usually includes all of the Torah mantles, the Ark curtain, and the cover on the reader's table. In our congregation we also adorn our *bimah* with white flowers.

Why do so many people go to the synagogue on the High Holy Days but not for the rest of the year?

Having served my congregation for almost three decades, the one thing I can be sure of is seeing my entire congregational family for the holy days of Rosh Hashanah and Yom Kippur. Unlike the other major Jewish holidays, the High Holy Days celebrate God's role as Creator of the world. They emphasize morality, spirituality, holiness, and self-examination.

The High Holy Days are also called the Days of Awe, and it is likely that they continue to inspire and move people (some out of fear) to be together as a Jewish community for these special and sacred days. On these Days of Awe, Jewish tradition teaches that God decides who shall live and who shall die during the coming year. This powerful tradition has succeeded in bringing people en masse during this time to use prayer in their attempt to influence God's decisions.

One powerful instrument used to motivate repentance during Rosh Hashanah is the ram's horn, which is blown in the synagogue one hundred times on each of the two days of Rosh Hashanah. For many worshippers, it is a highlight of the service, acting as their wake-up call to search their deeds and turn in repentance.

I am constantly amazed at the power of Yom Kippur as well. Many of my congregants who rarely attend services on Shabbat and festivals during the year come on Yom Kippur at the beginning of services and stay throughout the day, while fasting. It seems that Jewish people collectively experience the strongest sense of partnership with God on this day. With its many moments of atonement, life and death issues dominate the day, and after the fast ends many people feel a deep sense of relief that they have observed the holiday properly.

ROSH HASHANAH

Why is Rosh Hashanah observed for two days?

The Bible prescribes that Rosh Hashanah be observed for one day, on the first of Tishri. Many centuries ago, the testimony of witnesses was used to determine the official date of arrival of the New Moon, the first of the month. Messengers were sent forth to notify outlining communities. If the witnesses were to arrive too late for the messengers to be sent out to notify the distant communities, those living far from the city of Jerusalem would miss the correct day of observance of the holiday. In addition, if clouds filled the sky, there could be no witnesses to the arrival of the New Moon. To protect against this, Rosh Hashanah was turned into a two-day holiday. In many Reform Temples, Rosh Hashanah still continues to be observed for only one day, as was done in biblical times.

Why do some Jews visit a body of water on Rosh Hashanah afternoon to empty their pockets of crumbs?

The custom of symbolically casting the sins, using breadcrumbs, into a running brook or stream on the afternoon of the first day of Rosh

Hashanah is said to date from the fourteenth century. It is called *Tashlich* (you will cast), a word borrowed from the Book of Micah 7:17: "You will throw all our sins into the depths of the sea."

Some have explained the custom as a reminder of Abraham's attempted sacrifice of Isaac. A Jewish legend relates that Satan, in an effort to prevent Abraham from fulfilling the divine command, transformed himself into a deep stream on the road leading to Mount Moriah. Plunging into the stream, Abraham and Isaac prayed for divine aid, whereupon the place became dry again.

Another explanation for Tashlich suggests that we are given a chance to reflect on water's purifying effect on the body and to be reminded that even as the body is purified by water, so ought our souls be purified by repentance and appeal to God's mercy.

There are local Tashlich customs in various communities. Some are quite strange. For example, Jews in Kurdistan were known to actually jump into the water to cleanse themselves of their sins. Some Oriental Jews have the custom of reciting Tashlich prayers in the synagogue around a basin of water that contains live fish!

In our Temple, we ask congregants to gather each year at 3:45 P.M., and we take a two-mile walk together to a brook that runs in a beautiful park. Each year, the number of walkers increases, and now more than 150 people are a part of our walking team. Before throwing our sins into the water, we ask each person to share with another in his family a new goal or two for the coming year. Then all parents and grandparents who have children with them are given an opportunity to bless them. It's one of the highlights of the entire year.

Why are round challahs served on Rosh Hashanah?

The bread that is eaten on Rosh Hashanah is often round. Some say this is a reminder of a King's crown, for on Rosh Hashanah we proclaim that God is the Sovereign One, the Ruler of all rulers. Others says that the round shape is symbolic of the eternal nature of life, expressing the hope that the coming year will be complete, unbroken by tragedy.

Over the centuries, in various communities other challah shapes and forms have emerged. In the Russian Ukraine, challot were made in the shape of a bird. The symbolism is based on a verse in Isaiah (31:5): "As hovering birds, so God will protect Jerusalem." Just as a bird flies into the skies, so too our hope is that our prayers will be carried swiftly to the heavens.

In some communities, challot were shaped in the form of a ladder, as if to indicate that on Rosh Hashanah it is decided who shall be lifted up, and who shall be brought low.

Whatever kind of challah you use on Rosh Hashanah, be sure to dip the first piece that you are going to eat in honey, and wish everyone a sweet year.

Why do we dip challah in honey on Rosh Hashanah?

Eating things that are sweet on Rosh Hashanah is an ancient custom, dating back more than a thousand years. The custom is for family members to dip challah (some dip apples) in honey, expressing the hope that sweetness and happiness will enter their lives. After one dips, the custom is to say: "May it be Your will, Adonai our God and God of our ancestors, to renew for us a new, sweet and good year."

Serving honey cake on Rosh Hashanah is another popular custom. Each year we have a congregant who, instead of sending us a Rosh Hashanah greeting, makes us a honey cake using her family's traditional recipe. Eating it is a tasty treat, and it certainly helps to sweeten my year.

What is the shofar, and why do we blow it?

The shofar, the ram's horn, is the oldest surviving type of musical wind instrument, mentioned more than sixty times in the Bible. It is first mentioned in Exodus 19:16 at the revelation of Mount Sinai, when a "dense cloud descended on the mountain and there was a very loud blast of the shofar." In Bible times, the shofar was also used to usher in a new Jewish month, and used at the coronation of a king.

There are a variety of reasons presented in rabbinic literature for sounding the shofar. According to Maimonides, the shofar was the way of awakening the sleepers and a call to examine one's deeds, as well as return in repentance. The shofar has always worked for me as an alarm clock, awakening me to the realization that another year has passed and reminding me of the possibility of doing even better in the forthcoming year.

How do you make a shofar?

A horn made from a ram is the acceptable choice for making a shofar in Jewish tradition. The ram's horn is intended to remind the listener of the story of the sacrifice of Isaac, which is read on the morning of Rosh Hashanah. Just before Abraham was about to sacrifice his own son on an altar, an angel stopped him. Abraham noticed a ram nearby in a thicket, and substituted it as a sacrifice instead of his son Isaac. To honor the ram, Jewish law requires that a ram's horn be used. A horn of a cow was rejected because that animal was associated with the worship of the golden calf by the Israelites in the desert.

There are several other requirements for the ram's horn. One is that the shofar be bent or curved in shape, symbolizing the bent and humbled spirit appropriate on Rosh Hashanah. A second requirement is that the shofar not be painted, though it may be decorated with carved designs. A shofar also cannot be used if it is cracked.

Each year, in many places across the country the *Chabad Hassidim* conduct shofar-making workshops in various synagogues and Jewish community centers. You may want to check and see whether such an opportunity exists in your area.

Why don't we blow the shofar when Rosh Hashanah falls on Saturday?

Centuries ago, when the Temple in Jerusalem existed, the shofar was blown on the Sabbath by the area kohanim, the Jewish Priests. However, it was not blown on that day elsewhere in the country.

After the destruction of the Second Temple in the year 70 A.D., Rabbi Yochanan ben Zakkai, the head of the great academy in Yavneh, permitted the shofar to be blown on the Sabbath wherever there existed a central *Bet Din* (court of law). Generally, however, the practice of not blowing the shofar on the Sabbath was followed until the eleventh century, when Rabbi Isaac ben Jacob Alfasi declared it permissible. He was of the opinion that blowing the shofar was not work, and therefore it was permissible.

Most authorities did not accept Alfasi's opinion because, they argued, if the shofar were to be blown on the Sabbath it might lead to an infraction of Sabbath law. For example, the person delegated as the shofar blower might wish last-minute instructions from an expert and would carry the shofar, in violation of the Sabbath.

YOM KIPPUR

Why do some Jewish people wear sneakers on Yom Kippur?

When my own children were younger, I used to read to them a children's book called *Sneakers to Shule*. It does seem a bit funny sometimes to see a man dressed in a fancy suit or a woman in an elegant dress, both of whom are wearing sneakers on Yom Kippur.

As a holy day, Yom Kippur has additional prohibitions that add to the solemnity of the day. We are forbidden to eat, drink, bathe, anoint ourselves, engage in sexual relations, or wear leather shoes. Because leather shoes were considered an apparel of luxury, abstaining from wearing them was deemed a suitable form of self-deprivation. Another reason for not wearing leather shoes is that the entire day serves as a vivid reliving of the Temple days. Leather shoes were forbidden in holy places; the kohanim had to remove their shoes when they went up to pronounce the Priestly Benediction.

Some rabbis have explained the practice of not wearing leather shoes on Yom Kippur as an expression of concern for the welfare of animals. On one of the holiest days of the year, we are to show our compassion to the animal kingdom.

When I fast on Yom Kippur, at a certain point all I think about is food. What good is that when I'm supposed to be praying?

It would not be normal for a person on Yom Kippur who is fasting to avoid thinking of food when feeling hungry, especially in the late afternoon when one has not eaten for almost twenty-four hours. It is important to know the reason and the meaning of fasting and refraining from food on this holy day. The Prophet Isaiah's message, part of the message of the haftarah on the morning of Yom Kippur, helps me answer your question.

The haftarah from the Book of Isaiah was designated for Yom Kippur because its main theme is the true purpose of fasting. Isaiah gives a powerful speech to the Israelites. It appears that his address was spoken during a convocation on a fast day, when the Jewish people performed all of the proper rituals, but without the emotions of self-cleansing. The prophet warns against a superficial religion, a religion of form and ritual without feeling and proper action. He declares that fasting and prayer are of no purpose if they do not induce just and merciful treatment of our fellow men. A true fast, he says, must result in breaking the shackles of evil and deep concern for those in need of help.

Thus it is not enough to think of food and your hunger while praying on Yom Kippur. Your abstaining from food must work to help arouse your sympathy for the plight of the hungry and needy.

Each year on Yom Kippur morning in our Temple, before this haftarah is chanted, I remind the congregation that there are really two fasts happening on Yom Kippur day. There is the fast of our congregants, who by fasting are trying to cleanse themselves and repent for their mistakes. At day's end, their fast will end, and they resume their daily affairs, along with their eating and drinking. There is another fast, one that did not begin on Yom Kippur eve and does not end with the setting of the sun at the end of the holy day. It is the involuntary fast of a billion people across God's earth, whose every day is a day of hunger. I remind our congregation that almost each and every day, forty thousand children under the age of five die of hunger.

What all of this means is that our Yom Kippur fast and our hunger for food are meant to help us never forget all of those who suffer from hunger and poverty. In our synagogue, and in many others, there is a project named after the Prophet Isaiah called "Operation Isaiah." Congregations send out several large vans, and members are encouraged throughout the High Holy Day Season to bring food donations to be given to a local food pantry. In addition, many congregants may choose to donate to an organization known as MAZON, which works to provide food for thousands who are in need.

Next year on Yom Kippur, when you begin to feel hungry and are thinking about food, don't forget to think about all of those who have no food to eat, and do your God-given part to help them in every way that you can.

❦ Sukkot ❦

What is the lulav and etrog?

The Bible designates four plants as essential for observance of the holy days of Sukkot: "On the first day you shall bring the fruit of goodly trees, branches of palm trees, boughs of leafy trees, and willows of the brook, and you shall rejoice before God seven days" (Leviticus 23:40). In Hebrew, these plants are called *arba minim*, the "four species." Each has its own special meaning.

The lulav (palm branch), tall and straight, represents the spine. Three sprigs of *hadasim* (myrtle leaves, symbolizing eyes) are tied to the right side of the lulav, and two sprigs of *aravot* (willow leaves, symbolizing the mouth) are tied to the left side of the lulav. The etrog (citron), representing the heart, looks like an enlarged lumpy lemon. The spine, as well as one's eyes, mouth, and heart, are all important to praying to God with fervor and enthusiasm.

There are many other explanations for use of the lulav and etrog on Sukkot. The Midrash compares them to types of Jews. For example, the etrog has both taste and fragrance, while the palm has taste but no fragrance. The myrtle has fragrance but no taste, and the willow has neither taste nor fragrance. Similarly, some Jews have both learning and good deeds, while some have learning but no good deeds. Others have good deeds but no learning, while still others have neither learning nor good deeds. Which type of person are you?

Why do some Jews eat and sleep in the sukkah?

The Bible (Leviticus 23:42) says "you shall dwell in booths for seven days, in order that your generations may know that I made the Israelites dwell in booths." Because of this biblical commandment,

Jewish people who choose to follow this mitzvah leave their elegant homes to dwell in the sukkah, which is reminiscent of desert life lacking in all convenience and comfort.

More observant families eat, and sometimes sleep, in their sukkah. These Jews take the words in Leviticus 23, "You shall live in booths," literally. They interpret the word *live* to mean that one should eat and sleep in the sukkah.

If your family has never built a sukkah before, you might want to offer them some encouragement, since eating in one can be so much fun. Today there are many companies that sell prefabricated ones that can be assembled easily and quickly. Many historians believe that the Pilgrims who came to America modeled their own celebration and feast after that of Sukkot—known to them as Tabernacles, which they knew about from reading the Bible.

Why is the lulav waved in various directions on Sukkot?

Sukkot always arrives in the autumn, marking the official start of the rainy season in Israel. Many centuries ago in Israel, farmers were anxious about having enough rainfall to properly irrigate their fields. The waving ritual of the lulav was a way of asking God to bless them with sufficient rain. To indicate that the presence of God is everywhere, the lulav is waved symbolically in all directions: three times each to the east, north, west, and south, and then upward toward heaven and downward to earth.

✻ Hanukkah ✻

Why do we celebrate Hanukkah?

Hanukkah commemorates the deliverance of the Jews from the oppression of the Syrian-Greeks in the second century B.C.E. Antiochus Epiphanes, the Hellenistic king of the Syrian branch of Alexander's empire, decreed that local religions, including Judaism, be rooted out. Circumcision, kosher food, and observing the Sabbath were outlawed on pain of death. Pagan rituals and sacrifices were instituted at the Holy Temple in Jerusalem and at shrines throughout the land.

Many Jews, filled with admiration for the power of worldly wisdom of Hellenistic culture, followed the direction and obeyed the decrees of Antiochus. But others, committed to Torah, were filled with fury at the oppressive decrees. They rallied under the leadership of Mattathias the priest, and his five sons, who came to be called the Maccabees.

In the year 165 B.C.E., the Syrian-Greek armies were defeated, after which the Temple was cleansed of impurities and rededicated. The Jews celebrated the rededication of the altar for eight days. Then Judah Maccabee and his brothers, and the whole congregation of Israel, decreed that the rededication of the altar should be observed with joy and gladness at the same season each year, for eight days, beginning on the twenty-fifth of Kislev. Jewish people throughout the world kindle the *hanukkiah*, the eight-branched Hanukkah candelabrum, which includes a ninth branch, called the *shamash*, used to light the other branches.

Why do we give gifts on Hanukkah?

Gift giving was originally part of the early Purim tradition, but not of the Hanukkah tradition. Some families from Eastern European Jewish communities, on the fifth night of Hanukkah, gathered for a special family night during which children were given Hanukkah money, called *gelt*. Among Sephardic Jews of Salonica, gifts of clothing and useful household items were traditionally given to newlyweds at Hanukkah, whereas children received candy and money.

Giving gifts on Hanukkah is not, as is sometimes implied, merely imitative of Christmas. Both customs undoubtedly originate from a similar human desire to add joyousness to the somber days of winter, each religion explaining its traditional gift giving by relating it to the origin of the respective holiday. But it may be true that Jews have increased the significance and character of gift giving in response to living in a secular and commercial culture that puts such an emphasis on this tradition during the Christmas season.

Many families in my congregation have a new tradition of dedicating each night of Hanukkah to a type of gift. For example, on one night children might choose to give to their grandparents. On another night, everyone recites an original poem. On the last night of Hanukkah, everyone bestows a gift to a charity of his or her choosing, with the children's gifts matched by the parents.

Why do Jews eat potato latkes on Hanukkah?

In America, potato latkes are customarily eaten on Hanukkah because they are fried in oil, and oil symbolizes the miracle of the cruse of oil that lasted for eight days instead of one. I was in for a rude awakening on Hanukkah a few years ago when I visited Israel during the holiday. There, instead of eating potato pancakes Israelis were giving out free jelly donuts on every street corner in Jerusalem. Called *sufganiyot* in Hebrew, Israelis are known to eat donuts on Hanukkah, because they too are fried in oil and it is symbolic of the miracle of the holiday.

You will probably be surprised to learn that eating cheese is another tradition in many Jewish households on Hanukkah. In the Book of Judith in the Apocrypha, Judith feeds the Syrian-Greek army leader Holofernes salty cheese to encourage him to drink wine, just before he was lulled to sleep, only to be killed by Judith. In honor of Judith's bravery, many communities feature cheese dishes on Hanukkah.

Among other communities, various food traditions arose. The Yemenites claim the Maccabees ate a carrot stew. In Eastern Europe, most of the geese were slaughtered before Hanukkah since they were about as fat as they were going to get before the winter. Some of the meat was salted and stored away, and the rest made a festive meal for the holiday.

What's the difference between a hanukkiah and a Hanukkah menorah?

A *hanukkiah* and a *Hanukkah menorah* are one and the same, referring to the candelabrum designed to hold the Hanukkah candles. Today the preferable term is hanukkiah, which is a created word combining hanukkah and menorah. The hanukkiah is an adaptation of the ancient seven-branched menorah of the Holy Temple, one of the earliest symbols of the Jewish people.

When Judah Maccabee decreed an eight-day holiday to commemorate the rededication of the Temple, our ancestors began to kindle the eight lights of the festival. At first, people would simply line up ordinary clay oil lamps. But since multiple lamps of this type were required, the need for a single lamp with multiple wicks became evident.

The major difference between the menorah of the Temple and the hanukkiah is the number of branches: the Temple menorah had seven, while the hanukkiah had nine. Today, the hanukkiah comes in many shapes, sizes, and designs. As a lover of the game of baseball, one of my favorites is a hanukkiah in the shape of a baseball field, with each candle one of the baseball players. When you press a button, it plays "Take me out to the ballgame."

Who invented the dreidel game?

The most popular Hanukkah game is dreidel, played with a spinning top. It is a game of luck, where landing a top on certain letters means receiving appropriate rewards. Some scholars theorize that games of luck were attached to Hanukkah to reflect the "luck" of the victorious Maccabees. Others point to the need for an amusement to pass away the long dark evenings of the midwinter season.

Although many people think of the dreidel as the prototypical Jewish toy, it is but a variation of the spinning top some historians believe to have developed into a plaything from the spindle whorl used for spinning thread in ancient Japan. Jews throughout the ages have usually adapted games played in the surrounding culture to their own needs. It may well be that Jews played with tops during the Greco-Roman period. We know with more certainty, however, that the four-sided dreidel with which we are familiar became common as a Hanukkah amusement among Ashkenazic Jews at the beginning of the Middle Ages.

You might be surprised to learn that the dreidel's four Hebrew letters stand for Yiddish words. The *nun* stands for *nisht* ("nothing"), the gimel stands for *gantz* ("all"), the hei stands for *halb* ("half"), and the shin stands for *shtel* ("put"). Later, greater dignity was given to the dreidel by interpreting the Hebrew letters to stand for *nes gadol haya sham* ("a great miracle happened there"). In Israel, dreidels are made with the Hebrew letter *pe* (standing for *po*—"here") replacing the *shin*. The substitution signifies that in Israel "a great miracle happened here." Thus a simple game is transformed into a reminder of the Hanukkah story and of the modern miracle of the reborn Israel.

Hanukkah seems like a Jewish Christmas: they have a tree and we light candles; they give gifts and we give gifts. What's the difference?

What both Hanukkah and Christmas have in common is the happiness and joy that each brings to the family, and the family togetherness and desire to help others that each holiday seems to generate every year. The festive lights of both holidays continue to break the darkness of the winter sky, reminding us of the ever-continuing obligation to serve all of those in need, thus bringing some light and hope into their lives as well.

But although it is true that both Hanukkah and Christmas use lights and often have exchanging of gifts, the two holidays are not very similar at all. Hanukkah means "rededication," which refers to the eight-day rededication of the ancient Temple in Jerusalem, which had been defiled by the Syrian-Greeks. When the rabbis sensed that the military victory of the Maccabees was taking precedence in the minds of the Jewish people, they introduced the notion of the miraculous cruse of oil. According to tradition, the oil burned for eight days—or, at least, the miraculous victory was so great it seemed as if the Temple menorah glowed throughout the eight-day festival of rededication. Gift giving was part of the early Purim tradition, but not of Hanukkah. In Eastern Europe, on the fifth night of Hanukkah, families gathered for a special family night during which children were given Hanukkah gelt (money). Later, when Christians and Jews mingled more freely, Jews were influenced by the Christian tradition of giving gifts to children at Christmas time. Soon, Jewish parents began the practice of giving gifts other than Hanukkah gelt to their children.

Unlike Hanukkah, which celebrates rededication of the Temple, Christians around the world celebrate Christmas as the birthday of Jesus. The word *Christmas* is actually a contraction of the phrase "Christ's mass," which is a service of worship honoring Jesus, known as the Christ child.

Although Christmas is celebrated on the twenty-fifth day of December each year, the exact date of Jesus' birth is unknown. Most biblical scholars agree that the birth, in fact, did not take place in December at all, but probably during the spring of the year. December 25 was supposedly chosen not by Christians but by Romans, the traditional antagonists of the Early Church. Each year, as the days became noticeably shorter in November and December, the Roman citizens feared that the earth might be "dying." With the return of the sun at the end of December resulting in longer days, the Romans celebrated the Feast of the Sol Invictus (Feast of the Unconquerable Sun) on December 25. In the fourth century, a Roman bishop ordered that all Christians celebrate the birth of Jesus on that day. Many scholars believe that the bishop chose this date so that Christians, still members of an outlaw religion in the eyes of the Romans, could celebrate the birth of their Savior without danger of revealing their religious conviction, while their Roman neighbors celebrated another event.

❧ Purim ❧

Why is God's name not mentioned in the Story of Esther?

There are two biblical books in which God's name does not appear. One is the Song of Songs, and the other is the Scroll of Esther, which is also known as the Megillah. There is a theory that since the Book of Esther was written in the form of a scroll and was sent out as a letter to all the outlying districts of Persia, the name of God was omitted lest the letter be desecrated or otherwise improperly handled.

Concealed in its chapters, rabbis have discovered many signs of God's presence. The signs take on numerous forms. For example, in at least four places in the Scroll of Esther the Hebrew letters of God's name (*yud, hey, vav, hey*) are formed by acrostics in final letters of words or initial letters of words, sometimes read forward, sometimes read backward. For example, in Esther 1:20, the name *YHVH* is formed by the initial letters of four successive words when read backward: *hee vechol hanashim yitnu* ("it, and all the women will give").

One new interpretation of God's whereabouts in the book concerns the Hebrew word *yehudim*, the word meaning Jews, which appears thirty-eight times in the Book of Esther. Thirty-two times it is spelled in the traditional way (*yod-he-vav-dalet-yod-mem*). The other six times, however, an extra *yod* is inserted before the final *mem*, so that there are two *yods* together. It has been explained by modern interpreters that the extra *yod* is trying to tell us something. Since the letter *yod* itself means *yad* ("a hand"), and since two *yods* are a common abbreviation for God, it has been argued that they stand for the name of God. Together, the combined meaning of the double *yod* could be the hand of God. Thus, according to this theory, "hand of God" appears six times in the word "Jews" because there are six separate occasions in the story of Esther where divine intervention rescues either a Jew or the Jews as a whole.

Whatever you believe or think about these interesting theories, you should always remember that at all times we must work hard to search for God's presence. If we seek hard enough, we shall find!

Why are hamantachen served on Purim?

One of the most popular foods eaten on Purim is *hamantachen*. This word is said to have derived from a German word meaning "Haman's pockets." Hamantachen are triangular pastries filled with fruit, cheese, or poppy seeds. My wife also likes to make them with raspberry, blueberry, peanut butter, and chocolate chip fillings. One explanation for the name hamantachen is that Haman stuffed his pockets with bribe money.

Originally, hamantachen were called *mohn taschen*, "poppy seed pockets." A seed filling was used because the Hebrew word for "seed" (poppy seed) is *mohn* (manna). Mohn sounds like the Hebrew pronunciation of the second syllable of the name Haman. It has been said that these three-cornered pastries are eaten as a reminder of the type of hat worn by Haman when he was second in command to the King of Persia. There is no evidence for this claim, and many believe the shape was introduced in the early nineteenth century to copy the Napoleonic triangular hat. The more traditional explanation is that the strength of Queen Esther was derived from her antecedents, and the three cornered hamantach represents the three Jewish patriarchs: Abraham, Isaac, and Jacob.

In Israel, hamantachen also go under the name of *oznay Haman*, meaning Haman's ears. It was once the practice to cut off the ears of criminals before hanging. Since the criminal Haman was hanged, a special holiday pastry called "ears of Haman" was introduced. In Holland, the pastry is called *Hamansoren*, and in Italy *orecchi d'Aman*.

What is the origin of the Purim noisemaker?

Haman was the archenemy of the Persian Jews. In a sense, he continues to epitomize all enemies of the Jewish people throughout the ages. Using a noisemaker, or *greggar*, whenever Haman's name is mentioned is a method of "erasing" his name and fulfills the verse in the Bible (Exodus 17:14) that says "I will utterly erase the remembrance of Amalek from under the heavens." Haman's ancestors were considered to be the Amalekites.

Among the variety of methods used to "erase" Haman's name, the most literal was to write the name of Haman on two smooth stones or slates and then rub them and knock them together whenever Haman's name was mentioned during the reading of the Megillah, or the Book of Esther. Some people like to write Haman's name on the bottom of their shoes and stomp their feet whenever they hear Haman's name as part of the Megillah reading.

Why do Jews have masquerading and carnivals on Purim?

The Talmud says that when Adar (the month in which Purim falls) arrives, joy should be increased. Because Purim is a time of ultimate joy and the Jewish people were saved from an enemy intent on totally destroying them, the custom has been to allow frivolity, masquerading, and carnivals. Carnivals and dressing up are a part of the Purim tradition around the world. When I was ten years old, I dressed up in a Queen Esther costume and won my first Purim contest!

In our Temple, we ask everyone to attend the reading of the Megillah in costume. Nowadays almost everyone obliges, and many in the congregation try to guess what my costume is going to be. One of my best was a couple of years ago, when I dressed up as the popular Harry Potter, using the original eyeglasses from my Bar Mitzvah!

In many communities, there are parades on Purim afternoon, with food, dance, and costumes galore. Some families invite others to their home for the traditional *Purim shpiel.* Families serve many delicacies and put on funny little skits to the delight of all the members, who poke fun at each other in a humorous way.

❧ Passover ❧

Why are firstborn required to fast before Passover?

The custom of the firstborn fasting on Passover eve is based on the biblical account in the Book of Exodus (12:21–28), in which all Egyptian firstborn were slain and the firstborn Israelites were spared. The Hebrew word *pasach* means to "pass over" or "to spare."

To commemorate and say thanks for the sparing of the Israelite firstborn, the day preceding Passover became a fast day for the firstborn male in each family. In time the requirement changed. The fast is excused if the firstborn undertook to study a Talmudic tractate and to complete its studies on the day before Passover.

Today that practice is often assumed by the local rabbi. In our congregation on the eve of Passover, after the morning prayer service, I gather all the participants and study and teach them the conclusion of the talmudic tractate I have been studying in anticipation of the event. The practice is called a *siyyum* in Hebrew, which means completing. Since eating at such an occasion is a *seudat mitzvah* (a mitzvah meal), the first born who are present at the study session may join in the festivities and eat. Each year, our ritual committee provides us with the goodies. It is quite common for firstborn daughters to attend the siyyum as well.

🌱 The Seder 🌱

Why do we eat matzah on Passover?

Eating matzah, or unleavened bread, on Passover symbolizes the haste with which the people of Israel had to leave Egypt. According to the Book of Exodus (12:24), the Israelites "took up their dough before it had time to leaven." Eating matzah reminds us of the poverty and affliction of our ancestors while under the oppression of tyrants.

The commandment of eating matzah is further amplified in Deuteronomy 16:3: "For seven days thereafter you shall eat unleavened bread, for you departed from the land of Egypt in a hurry—so that you may remember the day of your departure from the land of Egypt as long as you live." The implication of this verse, as interpreted by the rabbis, is that it is mandatory to eat matzah on the first night of Passover, and it is optional to eat it for the balance of the week so long as *hametz* (leaven) is not eaten. In our congregation, most people choose to eat matzah all through the festival of Passover.

Every family probably has its favorite brand of matzah. Ours is Rakusen, a British-made matzah. We like it because it is very crispy, and comes in a smaller size than most other matzahs. We also like to serve *matzah shemurah* (guarded matzah) at both seder meals. This matzah, which is round in shape and handmade, is specially prepared from wheat that is watched from the moment of harvesting so that no moisture should touch it. Although at times it can taste like cardboard, we at our Seder like it because it looks absolutely authentic and each piece is different from the next.

Why do Jews celebrate Passover with a seder?

The original Passover service (not yet called a seder) is described in Exodus: a lamb was to be slaughtered and was to be consumed by families. It is not clear when the first "modern" formal seder was conducted. Some have said that Rabbi Gamaliel II, at the end of the first century C.E., may have begun the tradition. It was he who said, "Anyone who has not said these three words on Passover has not done his duty: *Pesach* (Passover lamb), matzah (unleavened bread), and *maror* (bitter herbs).

The seder has often been described as a "talk-feast." Conducted around a table with family, relatives, and friends, it is people spending a leisurely evening engaged in good talk and food.

The word *seder* means order and refers both to the Passover meal and the order of the essential parts of the seder service, found in the Haggadah, the book that contains the readings and prayers that are sung at the meal.

The seder is celebrated on the first and second evenings of Passover. Essentially the ceremony consists of telling the story of the Israelite escape from Egypt after four hundred years of slavery. Various food items each have their own lesson: the hard-boiled egg is the symbol of life, and it is dipped in salt water in sympathy with the bitter lot of our ancestors. For the same reason, bitter herbs are eaten. A mixture of nuts and apples reminds the family of the mortar used by the Hebrew slaves in building cities for the cruel taskmasters. The number four is prominent throughout the seder service. There are four questions, four sons, and four cups of wine, symbolizing the fourfold divine promise of liberation. Matzah, perhaps the most essential food at the seder, is a reminder of the joyous eagerness that marked the departure from slavery into freedom.

In addition to family, relatives, and friends, there is also a custom to welcome any person who has no place to go to celebrate a seder. At our Temple, we make sure to publicize that our homes are open to any person or family in need of a place to celebrate.

One of my most memorable seders was when I invited our local United Methodist minister, who happens to be a close friend of mine. It was his first seder ever, and was I surprised when he was able to follow and even read some of the Hebrew. For my two children, their seder highlight was when we invited a member of Temple Sholom who just happened to be a professional clown and magician. You can't image the fun that we all had as he did all kinds of magic tricks and stunts throughout the entire seder meal!

Why does Elijah appear at the Passover seder?

One of the highlights at our Passover seder each year is the opening of the door for Elijah. Each year we have a different person dress up as Elijah and wait outside the door for the grand entrance. When Elijah enters, each seder participant is allowed to ask him questions.

Elijah was a prophet from Gilead who was the outstanding religious leader of his time. The Bible (Kings II 2:1–11) records that he did not die but was carried to heaven in a chariot pulled by horses of fire. A later prophet, Malachi, built onto this legend with his prophecy that Elijah would be sent by God before the coming of the great and terrible days of God. Thus began the connection between Elijah and the promise of the Messianic age.

For centuries, many legends and much folklore surrounding Elijah have firmly established him as the forerunner of the Messiah. He is not considered to be the actual Messiah, but he will herald the future redemption of Israel. We remember Elijah daily in the *Birkat HaMazon*, the blessing after the meal, and weekly at the end of the service during the service known as *Havdalah*.

The popular legend of Elijah quickly became associated with the Passover seder and its theme of redemption. Stories of visiting the homes of every Jewish family on Passover probably stem from another popular view of Elijah as a kind of heavenly messenger sent to earth to combat injustice. On Passover eve, he is said to punish misers and provide necessities for the seder to the poor. His appearance at the seder is to announce the coming of the Messiah.

Today it is customary to have a special cup filled with wine, called Elijah's cup, which sits on the Passover table awaiting Elijah's grand entrance at the end of the seder, after the meal, when most families open their front door so he may enter. Many children in our congregation have spoken of how they have seen the wine in the cup disappearing when Elijah makes his entrance into their homes.

How many different Passover Haggadahs are there?

Since the first Haggadah appeared in book form in approximately the thirteenth century, more than four thousand Haggadot have been published in almost every country where Jews live in substantial numbers. Usually the Hebrew text has been accompanied by a translation into the language of its own country, along with commentary and illustrations.

The Haggadah is basically an anthology of prayers and readings. Some of the prayers date back to the time of King David, who was said to have written many of the Psalms in the Book of Psalms. Newer prayers include those for the state of Israel and prayers in memory of those who died in the Holocaust.

I enjoy collecting Haggadot, and I probably have more than one hundred. Among my special ones is a pop-up Haggadah for children, with pictures that pop up and objects that can move across the page. I also have an amazing one called the Moss Haggadah. This Haggadah was written and illustrated by David Moss, a friend of mine from college, who spent three years working on the project. Along with an original commentary, it also has original artwork, pictures, and even some mirrors built into some of its pages.

One of the highlights of my writing career was the creation of a Haggadah that I coauthored with a reform rabbi. It's called the Discovery Haggadah, and it is enjoyed in many synagogue school seders as well as family seders throughout the country. The Haggadah consists of many questions, games to play, new songs, and other activities that allow people to discover many new things about Passover and its celebration. It even has an original rap song written by one of our Hebrew schoolteachers and her students. So it's not uncommon for many new Haggadahs to be written every year by individuals, families, and other educational and spiritual groups who want to create their own tradition and way of having a seder.

Why do we hide the afikoman?

Afikoman, first mentioned in the Talmud (Mishna, Pesachim 10:8), is the piece of matzah broken off from the central of the three matzahs used in the seder service. The word itself is of Greek origin and denotes something served after the meal in the form of entertainment or food.

Breaking the middle matzah in two and hiding the afikoman, which is shared by all at the table at the conclusion of the meal, are intended to awaken the children's curiosity. It has been suggested that the afikoman is wrapped in a napkin as a symbol of the unleavened dough that, wrapped in their garments, the Israelites carried on their shoulders out of Egypt. In many Sephardic homes, there is a moment during the Passover seder when participants actually place a piece of matzah on their shoulders to recall this event.

The custom of encouraging children to snatch the afikoman and make it disappear for a while, until a promise of a gift has been obtained, is said to be based on a misinterpretation of the talmudic statement (Pesachim 109a), which reads, "The matzot are eaten hastily on the nights of Passover so that the children shall not fall asleep."

At our Passover Seder we employ a really fun way of letting the kids search for the afikoman. Instead of kids having to find the afikoman, they look for various letters of the English alphabet hidden throughout the living and dining rooms. They are told how many letters are hidden, and that when they find them and unscramble them, the answer will spell out the place where the afikoman has been hidden.

Chapter 5

❧ ❧

Circumcision

Why do we still observe *brit milah*? Isn't it barbaric? If we're against cultures doing female circumcision, why do we do male circumcision?

A few years ago, a member of our congregation who gave birth to a boy called me to tell me she did not intend to have her son circumcised, because "she thought it was dangerous and barbaric" to do so. I was successful in convincing her that circumcision was a safe procedure, and that we have been doing it as a people ever since Abraham was circumcised back in Bible times. Female circumcision, often done against the will of young women in many African countries, is a dangerous and painful procedure; in no way can it be compared to ritual circumcision.

According to the Bible, Abraham was commanded by God to be circumcised as a sign of God's covenant. He was ninety-nine years old at the time and did his own circumcision in addition to circumcising his children. The circumcision became a symbol for Abraham and his descendants that they would continue to follow in God's ways and obey God's commandments. Since that time brit milah continues to be performed on the eighth day after birth as a sign of the covenant, and not merely as a surgical procedure. The baby boy is also given his official Hebrew name at this ceremony.

Throughout Jewish history, circumcision has held a powerful religious influence on the Jewish people. The first major crisis in connection with the brit milah occurred during the reign of King Antiochus (in the Book of the Maccabees). Although the king prohibited the Jews from circumcising their children, they persisted, even at the risk of losing their lives. It continues to have survived every challenge put to it, including a major one from anticircumcision movements in the world today.

Brit milah may be held in the synagogue, the hospital, or the home. Today the home seems to be everyone's first choice, since its environment is warm and most conducive to a family gathering.

Does a baby have to be circumcised to become Jewish?

According to *halacha*, traditional Jewish law, a baby born to a Jewish mother is considered a Jew whether or not he is circumcised. Failure of the parents to perform the mitzvah of circumcision does not alter the child's identity as a Jew.

Chapter 6

❧ ❧

Bar Mitzvah and Bat Mitzvah

Why do we say that a Jew is a man at thirteen or a woman at twelve when we don't treat twelve- and thirteen-year-olds as adults?

This question is based on a common misconception. We don't actually say that a Jew is a man or a woman at that age, but rather that he or she is "becoming a man" or "becoming a woman." According to Jewish law, when a girl reaches age twelve (according to her Hebrew birthday) and when a boy is thirteen (according to his Hebrew birthday), the young person has reached the age of being responsible for performance of mitzvot, or religious obligations. Instead of calling the young person a man or a woman on achieving this milestone, I prefer to use the word "young adult," which is much less misleading.

Beginning in the second or third century C.E., Jewish girls at age twelve took on legal responsibility for performing these commandments. As with age thirteen for boys, twelve likely corresponded to the age of the onset of puberty. Today the custom is usually to allow both boys and girls to have their Bar Mitzvah or Bat Mitzvah sometime within the thirteenth year. When this occurs, they are officially obligated in Jewish tradition to accept upon themselves the many new privileges and obligations that await them.

At our Temple, becoming a Bar Mitzvah or Bat Mitzvah does not only mean chanting a haftarah or reading from the Torah at a synagogue service. It also means assuming new and greater responsibility. As do many other synagogues, we require each student in the last year of elementary Hebrew school to do a mitzvah project, involving many types of obligation. Students choose to visit and perform services for a nursing home, or go to a local food kitchen to give or serve food to the hungry; some sponsor a clothing drive and collect all kinds of apparel to be donated to people in need of clothing.

These are clearly activities that grown-ups are also involved in, and by requiring them of our students we tell them they have now entered into adult-type activity. It is true that becoming a Bar Mitzvah or Bat Mitzvah does not entitle a student to get a driver's license and drive a car as an adult. Nor can a thirteen-year-old order a beer at a bar, just because he or she has become a Bar Mitzvah or Bat Mitzvah. But at our Temple we do try to treat our twelve- and thirteen-year-olds as young adults, expecting them to take on added responsibility as they continue to grow into mature adulthood.

Is it true that a person automatically becomes a Bar Mitzvah or Bat Mitzvah on reaching thirteen or twelve, and that the synagogue service has little, if anything, to do with it?

Historically, the Bar Mitzvah and then later the Bat Mitzvah represented a Jewish rite of passage when a child reached the age of being responsible for performing mitzvot. According to Jewish law, these new responsibilities occurred when a boy reached age thirteen and a girl twelve. Technically speaking, then, whether children at age twelve or thirteen choose to have a Bar Mitzvah or Bat Mitzvah in the synagogue, they are still obligated to fulfill religious obligations. The problem is, how will they be able to do it without formal study, training, and preparation?

For this reason, synagogues require formal religious study along with a year of Bar Mitzvah and Bat Mitzvah training as a requirement for the privilege of having one's Bar Mitzvah or Bat Mitzvah at a synagogue service. It is also highly advisable that children studying for their Bar Mitzvah or Bat Mitzvah attend worship services regularly, enabling them to completely familiarize themselves with the prayers and the customs of their particular synagogue.

A few years ago, I wrote a book with a Reform colleague, Rabbi Kerry Olitzky, called *Doing Mitzvot*. The book contains a series of mitzvah projects that we require of all of our students, in order that they truly understand the meaning of becoming a responsible Jewish adult.

Also, it is never too late to celebrate a Bar Mitzvah or Bat Mitzvah. In our congregation, there are both men and women who for whatever reason never had a formal Bar Mitzvah or Bat Mitzvah observance and celebration in a synagogue. Over the years, we have offered an adult Bar Mitzvah and Bat Mitzvah class that has allowed more than one hundred men and women to become a Bar Mitzvah or Bat Mitzvah during a synagogue service. A member of our Temple who was already well into her eighties is our oldest Bat Mitzvah to date.

Chapter 7

❧ ❧

Marriage

Why shouldn't Jews marry non-Jews?

A cry of anguish was heard from a rabbi in a southwestern city. "Woe," he wrote, "we are intermarrying out of existence." Of every four Jews who marry, two are marrying non-Jews. Because of these developments, many Jews have become deeply concerned about marriage outside of the faith.

The topic has spilled out beyond those who decided they wanted to convert to Judaism. It is estimated that more than ten thousand people convert to Judaism each year in the United States. Although many conversions occur prior to marriage, some others occur after a marriage but prior to the birth of a child. Others are precipitated by a desire for family togetherness and the need of people in love to share every aspect of their lives with each other. Still others choose Judaism out of personal conviction that it is the most meaningful way of life for them, and that being a Jew is right for their own sense of identity and the definition of their personality.

My personal experience with Jews by choice, those who convert to Judaism, is that they tend to be the most "serious-minded" when it comes to religious practice. Many are leaders in our congregation and take an active role in a variety of synagogue committees. One woman in our congregation, a Jew-by-choice who is the daughter of a Presbyterian minister, was the chairperson for many years of our Jewish

Family Matters committee, responsible for designing and implementing all family programs in the synagogue.

There are many advantages to a Jewish marriage over a mixed marriage. A Jewish couple is able to share the warmth and strength of Jewish customs and observances, song and prayer, food and literature without the need for constant explanation and interpretation. When having a family, the children are not torn between two religious traditions, nor are they denied religious training because of conflicting beliefs that can sometimes lead to total avoidance. Growing up in a household with two faiths, and having to choose one over the other, is very difficult. When young people raised in a mixed marriage set out to establish their own religious identity, they often feel as if they are being forced to choose one parent over another.

Is it true that Judaism allows polygamy? Why weren't women allowed to have more than one husband?

In Biblical times there were patriarchal societies. Men were the acquiring agents of women, not the other way around. Therefore it stands to reason that biblical law would not allow a woman to have more than one husband.

In Bible times, men were allowed to be polygamous and have more than one wife. Abraham not only had Sarah and Hagar as wives but there were others too, including Keturah, after whom a kibbutz in the south of Israel is named. The wives had differing status back in biblical times. When a man took a second wife or concubine, it was often because of infertility. Thus Abraham took Sarah's handmaid, Hagar, as his concubine when Sarah seemed hopelessly sterile.

His unscrupulous father-in-law, Laban, tricked Jacob into marrying Leah. He ultimately was able to marry his beloved Rachel, Leah's sister, thus marrying two sisters—a practice later outlawed by the Torah. Kings of Israel were permitted by the Bible to marry several wives and maintain a harem; David and Solomon followed this system. Solomon had more than one thousand wives. It has been theorized that he did this for political reasons, since each wife had a father who would now be officially connected to the kingship.

The system of polygamy was fraught with tension and jealousy, as is clearly seen in the conflicts between Sarah and Hagar, Rachel and Leah, Hannah and Peninah, and others. The ideal marriage is a monogamous union with a single wife only, as evidenced by the Adam and Eve story.

In approximately the year 1000 C.E., the highly respected German authority Rabbenu Gershom ben Yehuda issued a ban on all polygamous marriage, but only the Ashkenazic communities abided by this edict. Jews who lived in Moslem countries continued to marry more than one woman until as recently as 1950, when the Chief Rabbinate of Israel extended the ban to all Jews.

You might be interested to know about some of the other enactments attributed to Rabbenu Gershom, which were far ahead of their time. People must respect the privacy of mail. The owner of a privately owned synagogue may not refuse admission to a worshiper because of a personal grievance. A divorce must not be forced upon a woman. If absence or poverty makes it impossible for a husband to support his wife, the community must provide for her. One who is summoned to court by a messenger must attend. These enactments are still in force today, almost a thousand years after they were initiated. But the enactment for which Rabbenu Gershom will be remembered forever is: only one wife per husband!

Chapter 8

🌿 🌿

Keeping Kosher

I love shrimp. Why should I stop eating it?

Back in my childhood days before I became kosher, I too liked eating shrimp, never thinking that I might one day want to stop eating it. If you ask most Jews why the laws of keeping kosher exist, you are likely to receive this authoritative reply: "It was a health measure. For example, pigs were forbidden to Jews so that Jews would not get trichinosis. But with modern health codes, we certainly don't need such measures today."

Unfortunately, this common opinion is an example of the "law of ignorant opinions authoritatively stated," which asserts that in politics and religion the less a person knows the more authoritatively he or she speaks.

Many of my own congregants are convinced that Jewish law does not constitute an ethical code but is really a health code. They tell me that *kashrut* is an ancient health measure that may have had its place in antiquity, but with modern methods of slaughtering, regular government inspection, and sanitary food preparation, is quite clearly an anachronism, which should be discarded along with the horse and carriage.

The facts, however, are different. The kosher laws are saturated with moral meaning. In Leviticus (11:44–45), after we are told which animals, fowl, and fish are permitted and which are forbidden, the reason for this long series of laws is at last given: "I am Adonai your God. Sanctify yourselves and be holy, for I am the Lord that brought you up out of the land of Egypt to be your God. You shall therefore be holy." This then is clearly the purpose and the goal of the kosher laws: not health but holiness. For me, the kosher laws are designed to hallow the act of eating by teaching us reverence for life.

First of all, kashrut teaches that eating meat is itself a sort of compromise. Adam, the first man, was not permitted to eat meat. As an inhabitant of the Garden of Eden, he and Eve were only permitted to eat fruits and vegetables (Genesis 1:27–29). After leaving the Garden of Eden, however, primitive man hunted and did so without consideration for the animal's suffering. Consequently, both for the animal's sake and for the sake of mankind's ethical development, laws were soon enacted to regulate the eating of animals.

First, people were forbidden to eat the limb of a living animal. Next, the Torah forbade eating an animal's blood. The purpose of this ancient law was to induce revulsion at bloodshed, and it seems that there is indeed a direct correlation between the Torah's prohibition of eating blood and a lower incidence of homicide among Jews.

Later, to prevent the Jews from going out and killing any animal they saw, the Torah, realistically compromising with its vegetarian ideal, divided the animal kingdom into permitted ones (kosher) and those not permitted. At the same time, Judaism instituted its laws of slaughter, the primary aim of which was to reduce the suffering of the slaughtered animals as much as possible. Thus, the laws that put half of the animal kingdom off limits to Jewish tables in conjunction with the laws ensuring humane slaughter of the permitted half make up the systematic ethics of Judaism with regard to food.

Every time a Jew sits down to eat a kosher meal, he or she is reminded that the animal to be eaten is a creature of God, that the death of such a creature cannot be taken lightly, that hunting for sport is forbidden, and that we cannot treat any living thing irresponsibly.

One of the most important books that I've read on kashrut is the *Jewish Dietary Laws: The Meaning for Our Time,* written by Rabbi Samuel Dresner. He wrote: "In eating a slice of bread, we can discover God, in drinking a cup of wine, we can sanctify the Sabbath, in preparing a piece of meat we can learn something of the reverence of life."

My father-in-law, a professor at the University of Houston, once told me a story about a student who would often join him for lunch. The university cafeteria was not kosher, so the only thing my father-in-law would eat each day was an all-vegetarian house salad. The student asked him, "Is there a reason why you only order and eat the salad every day?" He answered: "I'm Jewish, and each day when I eat the salad, I am reminded of who I am and what being Jewish means to me."

Is it true that killing animals the kosher way is painful for the animal?

On the contrary! Judaism has a distinguished record on the issue of proper treatment of animals. We may use animals for our benefit and are even permitted to kill them for food, but at the same time it is an absolute requirement to minimize their pain and suffering. Thus, with regard to the laws of kosher slaughtering, we must be meticulous in seeing that the sharpness of the knife causes as speedy and painless a death to an animal as possible.

Any extending of the animal's death agony renders its meat *treif*, strictly forbidden. The Jewish ritual slaughterer thus has both an economic and a moral incentive to hasten the animal's death. Concern for animal welfare is as a result cited as one good reason to keep kosher. In fact, the laws of kashrut are traditionally cited as yielding the most humane methods of slaughter.

Treating animals with kindness is one of the most important values in Judaism. The concept in Hebrew is known as *tzaar baalei hayyim* and is derived in part from the biblical passages suggesting that we assist in unloading burdens from beasts and returning lost animals to their rightful owners. Animals do possess sensitivity and the capacity for feeling pain, and because God is concerned with all of creation, God wants them to be protected and treated with compassion and justice.

I've always felt that the ideal Jewish diet is vegetarian. After all, it was only after the Flood that human beings were permitted to eat meat. Adam and Eve, in the ideal Garden of Eden, were only permitted the produce of the fruit trees as food to be eaten. However, the advent of the dietary laws of keeping kosher has created a good working compromise, allowing us to eat animal flesh while creating limits that spare the animal undue pain, while at the same time refining our sense of compassion.

What do the little letters on food packages mean, signifying food is kosher?

Various organizations, generally in cooperation with well-trained Orthodox rabbis, supervise the manufacture of and processing of kosher foods. A company wishing to have its food certified kosher must apply to one of these organizations; they carefully investigate manufacturing techniques and ingredients to determine whether they meet the kashrut standards of the kosher certifying organization. There are currently more than ten thousand food products certified kosher by these various organizations.

More than one hundred organizations nationwide offer rabbinic certification, and each has its own symbol that appears on a food product. One of the most popular and largest is the Union of Orthodox Congregations, which certifies thousands of products manufactured by more than one thousand firms. They are known as the OU; their symbol is a letter *U* with a circle around it. One of the smallest operations is an individual rabbi in Pittsburgh who certifies a brand of soft drink.

Occasionally a *P* or *D* appears near the symbol of the certifier. The *P* stands for *pareve* (indicating the food is not a dairy product and can therefore be eaten with a dairy meal or a meat meal) and the *D* for *dairy*. For foods that are kosher for Passover, one sometimes find a *P* next to the symbol, which stands for Passover. Food items certified as kosher are not necessarily kosher for Passover, unless so stated on the box or label.

Some kosher products simply carry the letter *K* on their packaging to indicate that they are under rabbinic supervision but not necessarily Orthodox supervision. The name of the certifying agent can be determined by writing directly to the manufacturer.

When I first became a rabbi, I became the rabbinic certifier of a local kosher bakery. One big thrill was making spot checks each week to examine the ingredients of the breads and cakes, and also to investigate the fillings used in the pastries. I created my own rubber stamp with my name on it, which I used to stamp the baked good packages as either "dairy" or "pareve" (nonmilk). I enjoyed visiting the bakery each week. What was even more fun was getting and eating the cherry pastries when they came out hot, right from the oven. That was the entire payment for my services!

Does keeping kosher have anything to do with health?

Some of my students have told me that many forbidden aquatic creatures (those that do not have scales) when eaten yield a higher level of cholesterol than kosher fish does. Although this may be, the Bible was clearly unconcerned with the hazards of too much cholesterol. In reality, there is no evidence that kosher eating is necessarily a healthier diet than nonkosher.

With the exception of holiness, the Bible does not present a rationale for the laws of keeping kosher. The most common misconception about the kosher laws is that they are an ancient health measure that may have had a place in antiquity but, what with modern methods of slaughtering, regular government inspection, and sanitary food preparation, are quite clearly an anachronism that should be discarded. Of course, one should not overlook concern for disease and the attempt to achieve purity in the kosher laws. However, if Jews have derived any healthy benefits from observing the dietary laws (such as a lower incidence of trichinosis, which can be traced to eating pork), they have been unexpected.

I've heard the term "eco-kosher." What does that mean?

Many modern-day Jewish environmentalists observe the ancient connection between the Jews and the land. For example, the Book of

Deuteronomy warns that when in war if you besiege a city you must not destroy its trees.

Today, some environmentally conscious Jews are even supplementing the biblical laws of kashrut. For instance, along with just avoiding *treif* (nonkosher) foods such as ham and shellfish, they buy neither tomatoes treated with pesticides nor ecologically harmful cleaning products.

In the United States, factory farming has become a popular method of choice for raising animals, both kosher and nonkosher. The animals are often kept in cramped, despicable conditions. In the case of veal, which comes from a calf and is kosher, the problem is more extreme. To ensure the tenderness of the meat, factory farmed calves are immobilized in a contraption that does not permit them to graze. Instead, the head is positioned over a trough so that the animal can be force-fed until its final days. Some Jews today refrain from eating any kind of meat when there is knowledge that the animal from which the meat is produced is treated without true concern for its welfare.

Jews who consider eating veal to be treif and who do not buy vegetables treated with pesticides are known as eco-kosher. The concept of eco-kosher mandates living and consuming in accordance with the spirit of Jewish law.

As the greening of Judaism takes root across the country, eco-kosher is just one of many earth-friendly trends gaining momentum. Synagogues of all denominations are beginning to look for more ways to integrate ideas coming from the eco-kosher movement. To give a small example, in our own synagogue we try to use cloth table coverings instead of the disposable variety.

If you are interested in more information about this fast-growing eco-kosher movement, you can contact the Coalition on the Environment and Jewish Life (COEJL), headquartered in New York City.

What is "glatt kosher"?

The word *glatt* is Yiddish and means smooth. Originally in Talmudic law, it referred to an animal's lung. If the lung of a slaughtered animal was found to be damaged or in some way scarred, the meat of that animal was considered nonkosher.

Misconceptions about the meaning of glatt are widespread. If I were to ask members of my congregation the meaning of glatt kosher, the most usual answer would be "extra kosher," meaning a higher standard. Today it is common to find fish, candy, and even dairy products with the stamp of glatt on them. It is technically inaccurate to do this, since glatt specifically relates to animal foods.

If I keep kosher, can I eat at a nonkosher restaurant and just have fish or salad?

Some Jews do not eat in a restaurant even if there is a kosher sign on the window, and other Jews say they keep kosher and eat only certain foods, such as broiled fish and salad, in a nonkosher establishment. It all depends on the level of observance.

Jews who are extremely careful about their dietary observance do not eat in a restaurant unless they are certain the owner is an observant Jew. They also require the restaurant to be closed on the Sabbath and Jewish holidays. Others may choose to eat in a kosher restaurant even if it stays open on the Sabbath.

Owing to the small number of kosher restaurants in the United States and Canada (unless of course one lives in New York City, where kosher abounds), situations frequently arise that make it necessary to relax the strict standards of kashrut observed in the home. When in such a predicament, there are several principles one ought to consider.

A thorough investigation should be made to ascertain whether there are kosher facilities available within a reasonable distance. This might be a vegetarian or dairy restaurant. As a Conservative rabbi, I would always prefer a kosher facility even if a nonkosher one appears more appealing.

If it were necessary and desirable to dine in a restaurant that does not have rabbinic supervision, those who keep kosher at home would not eat meat and dishes containing meat. Some kashrut observers sanction eating cold foods, such as salads, if it contains no forbidden ingredients. Some approve eating permitted fish and other foods, even if cooked.

When students who observe the kosher laws choose a college, I am usually able to advise them about the availability of kosher food or facilities for doing one's own cooking. All national and international airlines provide kosher or vegetarian meals if requested ahead of time. This is also true of many hospitals, hotels, and resorts.

Chapter 9

❧ ❧

Women's Issues

Are women second-class citizens in Judaism?

One of the most sexist sit-com characters ever to appear on television was Archie Bunker, from "All in the Family." To prove his point that men were superior to women, Archie quoted one of the Jewish morning blessings: "Thank God I'm not a woman."

At first blush, this blessing certainly seems to imply male superiority over women. But in looking at the blessing in the context in which it was written, it essentially is a prayer that says thank-you to God for allowing me the privilege of performing all religious rites. Women did not have such a requirement because, according to our tradition, Jewish women are given an exemption from most religious duties that have to be carried out at a fixed time. Since women were so fully occupied in bygone years with their domestic duties, it was next to impossible for them to become involved in the social and religious affairs of the community. For this reason, they were excused from those rituals having a specific time of performance. Their responsibilities to children and family needed to take priority.

Thus the blessing "who has not made me a woman" was not intended to offend or imply inferiority, but to show gratitude for the full load of mitzvot that the Torah placed upon the Jewish male. Today, because of the potential negative connotation of that blessing, it has often been changed to read "Praised are You, God, who has made me in the divine image."

90

The more enlightened attitude of the talmudic sages to women is best reflected in such statements as "The Holy Blessed One gave a greater measure of understanding to woman than to man" (Talmud, Niddah 45b) or "a man, to know peace in his home, should honor his wife even more than his own self" (Talmud, Yevamot 62b). Throughout history, the status of the Jewish woman, though more limited than that of the Jewish man, was historically always higher and more privileged than in the case of her non-Jewish counterpart.

In the Western world over time, the social and communal role of Jewish women rose to greater and greater equality. In religious matters, however, change has been slower. In Orthodox practice (and in some traditional Conservative movement settings as well), women are not allowed to make up part of the minyan, and in Orthodox settings women are not allowed to sit with men (and vice versa). However, in most Conservative, Reform, and Reconstructionist branches of Judaism today, women are given full religious equality. Although traditional Orthodox rabbinic academies still do not allow ordination of female rabbis, all other branches of Judaism admit men and women into their cantorial and rabbinical schools. Like many other parts of world society, Judaism is gradually but definitely reducing the amount of sexism in its religious and secular culture.

Does a woman go to a mikveh after she menstruates because she is considered unclean?

First, let me tell you a little bit about the *mikveh* and its history. The word means a gathering of water. The Torah requires a purifying bath to remove the uncleanness caused by leprosy, discharge of semen, menstruation, childbirth, or contact with a corpse. Before officiating at the Yom Kippur services, the high priest had to bathe in a mikveh to be ritually fit for his tasks. The water had to come from a natural spring or river, and the mikveh itself must have a minimum capacity of 120 gallons of water.

From ancient times until the present day, the mikveh prescribed in the Bible has played a most important part in maintaining what is called family purity. Essentially the family purity laws require a husband, and wife who is experiencing her menstrual cycle, to be separated.

Throughout the woman's period, and for seven days after that, she is called *tamay*. It is unfortunate that the only translation for tamay is "impure," a word that carries a negative connotation. It is simply an ancient term applied to anyone who is forbidden to have contact with sacred food, or to enter the Temple precincts in Jerusalem. For example, if a man or a woman comes into direct contact with a corpse, then the Torah legislates that they are tamay for seven days. Certainly no stigma of impurity is attached to them for having touched a dead body. Nonetheless, because they are tamay, certain ritual acts are prohibited.

Before sexual relations resume, a woman who has menstruated is required to go to the mikveh. Most *mikva'ot* are located in a building, although a lake, river, or any body of natural water may be used. Traditional Jewish women go to the mikveh on the first evening on which they are permitted to resume sexual relations. No men are present when women use it. The woman, totally unclothed, immerses in the mikveh and recites the blessing "who has sanctified us with His commandments and commanded us concerning immersion." Unmarried women are not required to immerse in the mikveh, with the exception of a bride-to-be, who customarily goes just before her wedding. Interestingly, the Christian ritual of baptism is based on the mikveh immersion.

Many psychologists who have studied the laws of family purity and use of mikveh have observed that the laws enhance Jewish marital and sexual happiness.

Why can't an Orthodox man shake hands with a woman? Isn't that rude?

Orthodox Jews believe in the separation of the sexes in a variety of ways. These practices are reflected in the fact that during Temple times there was a special Women's Court, and men and women were separated. Women occupied their separate section to avoid any possible frivolity resulting from contact with men. Today, in Orthodox synagogues, men and women continue to sit separately. I have attended

Orthodox parties where men and women sit separately and the dancing is separate too. I even attended the funeral of an Orthodox man
where men and women were sitting on their own side of the room.

There is a concept in Judaism called *siyug laTorah*, safeguard-
ing the Torah. Essentially this concept holds that there are times
when, although something is theoretically permissible according to
Jewish law, one ought to refrain from doing it because it might in
turn lead to a violation of the law. An Orthodox man not shaking
hands with a woman might well fall into the category of safeguard-
ing. The fear, here, is that by touching the hand of a woman, there
is always the possibility of becoming sexually aroused or interested
romantically in that woman. Since in Orthodox Judaism a man is
permitted to have sexual relations only with his own wife, the fear
would be that even touching the hand of a woman (other than his
wife) could lead to temptation.

Because there are varying degrees of being Orthodox, I know
quite a number of Orthodox Jews who might be more flexible about
shaking hands with a woman. It all depends on each person's personal custom and level of comfort.

Is it true that women are not supposed to touch a Torah?

The question of whether or not a woman can touch a Torah was asked
of me at my first interview for a rabbinic position. The argument has
been that a menstruating woman, who is in a state of ritual unclean-
liness, may not touch or hold a Torah lest she transmit her "impurity"
to a sacred object. Rabbinic law, however, never objected to a woman
coming into physical contact with a Torah, even if she were a men-
struant. The Talmud (Berachot 22a) is quite clear on this issue when
it says "words of the Torah are not susceptible to uncleanness." This essentially means that a Torah is beyond being defiled, since it has such
a high degree of holiness. Thus it is permissible for women to carry the
Torah, and in many synagogues, including modern Orthodox ones,
this is the case.

What is the controversy about counting women in a minyan?

Jewish law has always preferred that Jews pray communally rather than privately. The rabbis always felt that public prayers are more likely to be offered for what benefits the entire community, whereas individuals often pray for things beneficial only to themselves or their family.

In traditional Jewish law, the minimum number necessary to form a community is ten adult males, known as a minyan. If ten men are not present, many of the important prayers in the service cannot be recited.

According to Orthodox interpretation, a minyan can only be composed of people who are obligated by Jewish law to participate in communal prayer. Jewish law has always excluded women from communal prayer because of their family duties in the home.

In 1973, the Conservative movement ruled that women could be counted in the minyan. The movement regarded exclusion of women from the minyan as discriminatory. Today, most (although not all) Conservative synagogues count women in the minyan. Since the Reform movement is not bound by the category of minyan, it conducts a complete prayer service even in the absence of ten adults.

When did women start becoming rabbis? Why do some Jews object to this?

Although the rabbinate has existed for more than twenty centuries, women rabbis in United States did not emerge until the decade of the 1970s. The first female rabbi to be ordained in America was Sally Preisand, who graduated from the Reform movement's Hebrew Union College in 1972—fifty years after the Reform Union of Rabbis endorsed the idea of a woman rabbi. Today, more than one hundred women have been ordained as Reform rabbis.

In 1985, the Jewish Theological Seminary ordained the first Conservative Rabbi, Amy Eilberg.

There were a variety of objections to ordaining women as rabbis, notably that women were traditionally exempted from certain positive time-related commandments and that Jewish law prohibited women from serving as witnesses in most cases. Since a rabbi is called upon to serve as a witness to a Jewish marriage or divorce, a woman rabbi would be expected to serve in a role that was once prohibited to her. Another objection to ordination of women was based on the opinion that a woman could not serve as a cantor.

In Germany, before the Holocaust, a liberal seminary ordained a woman named Regina Jonas, making her the first woman in history to be ordained as a rabbi. Jonas perished during the Holocaust, but her papers, including her sermons, dissertation (on why it should be permissible to ordain women as rabbis), and even some love letters have survived.

Chapter 10

❧ ❧

Sex

Is it true that some Orthodox people have sex through a hole in a sheet?

As a teenager, I studied privately with an Orthodox rabbi and focused on many of the laws in the Code of Jewish Law. In one of the chapters named "Laws of Chastity," there are a whole group of statements related to making love and how to do it in a way that would satisfy Jewish tradition. For example, in the chapter we are told that a person should accustom oneself to be in a mood of supreme holiness and to have pure thoughts when having sex. The law states that it is forbidden to have intercourse by light, and one must make love with another in complete privacy, with no other people around. Nowhere, however, did I hear anything about needing to have sex through a hole in the sheet.

Although I too have heard stories that there are some Orthodox people who (for reasons of their own that I don't understand) use that method, the truth of the matter is that Jewish law does not mandate that a sheet be used. In fact, the ancient rabbis do not allow any articles of clothing to be worn during lovemaking. Clothing is seen as a barrier to intimacy.

Some people have speculated that this "urban myth" is based on a misunderstanding of a *tallit katan*, the item worn under the shirt by many Orthodox Jewish boys and men. This ritual item has fringes on each of four corners. The explanation indicates that when seen hanging from a clothesline, the tallit katan can look like a sheet with a hole in it!

What does Judaism say about nonmarital sex?

One of the most important lessons of the Jewish vision of life is that sex is not merely physical. God created each one of us as an integrated whole, with no part of us capable of living independently from any other. Therefore our sexual acts ought to reflect our values as individuals and as Jews.

Adam and Eve, the father and mother of all humanity, were specifically created for each other. They were told, "a man leaves his father and his mother and clings to his wife so that they become one flesh" (Genesis 2:24). Thus the Torah recognizes the basic need for intimate companionship and seeks to satisfy that need through marriage.

Although the Torah never explicitly outlaws nonmarital sex (except in the case of adultery and incest), the rabbis forbade it. Sex outside marriage simply did not fit their ideal of holiness and could lead to continued promiscuity after marriage. The only Mishnaic rabbi to explicitly outlaw nonmarital sex was Rabbi Eliezer, who wrote: "He sleeps with many women and does not know who they all are. She receives many men and does not know whom she received. It will turn out that a man will err and marry his sister, and a woman will err and marry her brother, and the world will be filled with *mamzerim*" (children born of forbidden marriages).

Marriage is no guarantee that sexual relations will be respectful and noncoercive. But the deep relationship that marriage fosters makes it more likely two partners care for each other in their sexual relations as well as in all of the other arenas of life.

It is probable that only a small minority of Jews maintain the ideal of chastity before marriage. Nevertheless, sex only within marriage continues to be the ideal, and I as well as many of my colleagues continue to promote this ideal in our life cycle courses.

Rabbi Michael Gold, a colleague who wrote *Does God Belong in the Bedroom?* relates how his own synagogue continues to promote the Jewish ideal. An unmarried couple who were living together applied to become members. After much discussion, the synagogue decided they could join as two singles but not as one family. In this way, the synagogue policy would reflect the ideals of Judaism.

Is masturbation a sin in Judaism?

Traditional Judaism forbids masturbation by males. It has little to say about masturbation by females.

In reality, almost all human beings masturbate at some point in their lives. Many sex experts see masturbation as natural and healthy.

Modern rabbinic views vary on the subject. The Orthodox rabbi and writer Reuven P. Bulka considers masturbation an instrument for focusing only on the self and strongly condemns it. Rabbi Elliot Dorff, in his book *Matters of Life and Death*, writes that masturbation in and of itself should no longer carry the shame it had for our ancestors, because the original grounds for opposing it (that a man has a finite amount of seed and spilling it is to sap a man's strength) are no longer tenable and it is a way of dealing with one's sexual energy before marriage. Others agree with him, positing that learning about one's body is permissible. Therefore they have declared masturbation as a form of permissible release, since it can work to discourage young people from sexual experimentation with others.

Finally, Shmuley Boteach, the rabbi of Oxford University and author of the book *Kosher Sex*, writes that every act of masturbation serves as a powerful release that in turn lessens our vital need for sex with another person. In the context of marriage, the lessening of need for sex can be disastrous.

Are Jews allowed to use birth control?

Since Judaism invests marriage and children with so much significance, it is not surprising that traditional Jewish texts look askance at interruption of the process of conception and birth. Jewish parents urge their children to marry and have their own children. But despite the traditional command to have two children (and the ideal of having more), contraception is permitted and even required under certain circumstances.

Jewish sources from as early as the second century C.E. describe methods of contraception and prescribe when they may or should be used. Until the latter half of the twentieth century, though, Jews never contemplated using contraceptives for purposes of family planning. Judaism, after all, values large families. But today there are a variety of reasons using birth control would be the responsible thing for a family.

In Jewish law, it is the male who is legally responsible for propagation. This argues against use of a condom, at least until he has fulfilled that duty. Nevertheless, many rabbinic authorities posit that condoms must be used if unprotected sexual intercourse poses a medical risk to either spouse, for condoms do offer some measure of protection against the spread of disease, and the duty to maintain health and life supersedes the positive duty of the male to propagate.

From the point of view of Jewish law, the diaphragm is the most favored form of contraception, for it prevents contraception and has little, if any, impact on the woman's health. If the contraceptive pill or implant is not contraindicated by a woman's age or body chemistry, it is usually the form of contraception next most favored by rabbinic authorities. Couples like these methods of birth control because they are easy to use and quite reliable. Jewish authorities recommend them because their success rate minimizes the possibility of the couple later considering an abortion as a form of retroactive birth control.

Since having children in Judaism is a religious obligation, it must be assumed that even the more liberal school among modern rabbis would limit use of contraceptives to those couples who have already fulfilled the commandment by having a boy and a girl—except, of course, if the medical condition of the woman requires it. In modern times, when couples frequently postpone marriage until after extended education and initiation of a career for one or both, rabbis of the branches of Judaism have varied widely in their response to the desirability and permissibility of family planning. Some allow contraception even before having children, and this has been the practice of the vast majority of Jews.

Today, Jewish religious leaders increasingly stress the need for Jews to have large families. Our numbers are down from eighteen million to twelve million worldwide, due to the loss in the Holocaust and Jews marrying out of the faith. The current reproductive rate among American Jews is between 1.7 and 1.8. This statistic essentially means that we are killing ourselves off as a people. Thus propagation is one of the most important mitzvot in our time!

Is there a Jewish view on homosexuality?

There are a variety of Jewish views on homosexuality. To begin, homosexual conduct between males is mentioned much more frequently and more heavily condemned in the traditional Jewish sources than such conduct between females. The emphasis is on the sexual act between males rather than mental homosexual tendencies, as in Leviticus 19:22: "You shall not lie with mankind, as with womankind, for it is an abomination" (Leviticus 19:22) and in Leviticus 20:13: "If a man lie with mankind, as with womankind, both of them have committed abomination. They shall surely be put to death."

Christianity and Islam shared this view, with really very little opposition, until recently. New medical knowledge about the origin of homosexuality has led some branches of Judaism and Christianity to rethink their stance against homosexuality, in some cases to the point of equating monogamous and loving homosexual relations with the same type of heterosexual relations. For some denominations of Judaism and Christianity, no change is called for, yet for others, the matter has become the source of deep controversy.

The Conservative movement, of which I am a member, is part of this last group. The discussion began in the mid-1980s, and it evolved into a resolution in May 1990. Here are some of the points of the resolution:

- Support of full civil equality for gays and lesbians in our national life
- Deploring violence against gays and lesbians in our society
- Reiteration that since they are all Jews, gay men and lesbians are welcome as members in our congregations

- A call upon our synagogues and the various arms of our movement to increase our awareness of, understanding of, and concern for our fellow Jews who are gay and lesbian

There is no question in my mind, having heard a lecture by a member of the Gay Synagogue in Manhattan, that we must all resolve to take positive steps to make gays and lesbians feel welcome in our synagogues and other institutions. In addition, Judaism has much to teach us about how we should think about sex and how we should behave sexually—whether single or married, heterosexual or homosexual.

Chapter 11

✤ ✤

Death and Dying

Does Judaism teach about reincarnation?

Yes, it certainly does. In Hebrew, the technical term for this idea is *gilgul neshamot*, the turning of souls. Jewish mystics who embrace a belief in reincarnation posit that the soul has an independent life, existing before and after the death of the body. The soul, they say, joins the body at an appropriate time, remains with it for a specified period, and then takes leave of the body about the time of death, prepared to assume its next assignment in the physical world. A soul can return again and again in different bodies, and how it conducts itself in each reincarnation determines its ascent or descent in the next visit.

Mystics often use reincarnation to explain odd or unusual occurrences of human characteristics. For example, if a person seems to be behaving like an animal, a kabbalist might well conclude that such a person is carrying the soul of a beast.

Mystics describe three types of reincarnation: *gilgul, ibbur,* and *dybbuk.* Gilgul takes place during pregnancy. Ibbur (impregnation) occurs when an "old" soul enters the body of another individual at any time during its lifetime. The soul dwells in a new body for a limited period of time and performs certain acts. Finally, when an evil soul enters a person, the invading soul is called a dybbuk (clinging soul). To eradicate such a soul, a Jewish exorcism must be performed. Kabbalistic literature is filled with stories of exorcisms and even describes the procedures with great detail.

Some of the greatest sages in Jewish history, including Rabbi Joseph Karo, author of *The Code of Jewish Law*, believed in reincarnation and wrote about it. In our day, Rabbi Adin Steinsaltz writes about the Jewish view of reincarnation in his book *The Thirteen Petalled Rose*.

Why and when do we light the candle in a glass?

There are several occasions throughout the year when Jews light a candle in memory of a loved one. Jewish tradition has special rituals to help the mourner meet the crisis of bereavement. One is the annual commemoration of the anniversary of death known as *yahrzeit* in Yiddish ("year time"); it is called *anos* among Sephardic Jews. Each year, on the anniversary of the death, a special day is consecrated to the loved one. Traditionally this is done on the anniversary of the death according to the Hebrew calendar, but some people use secular dates to mark the yahrzeit. If one is not certain of the exact day when a loved one died, one should select an approximate date to observe yahrzeit each year.

The yahrzeit officially begins with the lighting of a twenty-four-hour candle (usually it's in a glass) on the night of the anniversary. Light is symbolic of a person's soul, suggesting immortality. "The soul of a person," says the Book of Proverbs (20:27), "is the lamp of God." On the day of the yahrzeit itself, the traditional custom also includes attending services, reciting the Mourner's Kaddish, and giving *tzedakah*.

On the Jewish holidays of Yom Kippur, Shemini Atzeret, Passover, and Shavuot, a remembrance service called Yizkor takes place in the synagogue. Participating in this service allows one to remember the loved one and the values the person cherished and transmitted while alive. In this way, participants are encouraged to continue to lead the good life that the loved one bequeathed to them. Many synagogues today add a special yizkor memorial for the six million Jews murdered in the Holocaust, many of whom left no one behind to recite either the Mourner's Kaddish or yizkor.

As with the yahrzeit, it is customary to kindle a twenty-four-hour candle on the evening preceding Yizkor. The custom is also to pledge charity and perform other kind deeds to honor the memory of the departed.

Why do rabbis recite eulogies about people they never met?

Frequently rabbis must deliver a eulogy for someone they have never met. This may be because the deceased is not a member of the rabbi's synagogue, or the person may be a parent or some other relative of the deceased with whom the rabbi has little or no contact.

When I am asked to eulogize someone I do not know, I try to encourage others who knew the person to do the eulogy in my stead. If they are unwilling to do so, then I try to get as much information from members of the family so as to make a dignified and honest presentation. When I deliver the eulogy, I make it a habit of always thanking those who gave me the information, so that those who listen to the eulogy are not misled into thinking that I knew the deceased personally.

When it comes to delivering a eulogy, honesty with compassion is a working combination for me. As a rabbi, I always try to introduce biblical and rabbinic sources as well, which help lend comfort to the family in mourning. In Jewish tradition, it is considered an honor and an important obligation for mourners and family members to offer insights for the eulogy of a loved one. Abraham, Israel's first patriarch, eulogized his own wife Sarah. Today at many funerals, in addition to the rabbi delivering a eulogy, family members as well are encouraged to speak words of tribute to their loved one.

The purpose of a eulogy is twofold: to praise the deceased for his or her worthy qualities, and to express the grief and sense of loss experienced by the mourners and the community at large.

Wisely, Jewish tradition requires that eulogizing of the deceased be balanced and appropriate. The eulogy may not invent or grossly exaggerate qualities that the deceased did not possess. In addition, even if a person was undistinguished, one is encouraged in a eulogy to find at least some positive attributes and qualities of which to make mention.

How do we know about the afterlife if nobody has ever come back?

During the rabbinic period, the afterlife began to assume a prominent place in Jewish faith. A doctrine of the immortality of the soul suggested that the body returns to the earth, dust to dust; but the soul, which is immortal, returns to God, who gave it. In addition, rabbinic Judaism also affirmed the eventual resurrection of the body with its soul that occurs with the coming of the Messiah.

Reform Judaism rejects the idea of resurrection, and both Reform and Reconstructionist Judaism understand the messianic idea in more abstract terms. This remains an area in which each of us must confront the wonder of existence on our own, and make peace on our own terms with the mystery of death.

There are many Jewish ideas about the precise meaning of immortality and what form it can take. Ultimately, each of us, on the basis of our faith and what we have been taught, must choose an understanding that fits with our faith and belief.

Here are several of the forms in which our people conceive of immortality and life after death today:

- Influence through family: we live in and through our children. This naturalistic view says that eternal life occurs biologically through the children that we bring into this world.
- Immortality through influence: when we influence others to the point that they fashion themselves after us, and use us as a role model, this kind of eternal significance is itself a form of immortality.
- Influence through deeds and creative works: we continue to live on through our work. This notion of immortality is expressed in the Midrash: "We need not erect monuments to the righteous; their deeds are their monuments (Genesis Rabbah 32:10).
- Reincarnation: Kabbalists taught that a person's soul returns again and again in different bodies.
- Resurrection: here the belief is that the physical body will be resurrected during the messianic era.

No matter which understanding resembles your own, the basic question always remains the same: How did you live your life?

Why do we put rocks on gravestones?

It is considered an act of love in Judaism to visit the grave of a friend or relative. Whenever one visits the cemetery, one is free to recite or read whatever prayer, psalm, or reading one chooses. Before leaving, there is a Jewish custom of placing a small stone or pebble on the tombstone. Laying stones on a monument is a sign that someone visited the cemetery and thus an acknowledgment that the deceased is still loved and remembered.

Is it true that when a person dies, someone watches the body constantly until the burial?

According to Jewish tradition, one who has died is not to be left alone before the funeral. Although some sources trace this practice to the necessity of protecting the body from harm, not leaving the body unattended is essentially another way of showing respect to the deceased. In traditional settings, a person called a *shomer* (literally, watchperson) stays with the deceased from the time of death until burial. A candle is placed near the deceased, and the shomer often reads Psalms.

I will never forget the day when, as a young counselor at a Jewish summer camp in the 1970s, the chef died of a sudden heart attack in the early morning. The staff took turns watching the body while reading from the Book of Psalms.

Preserving the dignity of life and the human body sets the tone for the Jewish response to death. Historically, every family had the responsibility to care for its own dead. Today, this task has been assumed by a group of caring men and women called the chevra kaddisha, meaning "holy society." We have such a group in our own congregation, and there are even several teenagers involved with it as well.

Caring for the body from the time of burial is considered the truest act of kindness, since one does it without any expectation of repayment. The body is clothed in plain white linen shrouds, called *tachrichim*, after being washed in the prescribed manner.

In more liberal Jewish settings, personal autonomy with regard to burial may allow the deceased to be buried in clothing other than white linen shrouds, without a shomer to watch over him or her.

Why isn't cremation allowed in Judaism?

Liberal Judaism allows cremation, but it is traditionally prohibited because it does not permit the body to naturally return to the earth. In the Book of Joshua (7:15), cremation, which was already known in biblical times, was considered to be a humiliation inflicted on criminals.

For the rabbis, cremation was a denial of the belief of bodily resurrection and an affront to the dignity of the human body. Today, too, rabbinic opinion often compares cremation to the destruction of Jews in the crematoria of the Holocaust, a horrendous reminder of the evil and savagery that one group of people can perpetrate upon another.

In traditional Jewish law, if a cremation of a Jewish person does take place, the ashes may not be buried in a Jewish cemetery. Some cemeteries allow burial of ashes.

Traditional Jewish law requires no mourning for the cremated. Shivah is not observed, and Kaddish is not recited for them. Those who are cremated are considered by Jewish tradition to have abandoned, unalterably, all of Jewish law and therefore to have surrendered their rights to posthumous honor. More liberal Jews, though, observe full mourning rites, even when cremation does occur.

Can non-Jews be buried in a Jewish cemetery?

The concept of a Jewish cemetery is an extension of Jewish communal identity and cohesion. It is therefore desirable for Jews to be buried in a Jewish cemetery, and for non-Jews to be buried in a non-Jewish cemetery. Israel's Orthodox rabbinate and the Orthodox and Conservative rabbinate in the United States and Canada do not permit non-Jews to be buried in the same cemetery as Jews. In the Reform and Reconstructionist movements, it is generally accepted practice to bury non-Jewish relatives in a Jewish cemetery. The thinking here is that the entire cemetery is not consecrated ground; rather, only the individual grave where a body rests is sacred. It is strongly suggested that when a non-Jewish relative is laid to rest in a Jewish cemetery no non-Jewish symbols be used on the tombstone.

Some people buy fancy coffins. Is it true that in Jewish tradition a plain pine box should be used? Is it an insult to the deceased to do that?

Some mourners are tempted to purchase a casket that "will last forever," but in Jewish tradition we are told to follow the lead in the text "For dust you are, and to dust you will return" (Genesis 3:19). In other words, whatever prevents the process of returning to dust is considered inconsistent with traditional Jewish practice. Thus the casket, according to Jewish tradition, should be made entirely of wood.

Centuries ago the Talmud (Moed Katan, 27a, 27b) records that at one time the bodies of the wealthy were brought to burial on a richly ornamented stately bed, while the bodies of the poor were brought to burial on a plain platform. This practice brought embarrassment to the poor, resulting in a law that was instituted to require all of the dead—rich and poor alike—to be brought to burial on a plain platform. The dead at that time were not buried in coffins.

One of the watchwords of a Jewish burial is simplicity, which is designed to avert a psychological pitfall. The religious prescription of an all-wooden coffin is also meant to avoid ostentation at the funeral and to remind us that death is the great equalizer. In the democracy of death, all are equal, no matter what their social or economic status.

An unpolished pine box is the preferred choice of the traditional Jew. It is a soft wood that decomposes more rapidly than a hardwood such as oak. Other, fancier wooden caskets made of oak, cherry, or maple are also considered acceptable for use. Generally, people who purchase one for their loved one tend to believe that a plain pine box is simply not dignified enough for their tastes. In Israel, where wood is scarce, no casket is used at all. Rather, the deceased is buried in a wrapped shroud.

Chapter 12

❦ ❧

Medical Ethics

If drugs were legal, would Judaism allow them?

According to Jewish law and rabbinic opinion, anything that is dangerous to life and limb must be avoided. Our bodies are considered on loan from God, and because we are made in God's image we must do everything to protect them and treat them with respect.

There are quite a number of references in the classical Jewish sources to use of drugs as medicine or a painkiller. All of the drugs were, of course, legal in the communities where they were authorized to be used. If certain drugs that are now illegal were made legal, I suppose that there might be some circumstances under which Judaism would allow their use.

A good example might be marijuana, which is illegal in most states, but in some cases it can be used under a doctor's supervision to help alleviate the pain of a life-threatening illness or for another medical application. The bottom line is that if a particular drug were legal, deemed to be noninjurious to one's health, and had the approval of a physician, it would surely be permissible for use according to most Jewish rabbinic authorities.

Is there a Jewish view on abortion?

The Jewish view of abortion is, in some ways, quite simple. If you ask rabbinic authorities the question of the Jewish view on abortion, the answer is always the same: "Tell me the case."

109

There are two extreme viewpoints in the abortion controversy. One says there is no moral justification for abortion. The other proclaims it is a woman's right to have an abortion on demand. The debate continues to be a heated one.

Jewish law and tradition have struggled with the question of abortion since the time of the Bible, and even as we move into the twenty-first century the struggle continues. The United States has not been exempt from this controversy. In 1973, the Supreme Court seemingly decided the abortion issue in the landmark case of *Roe* v. *Wade*; the Court struck down all state laws that prohibited abortion. Yet the debate rages. Encouraged by political and religious leaders, antiabortion groups continue to push for a Constitutional amendment that would prohibit abortion. At the same time, other groups continue to uphold the *Roe* v. *Wade* decision and the legal right to secure an abortion.

In Canada, existing federal law prohibits abortion on demand. A legal abortion, however, may be performed if a doctor certifies that it is in the best physical and mental interests of the mother.

The main rabbinic statement regarding abortion occurs in the Talmud (Mishnah Oholot 7:6). The passage reads:

> If a woman is in hard travail [that is, she finds it very hard to give birth to her child and there is danger to her life], her child must be cut up while it is in her womb and brought out limb by limb, since the life of the mother has priority over the life of the child. But, if the greater part of it has already emerged from the womb, it may not be touched, since the claim of one life cannot override the claim of another.

The meaning of the Mishnah is clear. It is not permitted to murder one person in order to save the life of another. While the child is still in the womb, it is not a person by Jewish law. To destroy it is not to commit an act of murder. Once the greater part of the child has emerged from the womb, it is considered as if the child has been born and the child is then a person in Jewish life. The life of the mother must be saved by destroying the fetus.

Today, there continue to be many rabbinic opinions written on the subject of abortion. Because life is so sacred, the writings point to a restriction of the legitimacy of abortion to a narrow range of cases. Jewish law requires abortion when the woman's life or health — physical or mental — is threatened by the pregnancy. Jewish law permits abortion when the risk to the woman's life or health (again, physical or mental) is greater than that of a normal pregnancy but not so great as to constitute a clear and present danger to her.

In practice, Jews in North America and in Israel engage in abortion almost indiscriminately. The high rate of abortion among Jews is particularly problematic, because Jews are barely reproducing themselves. Today, many rabbis and Jewish communal leaders are calling for Jews to marry and have children so that the Jewish people and Judaism can continue for more than another generation or two.

How do Jews feel about assisted suicide?

Jewish tradition teaches that life is a gift from God, and God alone has the right to make decisions about life and death; therefore suicide is morally wrong. Since suicide itself is prohibited, aiding a suicide is also forbidden.

Assisted suicide combines active euthanasia (acting with the intention of taking another's life, but for a benign purpose such as relieving agonizing and incurable pain) with suicide. In assisted suicide, both the person who wants to die and his or her assistant contribute to executing the death.

I sympathize enormously with people going through an agonizing process of dying. Some Jewish ethicists take a more liberal stance on withholding or withdrawing life support systems, including artificial nutrition and hydration, to enable nature to take its course. However, the bottom line is that Jewish law does not permit suicide or assisted suicide.

Jewish law has always demanded that we take a much more active role in ensuring that the dying are not abandoned to physical pain or social ostracism, and that we make the mitzvah of *bikkur cholim* (visiting the sick) a critical part of our mission as Jews. Hospice care has also been an important system whereby the patient is supported physically, psychologically, and socially by a whole team of people, including family and friends.

Does Jewish law permit stem cell research?

The question of whether or not to permit stem cell research has at its core understanding of the moral status of tiny human embryos no larger than a pinprick. In each of these embryos are so-called stem cells, which can grow into any kind of human tissue. Scientists have posited that these cells can help find a cure for severe illness. But harvesting them kills the embryo, and therein lies the ethical issue and the question of when life begins, and when a life is a life.

There is no single view that can answer whether Jewish law permits stem cell research. There are, however, a multitude of opinions on the subject. Rabbis of the Reform movement, for example, posits that an isolated fertilized egg does not enjoy the full status of personhood. They wrote a letter to President George W. Bush supporting federal funding for stem cell research, on the basis of the primary responsibility to save human life, a supreme Jewish value.

Personally, I am in favor of stem cell research that is funded under strict guidelines. With an estimated 128 million Americans afflicted with conditions that may benefit, it seems to me the right thing to do.

When does Jewish law say a person is officially dead?

The definition of death in Jewish law is first mentioned in the fifth-century Babylonian Talmud (Yoma 85a). It was understood then that when the heart stops beating and no air emanates from the nose, one is no longer alive. The classical Jewish breath test consists of placing a feather beneath a person's nostrils. Lack of movement of the feather signifies death.

In the sixteenth century, the important codifier Rabbi Moses Isserles ruled that "nowadays" we do not know how to distinguish death with accuracy from a fainting spell; consequently, even after cessation of breath and heartbeat we should wait a period of time before assuming that a person is dead.

Waiting even a short time, however, is generally too long today if doctors are to be able to use a dying person's heart to save the life of an awaiting transplant patient. Consequently, many rabbis—including my professor, the late Rabbi Seymour Siegel of the Jewish Theological Seminary—suggested that a flat electroencephalogram, indicating cessation of spontaneous brain activity, be sufficient to determine death. In 1988, the Chief Rabbinate of Israel approved heart transplantation, effectively accepting that a flat electroencephalogram guarantees the patient can no longer independently breathe or produce a heartbeat. This has become the accepted opinion of virtually all modern Jewish authorities, with the exception of a few Orthodox rabbis.

Chapter 13

❦ ❦

Jewish Belief

What, according to Judaism, is the meaning of life?

Judaism sees the life that is given to each human being as a gift to be used for the benefit of all humanity.

Being a good person is clearly at the core of Judaism, and God's first concern is with a person's decency.

In an interesting Talmudic passage (Talmud, Shabbat 31a) that I have studied, a person is brought before the heavenly court for judgment and asked a series of questions. One might think the question would be, "Did you observe the Jewish holidays and pray a lot?"

I was so surprised to learn that the first question quoted in the Talmud was instead, "Did you conduct your affairs honestly?"

A Jewish person is to stay honest and learn to be good and honorable by adhering to Judaism's special system of mitzvot. God gave us a variety of religious obligations, and if we are diligent, I believe, they will help us do our part in bringing more mercy, loving kindness, and peace into the world.

The Book of Deuteronomy tells us to "follow God and walk in God's ways." I understand this phrase to mean that we should follow the attributes of God. Just as God clothed Adam and Eve, so should we give clothing to those in need. Just as God visited Abraham when he was sick after his circumcision, so we too should make it our duty to

114

visit sick people. All acts of justice and goodness are closely connected with the concept of honoring God's name by following God's ways.

A few years ago I was chosen to host a local radio program called "The Jewish American Hour." As host, I decided to end each program by going off the air with a verse from the Bible that was so important to me that I wanted my listeners to always remember it. The verse I chose is one of my favorites (it even adorns my office wall). The verse is from the Book of Micah, a prophet, and sums up for me what God requires of us, and thus how God intended for us to find life's meaning:

> God has told you what is good, and what God wants of you:
> Only to do justice, to love goodness, and to walk modestly with
> your God. (Micah, 6:8)

Is it ever permissible to lie?

Have you ever thought about what it would be like to be obliged to tell the truth for twenty-four hours? Many have tried and failed. Some have gotten themselves into trouble in the effort. No doubt you know the story of Pinocchio, whose nose grew every time he lied, until it became grotesque. Social scientists have pointed out that Americans tell many lies each day, in normal life, including white lies and false excuses.

This is why all religions extol the virtue of truth. Without truthfulness, morality cannot exist, and it is said that where truth abides, God's presence is felt. The Bible leaves no doubt about the fundamental virtue of truth: "You shall not deal falsely, nor lie to one another." Moses chooses "men of truth" to serve as judges over the Israelites. Bearing false witness against one's neighbor is condemned in the ninth of the Ten Commandments.

The Talmud is also unwavering in its support of truthfulness. False speech is compared to idolatry. God despises the person who says one thing with his mouth and another with his mind.

Jewish tradition is concerned with more than the mere uttering of truth when one speaks. A person is not permitted to withhold the truth by remaining silent. To protect a criminal by maintaining silence when one can assist the law is as serious a transgression as outright lying. Likewise, to create a false impression without directly lying is to distort the virtue of truth. For example, inviting someone to your home when you are certain that he will refuse is a kind of insincerity that the Talmud criticizes.

People have long debated whether a white lie is a departure from the truth. There are always dangers that a white lie, like petty stealing, leads in time to more serious dishonesty. But there are times when even the Jewish tradition recognizes that the white lie is permissible, especially if the interests of peace are involved. For example, if a separation can be prevented between husband and wife or between two friends, then for the sake of peace the truth may be withheld. In other words, only when a virtue higher than truth is served may truth be set aside.

The Talmud (Baba Metzia 23b, 24a) observes several instances when lying is permissible. It says that a scholar will never tell a lie except in the three instances of "tractate," "bed," and "hospitality." The commentators explain the first to mean that a modest scholar is permitted to declare he is unfamiliar with a tractate of the Mishnah in order not to flaunt his learning. The second is understood to mean that if a person is asked intimate questions regarding his marital life she need not answer truthfully. The third is understood to mean that a person who has been generously treated by a host may decide not to tell the truth about her reception if she fears that as a result the host will be embarrassed by unwelcome guests.

Finally, the question has often been asked, "Should a doctor let a person who is seriously ill know about his or her condition?" According to most rabbinic authorities, one should make a seriously ill person aware of his or her illness, without issuing any definitive pronouncement that deprives him or her of hope.

Do Jews believe in hell?

The word *hell* is not part of the Jewish vocabulary. The Tanach, the Hebrew Bible, uses a term, *Gehinom*, that in some circles has been understood as hell. In fact, Gehinom is a term borrowed from an actual place name, *Gei-Ben Hinom,* located south of Jerusalem, in a valley where the wicked once sacrificed their children to false gods. Thus when a Jew learned about the concept of hell from his neighbors, he often used this appropriate name to signify the home of the wicked beyond the grave.

Gehinom, or Gehenna, passed into use as a metaphoric designation for the place of punishment in the hereafter. According to a Talmudic view, the doors of Gehenna close behind apostates, informers, promoters of sin, and tyrants for many generations. According to the mystical holy book, the Zohar, sinners are punished for twelve months, half of the time in fire and half in snow. Among those who do not face Gehenna, a Talmudic passage includes the very poor and diseased.

Despite the many differences of opinion as to the meaning of Gehenna, it is nowhere considered to be a dogma or a doctrine of faith that Jews are required to profess. Even those rabbinic sages who delighted in describing the torments of Gehenna and other shadowy places were usually aware that they were permitting their imagination to roam freely.

During the Middle Ages, when Jews were susceptible to the folklore of their neighbors, belief in Gehenna was most evident. The Jewish scholars, however, sought to discourage belief in physical torture and punishment after life. They interpreted reward and punishment in the hereafter in a spiritual way. To the kabbalist Judah Lowe of Prague, the hereafter was a purely spiritual state. Neither rewards nor punishments were physical. Its joys consisted of union with God, its tortures alienation from God. Heaven was the satisfaction of life well lived, and Gehenna was the pain or remorse of having failed to live the good life.

Do Jews believe in an eye for an eye?

Few references in the Bible are more misunderstood than the ancient Hebrew law of an eye for an eye.

In Israel, for example, it is often understood in a pejorative manner. Critics often accuse the Israeli army of practicing eye-for-an-eye morality for immediate retaliation against a terrorist attack.

The Book of Exodus 21:24 states "an eye for an eye, tooth for tooth, hand for hand, foot for foot." Critics of the Torah point to lines such as this in an attempt to indict the Scriptures for a so-called primitive nature.

The rule of an eye for an eye, which appears to lay down the principle of literal retribution, was not at all formulated for such a purpose. In fact, no case of physical retaliation is recorded in the Bible where a penalty was ever exacted.

The Talmudic rabbis pointed out that, inasmuch as the law seeks equity, its literal enforcement would frequently lead to gross inequity. For instance, they said, taking the eye of a one-eyed assailant would not be just retribution but excessive punishment. Or, how is one to guard against the fatal effect of retribution upon the offender? If he dies he gives a life for an eye or a hand, and the objective of the law is thwarted. Therefore Jewish law made detailed stipulations for monetary compensation, much as modern insurance contracts are apt to do today.

In all likelihood, an eye for an eye is a graphic way of expressing the abstract idea that the punishment should not be too lenient or too harsh but should fit the crime and the circumstances. Both in insisting that evil must be punished and in equally insisting on setting limits to the punishment, an eye for an eye is a basic principle of biblical justice.

Do Jews believe in the devil?

There are a number of references to Satan in the Jewish Bible. It is doubtful if Jews ever took these references literally. In Judaism, Satan was the mythical figure of all the evil forces in the world. At times, he was identified with the Tempter, the evil impulse, which prompts people to heed the worst side of his nature. But even this notion was never too deeply rooted, for Judaism teaches that God is the Creator of both good and evil, and God's dominion alone is real.

In the Book of Job the character of Satan is more real. He is portrayed as an adversary (God's black humor, if you will) who begrudges man's contentment and well-being and is the indirect cause of Job's misery. But the Talmudic rabbis debated whether the Book of Job was fact or fiction; a number of rabbis contended that the entire book was actually a product of the imagination of some of our ancestors—a parable or allegory.

By and large, Satan in Jewish lore is most identified with the evil impulse, the lower passions that are a hindrance to man's pursuit of the nobler things in life. This can serve as a useful reminder of the all-too-frequent human tendency of rationalizing sinful conduct into saintly behavior, or of seeking the line of least resistance in a situation that calls for tenacity and courage. Eradicating Satan in our lives can symbolize for us the need to wage war against the evil in ourselves.

Satan is also sometimes identified with the angel of death. He leads souls astray and brings accusations against people. His chief functions are those of temptation, accusation, and punishment. Under the control of God, he always acts solely with the divine permission to carry out his plots. Even though he seems to have a will of his own in the Book of Job, he still keeps within the limits that God has fixed for him.

It is the genius of Judaism to draw on elements of popular folklore for moral instruction. Among the Jewish people there persisted vestiges of a primitive belief that the sounding of the shofar, the ram's horn, was intended to destroy Satan and other evil spirits. This accounts for Rabbi Isaac's explanation (Talmud, Rosh Hashanah 16b) that the purpose of blowing the shofar twice during the Rosh Hashanah service is to confound Satan. Rabbi Isaac's comment is also reflected in the later practice of reciting, before the first series of shofar sounds, six biblical verses that form an acrostic of the words *kera Satan* (destroy Satan).

Finally, in the prayer *hashkeveynu* the Hebrew word *Satan* appears. This prayer for peace, recited in the evening, asks God to remove Satan (often translated as "evil forces"), which surrounds us. It is comforting to have a prayer for tranquility, and for many in my congregation this prayer is a must to be recited before going to sleep at night.

Is it possible to be excommunicated from Judaism?

The Hebrew term for excommunication is *cherem*, a word that is said to be related to the Arabic word *harem*. The two words have a similar connotation. In Jewish tradition, excommunication means setting apart people who are guilty of crimes of Jewish law.

In the Middle Ages, when Jews were granted considerable autonomy and civil and religious transgressions were left to the rabbis to deal with, rabbinical courts were established and excommunication or banishment from the social and religious life of the community was meted out as a severe punishment.

In seventeenth-century Amsterdam, the Jewish community was so intolerant of any deviation from traditional teachings that the Dutch Jew Uriel da Costa (who had written an anti-Jewish ritual treatise) was excommunicated in a ritual that required people to step over his prostrate form on the threshold of the synagogue. Eventually he committed suicide.

The philosopher Baruch Spinoza came under a similar ban for his highly unorthodox writings, including his denial of angels, immortality of the soul, and God's authorship of the Torah. His exile from the community was a total ban; no Jew was ever to conduct business with him—or for that matter, ever speak to him. There is no evidence that he ever did again speak to another Jew.

During the past century, a ban of excommunication has rarely been issued in Jewish life. Today the ban might be seen in traditional Orthodox communities, when a man refuses to give his wife a *get*, a Jewish divorce. In Israel, religious courts are empowered to imprison a recalcitrant husband who refuses to give his wife a divorce, although women's groups complain that the courts rarely use their power.

Does anyone really believe that the world was created in six days?

Yes, there are certain Jewish traditionalists, fundamentalists, and others who believe in the world literally having been created in six days. For those who do, that's perfectly fine. I do not and never did. Great Jewish scholars and commentators of the medieval period did not consider the details of the biblical account of creation theologically binding. The great medieval philosopher Maimonides declared that it was not to be taken literally; the medieval commentator Joseph Albo and Rav Kook, a contemporary sage, agreed.

How the world came into being in Jewish texts is presented in varying forms and is expressed in several ways. The Bible itself contains at least three descriptions. The first chapters of Genesis give us the creation story in the form of a divine drama unfolding in six momentous acts in the course of six days. Psalm 104 presents a poetic description, and Proverbs 8 gives still another picture of the birth of nature.

In the writings of the rabbis, there is considerable speculation as to the manner of creation. Some expressed the view of successive creations, where God experimented with and destroyed many worlds before this world was finally established. Others held to the view of continuing re-creation; that is, God renews each day the work of creation.

According to Genesis, God created the world in six days and rested on the seventh. What is most interesting is that in the Babylonian Genesis story the world is also created in six days, with the gods throwing a big party on the seventh day. Other ancient creation stories have the six-day model of creation too.

Evolution and scientific data need not be considered in contradiction to any of the moral and spiritual views of the biblical creation story, and numbers in the Bible were rarely ever taken literally. A single day in the creation story might well symbolize several million years.

From the beginning, when God willed it into being, the world held the seeds of its own future development. Scientists can explain only how the potential became actual; the *why* falls into the province of religion. Science cannot and does not deny the belief that the universe is God's creation.

For me, the creation story is meant to teach us a number of things that we cannot learn from science—for example, the God that creates the universe is eternal and the universe was conceived by God's will for a reason, and it is still evolving according to God's words. The sanctity of the Sabbath, the seventh day, is divinely established. Last and perhaps most important, we learn that people are made in God's image, with the power to choose and transcend themselves.

Do Jews believe in Armageddon?

In chapter thirty-eight of the Book of Ezekiel (read as a Haftarah on the Intermediate Sabbath of Sukkot), there is a prophecy of messianic days called the "War of God and Magog," which bears a similarity to the Armageddon of the New Testament. Ezekiel foretells that the restoration of Israel to the land of his fathers will not pass unchallenged. Formidable armies from the extreme north, under the leadership of Gog, will invade Israel, but the invasion will end in the utter destruction of Gog and his confederate forces. The identity of Gog is obscure, and he is probably to be understood as an apocalyptic figure, personifying the forces hostile to Israel, rather than as a particular person. Magog in Ezekiel is the country of Gog, but in rabbinic literature Magog becomes his inseparable partner, and the war of God and Magog appears to be the great Armageddon that will immediately precede the messianic age. Note that the words Gog and Magog are similar in sound to Armageddon. An old tradition to the effect that this final war would be waged during the festival of Sukkot determined the choice of this passage as the Haftarah for the Intermediate Sabbath of Sukkot.

Armageddon is not mentioned prior to the New Testament, but it is believed by some to be a corrupt spelling of Megiddo, a city mentioned many times in the Tanach, the Jewish Bible. The Book of Revelation in the New Testament refers to Armageddon as the site of the final and conclusive battle between good and evil, involving "the kings of the earth and the whole world," on the "great day of God Almighty."

What is considered the holiest day of all for Jews?

Although the Day of Atonement, Yom Kippur, has been called the Sabbath of Sabbaths, I believe that each Sabbath itself is the holiest of all days. The Sabbath is the only day that is mentioned as being holy in the Ten Commandments, and its origin goes back to the beginning of creation. The Bible relates that God made the world in six days and rested on the seventh, thereby blessing it. Since that time, the Sabbath has remained the holiest day of the year for Jews, despite its occurring fifty-two successive times.

The Sabbath has many work restrictions. Observing the Sabbath gives people an opportunity to rest their mind and body, as well as an opportunity to express their appreciation for many of the things they are often too busy to notice during the week. My philosophy teacher at the Jewish Theological Seminary, Rabbi Abraham Joshua Heschel, once said that the most important ingredient in creating a Jewish home is the celebration of Shabbat.

I began observing the Sabbath in all its detail just before my Bar Mitzvah. In 1960, a couple of months beforehand, my parents sent me to the sleep-away camp that was one of a network of such camps run by the Conservative movement. The camp offered me a community of observant people who each day expressed their love of Judaism, Jewish study, and Jewish values. We had lively prayer services each day, and on Friday evening and Saturday morning the entire camp prayed outdoors in an amphitheater that was on the shore of a beautiful lake. I was so moved by the spirited singing and fervor I experienced every Shabbat at camp that, upon returning home, I too was devoted to Sabbath observance and became a regular worshipper at my synagogue.

I can honestly say that the Sabbath is my special day of rest and relaxation. I love to take walks on the Sabbath in the afternoon with my family and dog. It's so nice to know that people will not phone or e-mail me, and that I can put aside all business concerns and requests, at least for one day, and have a Shabbat Shalom, a day of Sabbath peace.

Chapter 14

🌿 🌿

Hasidim

Who are the Hasidim, and why do they dress like that?

Hasidism, the religious movement of the Hasidim, arose in eighteenth-century Europe. Its founder, Rabbi Israel, was known to spend much time in the forest in meditation and solitude. He preached that the ideal worship of God was in simplicity and with joy; it was a devout spirit that counted most. Around 1736, Rabbi Israel revealed himself as a healer and leader. He was also known as the Ba'al Shem Tov, which literally means "Master of the Good Name." This name was often applied in Jewish life to miracle workers and healers. The Ba'al Shem Tov's talks to his disciples tended to focus on an individual's personal relationship with God and with his fellow men rather than on the intricacies of Jewish law.

Many of the themes of the Ba'al Shem Tov's teachings became the central emphases in the Hasidic movement that his followers developed. One of his fondest teachings was that God desires the heart, which is interpreted to mean that God prefers a pure religious spirit to one having only knowledge of Talmud.

In my favorite Ba'al Shem Tov tale, an illiterate shepherd boy enters a synagogue where people are praying. Unable to pray himself, because he cannot read the words, he starts to whistle a tune, the one thing he does know how to do. His whistling is a gift that he offers to

God. The worshippers are horrified by what he is doing and yell at the boy. The Ba'al Shem Tov stops them in their tracks, telling the congregation "until now the prayers being offered were blocked and were not reaching the heavenly court. But the young boy's whistling was able to break through the blockage, and his prayers ascended directly to God."

The best-known group of Hasidim in the United States is the Lubavitcher, headquartered in Brooklyn. Their most recent Rebbe was Rabbi Menachem Mendel Schneersohn (only the seventh leader since the movement was founded in the late 1700s). He died in the 1990s, and no successor to him has yet been proclaimed.

Hasidic dress for men generally consists of a white shirt, and a long black frock coat with a black hat, sometimes with fur adorning it. This replicates the dress of Eastern European Jews in the sixteenth century. Hasidic women wear long-sleeve dresses that extend down past their ankles as a sign of modesty and humility.

Some thirty years ago, I spent a weekend in the Hasidic village of New Square in New York. It was one of the highlights of my youth. I got to meet the Rebbe in person and experience the joyous singing and dancing of the Hasidim, which lasted into the early morning hours.

Why do Hasidim wear curls at their ears?

The Torah (Leviticus 19:27) says, "You shall not clip your hair at the temples or mar the edges of your beard." This biblical commandment has given rise to the practice among many Orthodox Jews as well as Hasidim not to shave their beard or their side locks, called *pe'ot* in Hebrew (also commonly pronounced the Yiddish way, as "peyis"), the length of which is to reach the lobes of the ears according to the Code of Jewish law.

Curling the side locks is an attempt to keep the pe'ot more aesthetically attractive. It has been explained that shaving one's sideburns was prohibited in Bible times because this was a pagan custom, and Israelites needed to be physically distinguished from the pagans.

There are several styles of pe'ot. Sometimes you see abbreviated side locks, short strands of hair hanging to midcheek, sometimes tucked behind the ears. Some are long, curled, and dangling as far down as the chest. Some are even tied together over the head and under the yarmulke or other head covering.

Whereas the commandment of not rounding the corners of one's head was originally meant to prohibit the Israelites from copying their pagan neighbors and their practices, it is also symbolic of the mandate to leave the corners (again, pe'ot) of a cultivated field unharvested, for collection and sustenance by the widow, the orphan, and the stranger.

Yemenite Jews leave the pe'ot intact when, according to the custom among Oriental Jews, they perform the ceremony of giving the first haircut to a boy of four years. They refer to their long pe'ot as *simanim* (signs), distinguishing them from non-Jews. Today, ear locks are now characteristic of Yemenite Jews and Hasidim.

Who was the late Lubavitcher Rebbe, and why do some people say he is the messiah and will return from the dead?

Menachem Schneersohn became the head of the Lubavitch Hasidim in Brooklyn in 1950. He served the community for more than forty years, until his death in 1994.

Even in death, the Rebbe, as he was customarily called, serves as a vital force among his Hasidic followers. Disciples continue to visit his grave and pray for his soul. Each year, on his yahrzeit (the anniversary of his death), there is a worldwide gathering of the Lubavitchers to preach his message and be reminded of his teachings. A segment of his followers continue to believe that the Rebbe was, and continues to be, the legendary redeemer, *moshiach*, the messiah, whose ultimate arrival is a central tenet of Orthodoxy.

Originally, the term *mashiach* was applied to any person anointed with the holy oil and consecrated to carry out the purposes of God, such as the high priest or the king. When David received the divine promise that the throne would remain in his family forever, the title acquired a special reference and signified the representative of the royal line of David. The prophetic vision of the eventual establishment of the divine kingship on earth came to be identified with the restoration of Israel under the leadership of the messiah, God's anointed one.

The traditional outlook of Judaism is that the messiah will be the dominating figure of an age of universal peace and plenty. Jewish tradition affirms several things about the messiah. He will be a descendant of King David, gain sovereignty over the land of Israel, gather the Jews to Israel from the four corners of the earth, restore them to full observance of the Torah, and bring peace to the entire world. The Jewish belief that the messiah's reign lies in the future has long distinguished Jews from Christians, who believe, of course, that the messiah came two thousand years ago in the person of Jesus.

In the modern world, Reform Judaism has long denied that there will be an individual messiah who carries out the task of perfecting the world. Instead, the Reform movement speaks of a future world in which the efforts of human beings will bring about a utopian age.

The Lubavitcher Hasidic movement has placed increasing emphasis on the imminence of the messiah's arrival. At many of the Lubavitcher rallies and in their youth movements, you will hear the chant "We want Moshiach now."

Several years ago, I took a trip to Brooklyn and toured several Hasidic communities with a Lubavitcher as the tour guide. One of the stops along the tour was 770 Eastern Parkway, the home of Schneersohn. I specifically wanted to know whether the adherents of the Lubavitcher movement believed that the Rebbe was the messiah. What prompted me to ask the question were yellow flags flying outside many homes with a picture of the Rebbe and the Hebrew word *mashiach* written below.

The answer I received from the Lubavitcher tour guide was one I will never forget. He said: "The Rebbe has all of the right criteria for being the messiah: intellect, charisma, and a desire to bring total peace to the world."

Knowing that the Rebbe had died and was buried in Queens, I then proceeded to ask, "So, is the Rebbe dead?" He answered, "The Rebbe is concealed." Concealment is a kabbalistic term, and I intuited from his answer that the Rebbe will in time uncover himself and make himself known to the world as the moshiach.

I guess we'll just have to wait and see.

Chapter 15

※ ※

Jewish Denominations

Why are there so many branches of Judaism?

A woman went to the post office to buy stamps for her Hanukkah cards.

"What denomination?" asked the clerk.

"Oh, good heavens! Have we come to this?" replied the woman. "Well, give me fifty Conservative, two Orthodox, and thirty-seven Reform ones."

All things in life evolve, and no two people are exactly alike. Similarly, when it comes to interests and religious behavior of the Jewish people, things change over time, resulting in the several major branches of Judaism that we have today.

Historically speaking, it happened in a unique way. In 1833, the first class of rabbinical students was graduated from the Reform movement's Hebrew Union College. The ceremony that marked the occasion, the first ordination of any rabbinical seminary in the United States, was held in the Bene Jeshurun Temple.

Following the ceremony, a festive dinner was held that drew representatives from more than one hundred synagogues across the country, members of the eight-year-old Union of American Hebrew Congregations. The founder of the union and president of the Hebrew Union College was Rabbi Isaac Mayer Wise, who hoped to fashion a broad congregational association that would unite all of American Judaism under one roof.

That vision ended with dinner. The meal commenced with half-shell clams and proceeded to soft-shell crabs and shrimp salad, as well as a number of kosher meats, before concluding with ice cream dessert. Unprepared for such a menu that was so blatantly nonkosher, the more traditional rabbis abruptly fled from what has come to be known in the annals of American Jewish history as the "Treifa Banquet" (recall discussion of treif in Chapter Eight, "Keeping Kosher"). The unintended legacy was the hardening of ideological divisions into denominational wings as we know them today.

The oldest denominational form of Judaism in America is Orthodoxy. In fact, it was the only type of religious Judaism in this country until the 1800s, when the Reform movement began to grow. The word *Orthodox* means right belief, and it was applied to Jews who firmly refused to change their beliefs and observances when they came to the New World. The earliest settlers brought it to America, and each wave of immigration added its own special flavor to the life of American Orthodoxy.

The roots of Reform Judaism come from the beginning of the modern age in Germany. Following the French Revolution and the Napoleonic Wars, Jews in much of Western Europe were given new freedoms. For a goodly number of Jews, Judaism suddenly seemed old-fashioned and out-of-date. Reform Judaism was born in the hope that changes would stop the terrible wave of assimilation and conversion that was stealing thousands of Jews away from their faith. The first Reform congregation was in Charleston, South Carolina, formed in 1824 with fewer than fifty worshippers. Reform synagogues spread quickly, and by 1900 Reform Judaism was a major branch of Judaism.

Conservative Judaism, the movement in which I serve, also had its beginnings in Germany. The early builders of the Conservative movement in America were rabbis who were neither Orthodox nor Reform. They might best be called "traditional" Jews. Although they disliked the extremes to which the Reform group was heading, they realized the need to change and update the Jewish laws and practices. Today there are more than nine hundred Conservative synagogues in North America.

The youngest of the religious movements in American Judaism is the Reconstructionist. It is particularly an American movement, unlike the other religious groups that began in Europe and were transplanted to America. Born in 1922, its leaders and thinkers are all American, and most of the ideas are rooted in American philosophy and thought.

The founder of the Reconstructionist movement was the late Rabbi Mordecai Kaplan, who was ordained in the Conservative movement in the early part of the twentieth century. In 1922, he founded a synagogue that he called the Society for the Advancement of Judaism. This synagogue became Kaplan's laboratory for developing his ideas about reconstructing Judaism and Jewish values. Today, Reconstructionist Judaism is the fourth and newest religious branch in Jewish life. It is still small and weak compared with the three major movements.

Why is there so much infighting in the Jewish community with so many "movements"? It seems as if Jews don't get along with each other so well.

We have a Jewish newspaper in our community that each week features a column entitled "One Minute With." The column asks the featured person many questions, such as "What is your favorite book?" or "What is your major accomplishment?" One of the questions is, "What is the greatest problem in the Jewish community?" Invariably, the answer is "Not enough cooperation among people and the various Jewish communal organizations."

As a former communication major at Columbia University, I believe that the inability to communicate properly with one another and really listen to what the other is saying is the reason there continues to be infighting among the various branches of Judaism and among the Jewish communal organizations themselves. Sometimes fear is a factor in this desire not to communicate.

For example, as a Conservative rabbi it has not been my privilege and pleasure for our union of rabbis, called the Rabbinical Assembly, to have a get-together and dialogue with the Orthodox union of Rabbis. Perhaps it has been as a result of no interest on either side, although I am told that there has been some outreach by the Conservative rabbinate to the Orthodox for dialogue, with little interest on their part. It is true that we certainly do have our religious differences, but I often hear and read less-than-affectionate things said about our branch of Judaism, and about some of the latest decisions or modifications to Jewish law that we have made. This is unfortunate, because I think first and foremost we need to be respectful of each other's existence and know that our ultimate mission and purpose as a rabbinic organization is similar to that of other rabbinic groups.

There is a lot of humor about the Jews' inability to get along with one another. There is one riddle joke that goes something like this: Did you hear about the rich Jew who set sail by himself and got stranded on a desert island? Needing a house of worship in which to pray, he decided to build two synagogues: one to pray in, and the other into which he would never set foot.

⚘ Reform Jews ⚘

Is there any truth to the view that Reform Judaism is watered-down Judaism?

Reform Judaism arose in Germany in the beginning of the 1800s as a reaction to Orthodox rigidity. It is true that at its inception the movement considerably altered the way traditional Jews had always viewed the Torah and Jewish peoplehood.

Mitzvot; customs such as keeping the kosher laws, strict Sabbath, and festival observance; and use of Hebrew alone for prayer were changed or abandoned. In its original platform, it also declared that the Jewish people were no longer a nation but a "religious community," and no longer expected to return to Palestine or a Jewish state.

Over the course of the years, the old opposition to mitzvot disappeared and more and more rabbis and congregations began to restore certain discarded practices such as use of Hebrew prayers, traditional Sabbath observances, and wearing of yarmulkes and prayer shawls.

Do Reform Jews believe that God wrote the Torah?

Reform thinkers generally do not believe that God wrote or gave the entire Torah word for word. Rather, they believe that the Torah is a collection of people's thoughts throughout the ages and may even contain primitive ideas and errors.

Reform thinkers also believe that only the moral and ethical laws of the Torah are binding forever. Thus, the Ten Commandments and the Golden Rule, "Love your neighbor as yourself," must never be forgotten. But human beings created ritual laws, such as kashrut and Sabbath restrictions, for a specific time in history, and so those laws are not divine and not necessarily binding on Jews today.

Finally, Reform thinkers teach that revelation is progressive. That is, God is self-revealing and communicates Divine will and laws to every new generation. In ancient times, God revealed rules that were necessary then. In our day, God reveals new rules through the people of Israel and their teachers and scholars. These new rules meet the needs of Jews today.

Which group is the largest: Reform, Conservative, or Orthodox?

The Orthodox movement claims the lion's share of synagogues in the United States, despite being the smallest of the three major branches, according to a new census by the American Jewish Committee.

Of the 3,727 synagogues in the United States, 40 percent are Orthodox, 26 percent are Reform, and 23 percent Conservative, according to the census. Other groups, including Reconstructionist, humanistic, and Sephardic, make up 3 percent or less of all synagogues.

It is important to note that many of the Orthodox synagogues are small *shteiblach* with only twenty or thirty members, compared to some two hundred to three hundred members in many Conservative and Reform synagogues.

The fifty U.S. metropolitan areas with the largest Jewish populations contain 82 percent of all synagogues. The New York–Northern New Jersey–Long Island area, which has the heaviest Jewish population in the United States, contains one-third of all the country's synagogues. Next comes the Los Angeles–Riverside–Orange County area, with 7 percent; and Boston–Worcester–Lawrence, with 5 percent.

Reform synagogues predominate in smaller and more rural communities, such as those in Arkansas, Idaho, and Mississippi, where 90 percent of all synagogues are Reform.

Can you describe the basic difference between Reform and Conservative Judaism?

One basic difference between Reform and Conservative Judaism is that there is much more personal autonomy in the former, while the latter adheres to rabbinic law and the later Jewish law codes and is much slower in making modifications. Thus, for example, Conservative Judaism stands for keeping the Jewish dietary laws, whereas in Reform Judaism one is not required to keep kosher, as it is understood in Jewish tradition.

Whereas Reform Jews deny a belief in resurrection of the dead, even omitting traditional references to it in their prayer books, Conservative Judaism continues to adhere to the belief in an afterlife.

Reform Jews have eliminated references to a human messiah in their prayer book (substituting for it "a time of redemption"); Conservative Judaism still believes in the possibility of the coming of a human messiah.

Conservative Rabbis do not perform interfaith marriage between a Jew and a Christian, but there are some Reform rabbis who will perform such a ceremony.

Regarding worship services, there is generally more Hebrew used in Conservative prayer services than in Reform ones. There was a time when most Reform synagogues would not require men to wear prayer shawls and yarmulkes. Today, one is likely to see more prayer shawls and yarmulkes worn (in Conservative synagogues, they are a requirement), but Reform rabbis still have the option of not requiring them. Musical instruments are more common in a Reform worship service.

Conservative Judaism still adheres to the concept of Jews as the chosen people; Reform Judaism does not. Conservative Judaism also recognizes the traditional Jewish concept that the moral behavior of a person grants him or her a reward. Such reward and punishment theology is rejected in Reform Judaism, and references to it in their prayer book are omitted.

What are Reform Jews trying to reform?

Of the three pillars of Judaism—God, Torah, and peoplehood—Reform Judaism at its inception attempted to radically alter and reform the last two. It dropped the belief that the Jews are a people, arguing that Judaism is only a religion and that Jews have no special feelings of kinship with other Jews. For example, in 1840 Abraham Geiger, Germany's leading Reform rabbi, opposed efforts to help the Damascus Jews who were falsely accused in a blood libel.

With regard to the Torah, or Jewish law, the Reform movement's earliest changes consisted of reforming the synagogue service. Prayers for a return to the Holy Land were dropped, organ music was used to enhance the service, and prayers were recited in the vernacular.

As Reform Judaism developed, it dropped many Jewish laws, rather than reforming or modifying them. Within several decades, few Reform Jews kept kosher, the prayer service was further abridged, and there was an almost exclusive stress on Judaism's ethical teachings.

❧ Conservative Jews ❧

What are Conservative Jews trying to conserve?

Conservative Judaism came into being to create a new synthesis in Jewish life. Rather than advocate assimilation or yearn for the isolation of a new ghetto, Conservative Judaism has attempted to become a creative force through which modernity and tradition inform and reshape each other. Its goal is to conserve Jewish tradition while at the same time realizing that some modifications may be necessary in light of changes in society in each generation.

First and foremost, Conservative Jews who observe the tenets and principles of the movement are trying to preserve their commitment to observe the mitzvot (including Sabbath and festival observance, the Jewish dietary laws, and the importance of daily worship). The moral imperatives of Jewish tradition are meant to impel a Conservative Jew to universal concern and deeds of social justice. The Jewish home must be conserved and sustained by the guiding ethical insights of the Jewish heritage.

Finally, the Conservative movement is trying to preserve the ideal of the Conservative Jew as a striving Jew. No matter the level at which one starts and no matter the heights of piety and knowledge that one attains, no one can perform or acquire everything there is to know. Thus the ideal Conservative Jew is intended to be a Jewish traveler always striving to ascend the ladder of holiness.

Why did you decide to be a Conservative rabbi? Did you consider the other movements?

I grew up in Toronto, Canada, in a home with parents who belonged to a Conservative synagogue. There was no question that when I first entertained the idea of becoming a rabbi (at age eight) the only rabbinical school I ever entertained applying to was the Jewish Theological Seminary, headquarters of the Conservative movement.

My interest in Judaism began when I was in third grade. I very much enjoyed learning the Hebrew language and the prayers and always did well on my tests. At age twelve, a new young rabbi came to town. He was a very friendly guy, and he spent considerable time visiting us at Junior Congregation services, which I regularly attended. He also played guitar, which I also greatly admired. Although he was the rabbi at my Bar Mitzvah and taught me for only a couple of years (after which he moved on to a large synagogue in Massachusetts), his charm, presence, and interest in me convinced me more than ever that I wanted to be a rabbi. I also learned to play the guitar!

One of the highlights of my career occurred a few years ago, when I met him again. This time, both of us found ourselves co-officiating at a wedding, and under the chuppa I talked to the bride and groom about the specialness of the rabbi who "barmitzvahed" me. It was quite an emotional moment for both of us.

Do Conservative Jews believe that God wrote the Torah?

Recently, in a confirmation class in which I teach tenth graders, I posed this same question to my class: "Who wrote the Torah?" I got a range of answers. Some students believed that God wrote the Torah, dictating it to Moses word for word. Others thought great rabbis wrote the Torah, while still others thought that prophets wrote it.

Whereas Orthodoxy builds its faith on the absolute belief that God gave every word of the Torah at Mount Sinai, and Reform believes that only the ethical rules were revealed there, Conservative Judaism tries to steer a course between the two.

Many Conservative thinkers accept the idea that God revealed the Torah to Israel. But there are some who believe that the revealing of Torah, or revelation, happened only once in history; others consider revelation to be an ongoing process by which each generation of Jews uncovers more and more of God's word.

Most Conservative thinkers do not believe that God actually spoke each word of Torah to Moses and Israel. Biblical studies have shown that there are different sources in the Bible text, and that Moses could not have been the sole writer. So the majority of Conservative thinkers do not believe the entire Bible is the word of God. But they do believe that the basic core, the important parts, of Torah is Divine.

✸ Orthodox Jews ✸

Why do some Jews wear beards?

As I young child, I would see a Jewish man with a long beard and think that he was a rabbi. This was because my grandmother used to take me on visits to her Rebbe, and he had an extremely long beard. I now know that growing a beard, usually among traditional Orthodox Jews, is in keeping with the biblical injunction (Leviticus 19:27) "You shall not shave the corner of your beard," which was apparently a practice of the idolatrous nations of biblical times.

Although Jewish law permits use of scissors and clippers, many Jews, particularly Hasidim, do not trim the side locks even of children. They understood the law of not shaving the corners of their beard to mean that one may not shave one's beard using a razor blade or a knife. However, in modern times, with the introduction of the electric razor (considered a scissors rather than a blade), shaving of the beard by strictly observant Jews has become more common, and among Jews who are not Orthodox there are no more beards than in any other demographic group.

Do Orthodox Jews believe that Jews who aren't Orthodox aren't Jewish?

One of the first laws passed by Israel's Parliament, known as the *Knesset*, was the so-called Law of Return, which guaranteed that all Jews had a right to claim immediate citizenship in Israel. Ironically, it is the Law of Return that has led to extraordinary infighting within the Jewish community, for although the law welcomes all Jews, it does not answer the question, "Who is a Jew?"

In 1958, the who-is-a-Jew issue came to light in the famous Brother Daniel Case. Brother Daniel, a Carmelite monk living in a monastery in Haifa, petitioned Israel's High Court of Justice to become a citizen as provided for by the Law of Return. Brother Daniel had been born to Polish Jewish parents. Reared and educated as a Jew in every respect, he was active in a Zionist youth movement in preparation for immigrating to Israel. During World War II, he escaped a Nazi prison and evaded recapture by using forged documents certifying that he was a German Christian. He eventually entered a Christian convent and in 1942 converted to Christianity. Following the war, he became a monk. In 1958, he applied for Israeli citizenship under the Law of Return, arguing that according to Jewish law a person born a Jew always remains a Jew. His lawyer recited the Talmudic dictum "A Jew, even if he has sinned, remains a Jew" (Talmud, Sanhedrin 44a) and contended that even the most Orthodox Jew could not deny that Brother Daniel was a Jew.

The High Court of Justice in Israel ruled that the term *Jew* in the Law of Return has a secular meaning. As the ordinary person understands it, a Jew who has become Christian is not a Jew. Thus, in refusing to accept the halachic (Jewish legal) definition, the High Court gave *Jew* a nationalist definition, reflecting the healthy instinct of the Jewish people and its thirst for survival.

I've heard people in my own congregation who went to a Reform congregation to attend a Bar Mitzvah or Bat Mitzvah tell me "they spent their Shabbat in a church." It is language such as that, which fosters a lack of respect for our brothers and sisters, that does a disservice to the respect for the branches of Judaism in our country.

I have no doubt there are some Orthodox individuals who are convinced that there are many Jews who profess Judaism who are not Jewish. Certainly, they believe that they are not authentic Jews, and some have said the Reform and Conservative movements are doing a disservice to the Jewish religion by teaching their members a distorted view of the religion that is not in accordance with Jewish law.

I am also quite certain that there are some Orthodox rabbis who think Conservative, Reform, and Reconstructionist rabbis are not really rabbis. A few years ago, a local mikveh I would use for candidates who were to become Jews by choice came under new management. Orthodox Jews who determined that the conversion procedures of any rabbi other than an Orthodox one were not kosher now ran the mikveh. Therefore I was no longer welcome there.

In Israel too, the question of who is a rabbi continues to fester. Throughout Israel's history, it has been the Orthodox Rabbinate that controls its religious affairs. With the beginning of the emergence of Reform and Conservative synagogues in Israel in the 1970s and 1980s, Orthodox rabbis ruled that people who were converted to Judaism by such rabbis were not Jewish, since conversion had to take place according to halacha, which they defined as Orthodox Jewish law. Reform and Conservative rabbis in Israel are not even permitted to officiate at wedding ceremonies, unless an approved Orthodox rabbi stands beside them and says some of the prayers too.

According to most dictionaries, a Jew is defined as "a person whose religion is Judaism." In reality, this definition is far from the real truth. The who-is-a-Jew question has continued to foster much bitter infighting and division within the Jewish community.

✻ Reconstructionist Jews ✺

What is Reconstructionism?

The youngest of the religious movements in American Judaism is the Reconstructionist. It is particularly an American movement, unlike the other religious groups that began in Europe and were transplanted to America. Born in 1922, its leaders and thinkers are all American and most of its ideas are rooted in American philosophy and thought.

The Reconstructionist movement is based on the work of Rabbi Mordecai M. Kaplan, who studied at my *alma mater*, the Jewish Theological Seminary in New York City. In 1922, Kaplan formed his own synagogue in New York, the Society for the Advancement of Judaism, which became Kaplan's laboratory for developing his ideas about reconstructing Judaism and Jewish values. With the opening of the society in 1922, the Reconstructionist movement was born.

What are Reconstructionists trying to reconstruct?

The most important of the Reconstructionist teachings is that Judaism is a changing, evolving, developing religious civilization. As important as religion is, it is only one part of a whole civilization. Kaplan, founder of the movement, viewed Judaism as much more than worship of God, prayer, and performance of mitzvot. The Jewish people have created their own art, music, language, folkways, and customs. In short, Judaism is not only a religion but also a total civilization.

Reconstructionists feel that Orthodoxy relies too much on its belief in a personal God. They are critical of the Reform movement because it neglects the religious meaning of peoplehood and the value of ritual. It also posits that Conservative Judaism is too concerned with the past and with its attempts to remain true to Jewish law, while at the same time changing it.

Since each movement and its philosophy has serious short-comings, the best hope, according to the Reconstructionists, is a re-construction of Jewish ideas, life, and philosophy. That is the essence of Kaplan's approach.

The seal of the Reconstructionist movement explains its basic goals. The form is that of a wheel. The hub of the wheel is Israel, the center of Jewish civilization. Religion, culture, and ethics are the spokes of the wheel by which the vital influence of Israel is felt on Jewish life everywhere. The wheel has an inner rim and an outer one. The inner rim represents the Jewish community tied to Israel by bonds of religion, ethics, and culture. The outer rim is the general community (for us, the community of America), with which the Jewish civilization maintains contact at every point. The seal thus symbolizes the whole philosophy of the Reconstructionist movement.

Is Reconstructionism even more liberal than Reform?

Reconstructionism differs from Reform, but I would not say that this means that it is more liberal.

Reform ideas about God, for example, are rich and diverse. Some Reform thinkers suggest that God is a part of nature, while others believe that God is a force that we feel as we struggle to evolve. Kaplan defines God as the power or process that makes for human salvation and fulfillment, for the realization of the highest ideals for which people strive. Reconstructionists also believe that there are things within God's power and things God cannot control, at least for now. This is why there is still much evil and suffering in the world.

Reform thinkers were negative toward the mitzvot, writing that they were old-fashioned; modern Reform thinkers often talk about the importance of mitzvot (especially the ethical ones) and even have mitzvah committees in their synagogues. Kaplan taught that the mitzvot seemed out of date, and if no new meanings could be found in them, they should be dropped.

Of course, this privilege to change the past also carries with it the responsibility to create new customs and practices to replace the old. Kaplan was in the forefront of this trend. He worked for women's liberation within Jewish life long before we used those words. He created the Bat Mitzvah ceremony for girls, and it was his daughter Judith in 1922 who was America's first Bat Mitzvah.

One of Kaplan's last proposals was his idea that people, not the rabbis, must have the final say in accepting or dropping mitzvot. In his congregation, the entire membership got to vote for or against ritual changes. This is surely the reason the Reconstructionist movement is deemed the most democratic of all Jewish groups.

Chapter 16

❧ ❧

Rabbis and Cantors

How does someone qualify to be a rabbi? Who gives the right to say that someone is a rabbi?

The Torah tells us how Moses symbolically transferred his authority to Joshua, his successor, by placing his hands (*semicha*) on him in the presence of the whole community and investing Joshua with some of Moses' own dignity. The custom of semicha, whereby the ancient sages conferred on their disciples the title rabbi, thus permitting them to make decisions in matters of civil and religious law, was practiced in the manner described in the Torah. The master, in the presence of two other teachers, transferred his authority to his disciple, who was to be the future teacher, by placing his hands on him. So until the early centuries of the common era, the ordaining rabbi would place his hands over the head of the man being ordained and confer upon him the title of rabbi or rav.

I am a Conservative rabbi, and as such I had to study in the rabbinical school of my *alma mater*, the Jewish Theological Seminary of America. Most rabbinical schools, including those of the Reform, Conservative, modern Orthodox, and Reconstructionist branches of Judaism, are graduate schools. This means one must have attained an undergraduate degree before entering these rabbinical schools.

To enter them, one must have good grades and a commitment to observe the tenets of Judaism as understood and interpreted by the school. I spent five years in rabbinical school, studying Jewish philosophy, Bible (my major), codes (Jewish law), and Jewish literature. I also had an opportunity to take courses in practical rabbinics, where I learned the practical aspects involved in the life of a rabbi—how to give a sermon, visit the sick, work with the board of a synagogue, teach adults and children, and the like.

Many changes are noteworthy in rabbinical schools today. Beginning in the 1980s, the Conservative and Reform movements' rabbinical schools began to admit women for the first time. Today, perhaps a third or more of all rabbinical school students in Reform, Conservative, and Reconstructionist schools are women. Orthodoxy opposes this tendency, although it has been predicted that eventually women will be Orthodox rabbis.

Why does the cantor in the synagogue sometimes sing in such a fancy way?

Most religious traditions have realized that a person must go beyond mere words in expressing himself or herself at a moment of deepest emotion. Music is perhaps the most expressive language known to human beings. It helps us when words are insufficient, and it assists us in renewing the meaning of words said again and again by filling them with new dynamism and movement.

Cantors are specially trained to bring the words of the prayer book to life. They have usually been carefully trained in vocal technique and various special styles of singing the prayers and services. They are also experts in musical motifs and always sense the proper musical key that is comfortable for the congregation. Our cantor has a powerful and mellifluous voice, and all enjoy singing with him the many beautiful melodies to the prayers, some of which he composed. Being fluent in Hebrew, he also fully understands each and every Hebrew word that he sings. Although he enjoys singing many of the prayers with the congregation, occasionally there is a prayer that he sings as a solo, with a more ornate style and prolonged melody. He does this to add to the feeling and spirituality of the prayer, and make it come to life. I can think of several prayers when he uses the fancier notes, as you call them.

For me, the most stirring moment in the year in which the cantor uses fancy notes is when he sings the prayer on the High Holy Days called *Hineni*. This prayer is said to have been composed by a cantor in the Middle Ages. It is a personal prayer in which the cantor pleads that his prayers on behalf of the entire congregation be acceptable. What is amazing about the way our cantor sings this prayer is that he makes his entrance from the back of the very large sanctuary, chanting the prayer as he walks down the aisle and later ascends the stairs to the bimah. His magnificent voice can be heard even without a microphone, and each year that I hear him I continue to be in awe of how he interprets the words of this ancient prayer.

Can gays and lesbians become rabbis?

Because the classical Jewish tradition saw homosexual relations as forbidden, rabbinical schools were reluctant to open the doors to gay and lesbian students. New medical knowledge about the etiology of homosexuality has led all denominations of Judaism to rethink their stance against homosexuality.

Currently, all four of the major denominations of Judaism stand on record for full civil rights for gays and lesbians, officially welcoming them into their congregation. With the exception of the Conservative and Orthodox rabbinical schools, the others now open their doors to gays who are interested in studying for the rabbinate.

The Conservative movement's ban on ordaining openly gay individuals stems from its understanding of the biblical prohibition against homosexual acts by men. The Torah calls such acts an "abomination." The majority opinion of the Conservative movement's Committee on Law and Standards, seeing such acts as against Jewish law and custom, banned homosexuals from spiritual leadership and counseled that they embrace celibacy. The minority opinion of the same body, following modern scientific opinion, views homosexuality as a natural, God-given condition entitling homosexuals to the same rights and protections as heterosexuals.

What are the differences among Reform, Conservative, and Orthodox rabbis?

Each major branch of Judaism has its own philosophy, theology, and way of understanding Jewish tradition. Orthodox rabbinic practice is the most to the right, adhering to Jewish tradition with little modification of past traditions. Thus, for example, Orthodox rabbis believe in the separation of the sexes; their synagogue seating places men and women in separate sections.

Reform rabbinic practice is the most to the left. In Reform rabbinic practice, there is much personal autonomy; one Reform rabbi might not adhere to all of the laws of keeping kosher, while another keeps kosher.

Conservative rabbis are often imagined to be somewhere in the middle between Reform and Orthodox when it comes to their religious practices and beliefs.

As a Conservative rabbi, I would have to say that many Conservative rabbis are more traditional than people think. Although it is quite true that various modifications have entered into the Conservative movement (for example, permission to drive to and from synagogue on the Sabbath, or permission to grant women full participation in services), Conservative rabbis still are Sabbath-observant, adhere to the Jewish dietary laws, and perform life cycle events in much the same way as an Orthodox rabbi would perform them, adhering to ancient customs and traditions.

One big difference between the Orthodox rabbinate and that of the Conservative and Reform branches is that many women now serve Reform and Conservative synagogues. The Orthodox movement is not ordaining females as rabbis.

Chapter 17

❧ ❧

Origins

Why do Jews like Chinese food?

Someone once told me that if you visit a new town or city and want to know how many Jews live there, look in the yellow pages and count the number of Chinese restaurants. Having received this question once before (and having been unable to answer it then), I decided to do some research. Now I do have an answer.

A friend read about the Jewish preference for Chinese food as the "wonton-kreplach" connection. The theory here is that there are many similarities between Jewish and Chinese food. For one, the Chinese wonton, a dumpling, looks very much like the Jewish dumpling, which is called a kreplach. In addition, the Chinese culture has many of the same values as the Jewish tradition: strong emphasis on family, education, achievement and productivity, commitment, and devotion to the group. Finally, of course, there has been a lot of wandering and a Diaspora for both groups too.

Recently, many diverse observers have also called attention to the phenomenon of Jewish people loving to eat Chinese food. A long line of Jewish comedians—Lenny Bruce, Buddy Hackett, Jackie Mason, and others—have created routines about Jews and Chinese food. Even Chinese restaurateurs whom I have spoken with agree.

Recently I searched the Internet for "Jewish Chinese Food." Was I ever surprised to discover numerous articles on the subject!

146

There was one I found especially interesting, called "'Safe Treyf': New York Jews and Chinese Food," written by Gaye Tuckman and Harry G. Levine.

According to the article, Jews like Chinese food for the same reasons given by people all over the world: it is available, delicious, and relatively inexpensive. In short, quality, price, and proximity are some of the reasons Chinese food became so important to New York Jews. But these factors appeal to anyone who eats out in a restaurant. There was certainly other restaurant food for New York City Jews to eat, including their own Eastern European foods.

To answer this question, Tuckman and Levine cite several themes in Chinese food that relate to their identity as modern Jews. First, Chinese food is unkosher, and therefore non-Jewish. But because of the specific ways in which Chinese food is prepared and served, immigrant Jews and their children found it to be more attractive and less threatening than other non-Jewish unkosher food. For instance, Chinese food does not mix milk and meat (a practice forbidden by Jewish law), and Chinese restaurant food also uses some ingredients that were familiar to Eastern European Jews: chicken, garlic, celery, and onions. In addition, with regard to the nonkosher meat and fish often used in Chinese food, Chinese cooking disguises them by cutting and finely chopping them, so they look less repulsive.

Second, Jews understood Chinese restaurant food as cosmopolitan. Eating in a Chinese restaurant signified that one was not a hick or a greenhorn, but rather that Chinese food was sophisticated in preparation. In other words, it "looked good" to be eating Chinese food, demonstrating a sophisticated palate.

Third, by the second and third generation, Jews identified eating Chinese food as something modern American Jews did together. In other words, it became a Jewish communal custom when eating out to frequent Chinese restaurants; thus eating Chinese became a New York Jewish custom, a part of daily life, that over time spread to other cities and towns across the country.

In recent years, many new kosher Chinese restaurants have emerged in central New Jersey, which has allowed my family and me, along with others who keep kosher, a chance to experience Chinese dining without the worry of forbidden ingredients. To my amazement, a kosher Chinese restaurant opened just a few weeks ago, only ten minutes from where I live. I have dined there several times, and during the intermediate days of Sukkot, where I ate outside in a portable sukkah they built just for the holiday. When I asked the owner of the restaurant, Mr. Lin, why he decided to open a kosher Chinese restaurant (his brother owns a nonkosher one in southern New Jersey) in a town that is predominantly non-Jewish, he said, "Don't worry—once the Jews find out, they will come." And come they have indeed. Even non-Jewish people (including two sisters from a local Catholic church) have been frequenting his restaurant, which is beginning to build an excellent reputation.

Why do Jews have Jewish-sounding last names?

At the beginning of the biblical period, Jews, like all members of ancient societies, had no surnames (last names). Men were known simply as Abraham, Isaac, Jacob, Moses. As the patriarchal families swelled into tribes, more definite identification was deemed necessary, and so-called patronymics came into use. Thus we find, Joshua the son of Nun, and Caleb the son of Yefuneh. Places of origin began to be used in Talmudic times: Nachum the Mede and Hillel the Babylonian.

In the tenth and eleventh centuries, family names became common, among Jews and non-Jews. There are several important reasons for this development. With the rise of cities, it became impossible for individuals to know one another as they did in villages, and a personal first name no longer sufficed. The increase in commerce too, necessitated a more exact system of naming.

In a number of countries, family names were often derived from Hebrew words, and thus was born the "Jewish-sounding" last name. An occupation often served as a source for a family name. Thus for example, in my own community we have a family whose last name is Chazin, deriving from the Hebrew *Chazan*, meaning "cantor." Grandpa Chazan is a retired cantor. The common Jewish family name Metzger means "butcher," and the last name Schneider means "tailor." In Italy, a common last name is Dayan (meaning "rabbinic judge"). The famous defense minister of Israel in the 1960s was Moshe Dayan.

Other last names related to the lineage of a Jewish family. For example, the last name Cohen or Kahn is a usual indication of priestly lineage, while Levine or Levy is an indication of Levitical lineage.

As Jews began to assimilate into American society in the twentieth century, it became quite common for families to change surnames that had many syllables into shorter-sounding names that would more likely blend into society. So, for example, Goldstein became Gold, Levinsky became Levine, Feinberg to Fine, and Kaganoff to Kagan.

One of the best books I've ever read on the subject of Jewish names is A *Dictionary of Jewish Names and Their History* by Benzion C. Kaganoff (who obviously chose not to shorten his surname). He reports in his book that the longest Jewish family name—Katzenellenbogen—was assumed by Meir ben Isaac, a renowned fifteenth-century Talmudic scholar. He derived it from the locality of Katzenelnbogen, the place of his birth. We have many Katz families in our congregation. I wonder whether there is any connection to that author.

How did the phrase "People of the Book" originate?

You may be surprised to find out that Mohammed, the Arab founder of Islam, is credited with naming the Jews "People of the Book," or in Hebrew *Am Hasefer*. Mohammed was impressed with the Jewish Bible and felt certain that the people who produced the Holy Scriptures must have qualities of greatness.

From the days of Ezra the Prophet, the Torah and the books added to it were so intimately a part of the Jewish people that they could not easily conceive of another way of life. They were aware that acceptance of the Book marked the birth of the Hebrew people. Without continued contact with the Book, the Jews instinctively knew they could not attain self-fulfillment, or even survive as a people. It was a non-Jew, then, who made explicit a concept they had long lived by implicitly.

The Torah exempted no one, not even a king of Israel, from studying the Book: "And it shall be, when he sits upon the throne of his kingdom, that he shall write a copy of this law in a book. And he shall read it all the days of his life" (Deuteronomy 17:18). Joshua, successor to Moses, was likewise instructed to apply himself to the Book: "This book of the law shall not depart from your mouth, but you shall meditate on it day and night, that you may observe to do according to all that is written in it" (Joshua 1:8).

How the Jewish people conceived their dedication to the Book is illustrated by a Talmudic legend:

> When the Israelites were gathered at Mount Sinai, an apparition of The Book and The Sword appeared before them. A heavenly voice demanded that they make a solemn choice: "You can have one or the other, but not both. If you choose The Book, you must renounce The Sword. Should you choose The Sword, then The Book will perish." The Israelites made one of their most memorable decisions. They chose The Book. Then God said to Israel: "If you observe what is written in The Book you will be delivered from The Sword, but should you refuse to observe it, The Sword will ultimately destroy you."

The Jews' attachment to the Bible has been carried over, in Judaism, to broad respect for the printed word. In synagogue schools, a child who has accidentally dropped a holy book will lift it from the floor to his lips and kiss it. Books are considered the fountain of learning, and they are to be embraced as something precious.

Are there Chinese Jews?

Yes, Jews not only enjoy eating Chinese food, but there are Chinese Jews too. More than forty-five hundred miles from Israel, a Jewish community of ten thousand people lived in central China during the Sung Dynasty (96 A.D.) A synagogue was said to have been constructed there in 1163. Under the declining Sung Dynasty, a cohesive group of some one thousand people settled in the ninth or tenth century at the invitation of the emperor in Kaifeng. They were expert in the production of dyed cotton fabrics. The Kaifeng synagogue was destroyed in a monstrous flood and restored in the late 1200s. Thereafter the community fell into rapid decay, mainly as a result of its complete isolation from other centers of Jewish life. By the middle of the nineteenth century, the Kaifeng Jews preserved only a rudimentary knowledge of Judaism and only the ruins of the former synagogue were left. At the end of World War II, just 200–250 traceable descendants of the original Kaifeng Jewish community still survived.

Mr. Leo Gabow, a former Hong Kong businessman and international trader, has served as a tour guide for Jewish Americans interested in visiting descendants of the Chinese Jews. He managed to gather memorabilia and other artifacts connected to the synagogue, and several years ago his collection became part of a show in Palo Alto, California, titled "At the End of the Silk Road: The Jews of Kaifeng, China." Today, a hospital has been built over the synagogue's original site. However, eight of the synagogue's thirteen Torah scrolls have been preserved in museums throughout the world.

If you asked Chinese Jews twenty years ago how many of their ranks remain, estimates ranged from one hundred to three hundred, although it is not clear if they mean individuals or only male heads of household, since Chinese Jews trace their descent that way, as is the Chinese custom. This, of course, raises problems for other Jews who define Jewishness matrilineally (through one's mother), according to Jewish law. By this criterion, Chinese Jews are not "really" Jewish, and haven't been so for hundreds of years.

A Ming emperor in the 1400s was said to have conferred upon the Jews seven surnames by which they are identifiable to this day: Ai, Lao, Jin, Li, Shi, Zhang, and Zhao. Although other Chinese may have one of these surnames, Chinese Jews and their descendants use only these seven names. Two names are of particular interest; Shi and Jin mean stone and gold, respectively—common surnames today among Western Jews.

There are many reasons for the assimilation of the Jews of China, including lack of rabbis, lack of translation of the Torah into Chinese, loss of the Hebrew language over the years, and several destructions of the synagogue from flooding of the Yellow River.

No new Jewish communities were formed in China until the middle of the nineteenth century. Jews settled in China in the 1840s with the cession of Hong Kong to Great Britain and establishment of foreign concessions in Shanghai, Tientsin, and other cities. By 1937, about ten thousand Jews were living in China.

Hitler caused the greatest influx of Jews in China. Some eighteen to twenty thousand victims of Nazism found a precarious shelter in Japanese-occupied Shanghai between 1938 and 1941.

The Japanese captured Shanghai in 1937 and closed it to further immigration in 1941. They deported most of their Jews to the Hong Kong district of Shanghai and kept them in unsanitary camps. After the war, most of the Shanghai Jews left for the United States, Britain, Israel, and Australia. Since 1948, more than one thousand Jews from China have immigrated to Israel.

Today, sources say that China's Jewish community numbers around two hundred, nearly all in Shanghai. But led by Chabad Lubavitch Rabbi Shalom Greenberg, efforts are under way to revive the small Jewish community.

What's the origin of the Jewish star?

Like the seven-branched menorah, the Jewish star (in Hebrew, *magen David*, meaning star of David) composed of two triangles, has been a symbolic ornament of Judaism for many centuries. It was found in the Capernaum synagogue of the third century and on a Jewish tombstone in southern Italy. Since the Star of David is not mentioned in rabbinic literature and has been found on Roman mosaic pavements, it is assumed that the star formed of two superimposed triangles is not of Jewish origin.

The first Zionist Congress adopted the star as a symbol, with the word Zion in the center. During the First World War, it was used by Jewish organizations doing military relief, describing them as the Red Magen David (*Magen David Adom*).

Today, the Magen David is a universally recognized symbol of Jewry. It appears on the flag of the state of Israel, and the Israeli equivalent of the Red Cross is known as the "Red Magen David."

What is a kike?

Kike is a derogatory word, slang for Jew. There are varying explanations as to its origin, but no one is certain of the derivation. One explanation is that the word *kike* originates from *keikl* which in Yiddish means "circle." At Ellis Island, one of the main immigration check-in points, immigrants were initially grouped by religion and language to make it easier for them to communicate with each other, and also to be identified more quickly by relatives waiting there to meet them. Christians were marked with an X, which was likely supposed to be a cross. Jews were marked with a circle, which was likely supposed to be the Star of David. It is easy to see how the staff could become sloppy at drawing these symbols as X and O. The word *keikl* was used by the Jews to make fun of the poorly drawn star; they referred to each other as being "circles." Unfortunately, from this innocent usage, the term acquired a derogatory meaning.

Robert L. Chapman's *American Slang* has a slight variation on the explanation. Rather than saying the circle was a mark made by the staff to symbolize the Star of David, the book says, "Jews who could not sign their names would make a circle." This suggests that it was Jews themselves who started using the circle—presumably to avoid the X, which was reminiscent of a cross.

According to *Our Crowd*, by Stephen Birmingham, the term *kike* was actually coined as a putdown by assimilated American German Jews for their Eastern European brethren: "Because many Russian Jewish names ended in 'ki', they were called 'kikes'—a German Jewish contribution to the American vernacular."

Chapter 18

❧ ❧

Black Jews

How do we know that the black people from Ethiopia who claim to be Jewish are really Jewish?

For centuries, the world Jewish community was not even aware of the existence of the Jewish community of Ethiopia in the northern province of Gondar. They called themselves Beta Israel—the house of Israel—and used the Torah to guide their prayers and memories of the heights of Jerusalem as they lived in their thatched huts in Ethiopia. But their neighbors called them Falashas—the alien ones, the invaders. Even three hundred years of rule and the black features that matched those of all the people around them did not make the Jews of Ethiopian secure governors of their own destiny in Africa.

According to an old Jewish tradition, Ethiopian Jews are descended from the Israelite tribe of Dan. There are several other theories as well concerning their beginnings. Some posit they may be descendants of Menelik I, son of King Solomon and the Queen of Sheba. Others have held that they may be descendants of Ethiopian Christians and pagans who converted to Judaism centuries ago. Still others have theorized that the Ethiopian Jews may be descendants of Jews who fled Israel from Egypt after the destruction of the First Temple in 586 B.C.E. and eventually settled in Ethiopia.

No matter which theory is actually correct, the authenticity of the "Jewishness" of the community became a major issue. As early as the sixteenth century, Egypt's Chief Rabbi, David ben Solomon ibn Avi Zimra (known as the Radbaz), declared that in Jewish legal issues the Beta Israel were indeed Jews. In 1855, Daniel ben Hamdya, a member of the Beta Israel, was the first Ethiopian Jew to visit Israel, meeting with a council of rabbis in Jerusalem concerning the authenticity of the Beta Israel. By 1864, almost all leading Jewish authorities accepted the Beta Israel as true Jews, and in 1908 the chief rabbis of forty-five countries officially recognized them as fellow Jews.

In the 1970s, Ethiopia turned Marxist and the situation of the Jews there deteriorated quickly. The leadership was anti-Israel, and the people of Ethiopia experienced massive famine. Soon Israel began to quietly smuggle out of Ethiopia as many Jews as it could. The program, known as Operation Moses, began in November 1984 and ended some six weeks later. In that short time, almost eight thousand Jews were rescued and brought to Israel. But the mission was not without its problems. Because of news leaks, the mission ended prematurely as Arab nations pressured the Sudanese government to prevent any more Jews from using Sudan to go to Israel. Thousands of Jews were left behind in Ethiopia.

The new arrivals spent between six months and two years in absorption centers, learning everything from the Hebrew language, to how to use a knife, spoon, and fork. Some years ago, when I took a group of families from our synagogue to Israel, we had a chance to visit one of the absorption centers and speak to the Ethiopian Jews. They were pleased to greet us and have us visit, and they even gave the group some of their handmade gifts, including Ethiopian yarmulkes!

The Ethiopian Jews' ignorance of Talmudic Judaism caused many Israeli rabbis to question the authenticity of their Jewishness. Nonetheless, in 1975 the Ashkenazic Chief Rabbi, Shlomo Goren, wrote to the Beta Israel, telling them: "You are our brothers, you are our blood and our flesh. You are true Jews." Later that same year, the Israel Interministerial Commission officially recognized the Beta Israel as Jews under Israel's Law of Return. The Beta Israel was ready to come home.

Indeed, the Beta Israel was strictly observant in pre-Talmudic Jewish traditions. The women went to mikveh just as observant women do to this day, and they continue to carry out ancient festivals, such as Seged, that have been passed down through the generations of Beta Israel. The *Kesim,* or religious leaders, are as widely revered and re-spected as the great rabbis in each community, passing the Jewish customs through storytelling and the like.

As time went on, an increasing number of rabbis in Israel tried to encourage the Ethiopians to undergo a pro forma ritual of conver-sion to Judaism, to forestall any possible questions about their status, which was still in doubt by some rabbis. Since the males had been cir-cumcised at birth, all that was asked was that a symbolic drop of blood be drawn from the male organ, and that men and women immerse in the mikveh. Recently, a growing number of Ethiopian Jews are refus-ing to take on these conversion procedures, arguing that to do so now would intimate they were not Jewish.

I have a black friend from Harlem who says he's Jewish. How could this be true?

When I was a student in rabbinical school, I used to visit the black synagogue in Harlem. Rabbi Wentworth Arthur Matthew, born in West India, was the founder of the Commandment Keepers Con-gregation in Harlem in 1919. He trained and ordained many of the rabbis who later founded synagogues in various places in the United States and the Caribbean.

The emergence of Judaism among people of African descent in the first half of the twentieth century is said to have been made possi-ble by a combination of factors. One was a strong religious tradition in the background of the person who became Jewish, embodying Jewish practices from an early but unclear source. When interviewed, many of the older members of this community recalled memories of their parents observing certain dietary laws, such as abstaining from pork. Others recalled traditions related to observing the Sabbath or festivals. In most cases, the practices were fragmentary and observed by people who simultaneously practiced Christianity.

The possible origins of these Hebraic traditions could be traced to West Africa, where a number of tribes have customs so similar to

Judaism that an ancient connection or maybe even descent from one of the Ten Lost Tribes is conjectured. Another possibility for these well-documented practices is association with Jewish slave owners and merchants in the Caribbean and North America.

Many African Americans who practice Judaism today maintain that they have always had a close affinity with the Hebrews of the Old Testament. Scholars such as Albert Raboteau (in his book *Slave Religion*) have described how the biblical struggles of the Hebrew people, particularly their slavery and exodus from Egypt, bore a strong similarity to the conditions of African slaves and was therefore of special importance to them. This close identification with the biblical Hebrews is clearly seen in the lyrics of gospel songs such as the popular "Go Down Moses."

What all this proves is that there was a foundation, be it psychological, spiritual, or historical, that made some black people receptive to the direct appeal to Judaism that Rabbi Matthew and others made to them.

Rabbi Matthew always maintained that the "original Jews" were black people—or at least European. However, he did not deny the existence or legitimacy of white Jews. When I visited his synagogue, there were many of the traditional rituals and customs. There was separate seating for men and women (typical of an Orthodox synagogue), worshippers wore prayer shawls and yarmulkes, they wore tefillin during the week, and they read from a Torah.

Toward the goal of greater integration, a group predominantly comprising young adult black Jews was organized in 1965, with some significant support from white Jews, calling itself *Hatza'ad Harishon* ("first step"). In addition to promoting contact between white and black Jews, this group has sought to enlarge Jewish educational opportunities among the black Jews.

Rabbi Matthew died in 1973, a year before my rabbinic ordination. Since his death, there has been virtually no dialogue between white and black Jews in America.

According to the *Encyclopedia Judaica*, no reliable statistics exist for the number of black Jewish congregations or for total membership, but estimates suggest a few dozen distinct groupings in such cities as New York, Chicago, Philadelphia, Boston, and Cincinnati, with membership between two and six thousand. Most of these groups consist of individuals who attach themselves to a charismatic figure generally proclaiming a rediscovery of the lost roots of the black nation in Judaism. The groups bear such names as Bnei Israel, Temple of the Gospel of the Kingdom, and Kahal Beth B'nai Yisrael. Their knowledge of Hebrew, ritual, and the Bible is quite rudimentary.

Chapter 19

❦ ❧

Jewish Professions

Why are so many comedians Jewish?

It has been said that when Jews immigrated to America in the early twentieth century they were able to integrate themselves into American life with influence more than any other minority group. From the 1920s onward, Jews held positions of status in science, literature, education, and business. Surprisingly though, it wasn't the brightest student but rather the class clown that was to define Americans' perceptions of the Jewish character. The overbearing Jewish mother, the cheapskate, and the wisecracking outsider caricatures imbedded themselves in mainstream America. Although stereotypes are certainly distasteful, it was precisely this self-criticism that made Jewish humor nonthreatening and desirable to the typical American audience.

Many who write about Jewish humor have said that because Jewish immigrants came from families that had to confront hatred and persecution, they were anxious and fearful. Needing a way to cope with their anxiety, the Jew turned to humor as a way of dealing with the anti-Semite. If Jews could deflect hatred with laughter and humor, people wouldn't hurt them.

Thus began Jewish vaudeville acts in the early twentieth century, with Jewish comedians incorporating their Yiddish wit into acts that dominated the American entertainment scene. Notable among these comedians were the famous Marx Brothers, Eddie Cantor, George Burns, and Jack Benny.

With the advent of television in the early 1950s, Jewish comedians made their biggest mark with humorists such as Milton Berle and Sid Caesar, who had as their writers such celebrities as Neil Simon, Woody Allen, Mel Brooks, and Carl Reiner. Along with television, Jewish humor was a part of the summer culture of New York's Catskill Mountains. The so-called Borscht belt hotels were a breeding ground for Jewish comic talent, including Danny Kaye and Jerry Lewis, and many others who would later make their names in film and television.

Today Jewish comics still dominate the comedy profession, including the likes of Jackie Mason, Jerry Seinfeld, and Adam Sandler to name just a few.

A childhood friend of mine, William Novak, coedited with Moshe Waldoks a wonderful book titled *The Big Book of Jewish Humor.* Consisting of Jewish jokes, quotations, and short stories, this collection still stands as one of the most influential books of Jewish humor ever published in English. I highly recommend it!

Why are there a lot of Jewish doctors?

The fact that the Torah already mandated medical care several thousand years ago might explain the attraction of the Jewish people to the art of healing. Judaism has always viewed seeking medical attention as a moral necessity. Jews are obligated to take care of their body and to seek medical care when necessary.

In Talmudic sources, there were a substantial number of practicing physicians. The Talmud (Sanhedrin 17b) enumerates ten things that must be found in a city where a scholar wishes to live, among them both a physician and a surgeon. Many outstanding Jewish scholars achieved fame as prominent doctors.

In the majority of cases, the art of healing was transmitted from father to son. Among the best known in ancient Jewish history was Mar Samuel, a judge and head of an academy of learning, who is credited with discovering an ointment for curing eye disease. One of the most famous sixth-century physicians was Asaf HaRofey, who wrote a book that constituted a source of information on Jewish medical ethics and all sorts of remedies for a variety of ailments.

In the twelfth century, the poet and philosopher Judah Halevi became a highly sought-after doctor in Spain. The twelfth-century philosopher Maimonides, considered by many to be the greatest of all Jewish scholars, wrote numerous medical works and served as the personal physician to the family of Sultan Saladin of Egypt. His original Medical Oath is often chosen by Jewish doctors and is also used in a number of medical schools as well.

Jewish doctors were overrepresented by a factor of ten in the cities of medieval Europe, frequently numbering 50–60 percent of physicians when the Jewish population was roughly 3–5 percent of the total. To cite one example, the municipal records of Perpignan, France, over a period of two centuries listed 67 Jewish physicians out of a total of 120! In many of these cases, the occupation was passed down as a family tradition from generation to generation.

It has been estimated that there are between 80,000 and 100,000 Jewish physicians, who are 12–15 percent of the 685,000 physicians in the United States, according to AMA statistics. In 1934, 60 percent of medical school applicants were Jewish, although the number has fallen substantially since then.

The reasons for the rise and decline of Jewish physicians at various periods in history are multiple and complex. It has been said that a more discriminatory quota system in medical school, coupled with a lessened interest in pursuing a medical career among young Jewish students, likely has resulted in a decline in the number of Jewish applicants to medical school.

Why aren't there more Jewish athletes?

Because interest in sports was not a high Jewish cultural priority, there are not a large percentage of Jews who play in professional sports. Over the years though, many famous Jewish athletes have done exceedingly well and even landed in the Sports Hall of Fame.

When I was a teenager, I remember watching on television the great Sandy Koufax, pitcher for the Brooklyn Dodgers. Koufax pitched in four All Star games and between 1962 and 1965 became the first pitcher to throw four no-hitters. Koufax always observed the High Holy

Days. When Yom Kippur occurred on the first day of the 1965 World Series with Minnesota, he missed his starting assignment to attend services at Temple of Aaron in St. Paul, Minnesota. He came back and pitched shutouts in the fifth and seventh games, and the Dodgers won the series four games to three.

Mark Spitz, a member of the Swimming Hall of Fame, is considered the greatest swimmer in the history of the sport. From 1965 to 1972, he won eleven Olympic medals.

Recently a documentary movie was made on the life of Hank Greenberg, a member of the Baseball Hall of Fame. All eyes were on Greenberg in 1938 when he challenged Babe Ruth's record of sixty home runs. His total of fifty-eight fell short but did tie the record for a right-hander. I am in possession of a wonderful early baseball card of his.

A few years ago, I learned that I had a cousin who played professional hockey in the 1930s and 1940s by the name of Alex Levinsky. I searched the library for old newspapers with his name and found that he played on several Stanley Cup hockey teams. He is now deceased, but I recently wrote his son and asked whether he could send me some more information about his father. I not only received the information, but several of his hockey cards as well as newspaper articles of his winning goals.

There is now a Jewish Sports Hall of Fame in several major cities in the United States, and many books are being published that describe in full detail the accomplishments of some of the greatest Jewish athletes who ever lived.

Is it true that there used to be Jewish gangsters?

Yes, and they had nicknames like Abe "Kid Twist" Reles, Benjamin "Bugsy" Siegel, and Arnold "The Brain" Rothstein. What they all had in common was being American Jewish gangsters, whose influence on organized crime in the United States in the 1920s and 1930s rivaled their Italian counterparts.

The period between the World Wars—the eras of Prohibition and the Great Depression—saw the rise of the American Jewish gangster. In 1919, the United States government, in an attempt to regulate morality, outlawed the manufacture and sale of alcoholic beverages. Prohibition was the perfect opportunity for the mobster to provide what society still wanted—namely, booze.

Jewish gangsters engaged in gambling, extortion, narcotics, peddling, and murder. For a time, they dominated the rackets in Cleveland, Detroit, Boston, Philadelphia, and New York. A composite portrait of the typical Jewish gangster of this period would show him to be a second-generation American male of Eastern European parentage, city-bred, and in his early twenties. He would not have finished high school and was often the only member of his family to choose a life of crime, because it was a quick way to material success.

The American Jewish community at large entertained ambivalent feelings about the Jewish gangster. Some were repelled because they epitomized the "bad Jew," while others harbored a grudging admiration for the Jewish mobster because he competed physically with the non-Jew and gave as good as he got.

A number of Jewish gangsters acquired respect because they assumed the role of protector of their people. In Chicago, the funeral of Samuel "Nails" Morton, the Jewish gangster, was attended by five thousand Jews who felt they owed him thanks for protecting their neighborhood from Jew baiters.

In spite of their own success in crime, most Jewish gangsters kept their families from being implicated in criminal enterprise. They often sent their children to the best schools and encouraged them to enter professions such as medicine and law. In this, they were very much like other Jewish parents of their generation.

Why are so many people in Hollywood Jewish?

Jews are conspicuous in the entertainment world. We find them in considerable numbers in the theater, radio, and motion pictures. They are actors, writers, producers, and theater owners. Jews are especially prominent in Hollywood. Some of them were among the early pioneers of the motion picture industry: the Warner Brothers, Harry Cohen, Samuel Goldwyn, Irving Thulberg, and Louis B. Mayer.

The motion picture was created at a time when Jews were seeking entry into the economic and cultural life of their host countries. Their involvement with film was due to a number of factors:

- The film business had not developed a tradition of its own and had no vested interests to defend.
- Participation in the movie business did not require knowledge of the native language.
- The film industry was initially regarded as a low-grade form of entertainment, suitable only for the immigrant or the uneducated masses, rather than a valid art form, and those connected with films were often held in contempt.
- New Jewish immigrants to America therefore found it relatively easy to enter this field, and they used the opportunity to transform the media from a marginal branch of entertainment into a multi-million dollar industry.

Today, films are a billion dollar industry, and there are still scores of Jewish writers, producers, studio owners, and directors.

Why do anti-Semites say that the Jews control the media?

There is no question that any list of the most influential people in movie and television studios and in the print media produces a significant number of Jewish names. The famous Disney studio, for example, which was founded by Walt Disney, now features Jewish personnel in nearly all its most powerful positions. There is no denying the reality of Jewish prominence in popular culture disproportionate to population statistics.

Jealousy of those who have become successful in high-profile positions (such as the media) has often led to virulent anti-Semitism and causeless hatred. It is especially exacerbated when famous people in the clergy and the arts and sciences make public remarks. In 1972, the Rev. Billy Graham complained to then-President Richard Nixon that Jews controlled the media. Recently he was reminded of this fact and said that he did not recall saying it—but he added that if he did, he now apologizes.

Actor Marlon Brando complained a few years ago on "Larry King Live" that the Jews have slandered every other racial group but are careful to ensure there is "never any negative image of the kike." For this he was branded as anti-Semitic, and he too was forced to apologize.

The Anti-Defamation League, established in 1913, has worked diligently to collect anti-Semitic data to fight anti-Semitism and anti-Jewish discrimination of this sort. Although it has had a modicum of success, it continues to fight an uphill battle.

Why are there a lot of Jewish lawyers?

For Jews, the halacha (Jewish law) establishes the structure of rules to govern interaction. The study of law is a tradition among Jews dating back many centuries. The ability to create and interpret law has always been seen in Jewish tradition as admirable, since only the most knowledgeable and learned were able to do it.

Although Jews were noted advocates in Spain as early as the fourteenth century, they were generally prevented from practicing law in most of the countries in which they settled until early in the nineteenth century. In many of these countries, their exclusion was based on the claim that they were an "alien" race to which citizenship and political rights had not been granted.

The very reasons that caused their exclusion acted as a spur to Jews to seek admission to the legal profession. On the one hand, the study of law was a tradition among Jews, while the fact that membership of the legal profession was a mark of distinction encouraged Jews who wished to integrate to become lawyers.

In most countries, Jews were permitted to practice law at about the time they were granted civil rights. Only in the United States and in the British colonies, where Jews always enjoyed civil rights, were they able to practice law without hindrance.

After World War II, Jews in the United States, France, and England constituted a high proportion of all the lawyers in the capital cities. One other notable feature of Jewish involvement in law was the large number of Jews prominent in the field of international law. Many of them were of German origin, such as Sir Hersch Lauterpacht, who became judge of the International Court of Justice at the Hague and edited the standard textbook on international law written by another German Jew, Lassa Oppenheim. Jews also served as legal advisers to the foreign ministries of various nations, notably the United States, Britain, and Holland. They also held chairs in international law at most of the European universities.

Various theories have been postulated for the Jewish prominence in international law. One influential factor would seem to be that Jews wandered from land to land and were rarely attached to any particular system of law for a long period of time.

Among the most famous American Jews in the legal profession were Louis Brandeis, Benjamin Cardozo, and Felix Frankfurter, who were successively appointed to the U.S. Supreme Court and established a tradition of the "Jewish seat" on the Supreme Court bench.

An interesting book on the subject of Jewish lawyers is called *Rabbis and Lawyers*, by Jerold Auerbach, professor of history at Wellesley College. He addresses the question of what it is about Jewish culture that has inspired so many men and women to pursue the legal profession.

Chapter 20

❦ ❦

What Others Think of the Jews

Why do Jews have a reputation for being smart?

There's no biological or statistical evidence that Jews are smarter than anyone else. So this reputation is probably a result of the emphasis Jews place on the value of education.

Giving a Jewish child an education has always been considered one of the most important religious obligations of a parent. The ideal education in Judaism is achieved when both the home and the school prepare a child to take his or her place in the world. Two thousand years ago, before there were synagogue schools, parents were the primary teachers of their children. When schools began to emerge, parents and schoolteachers shared the role of educating children.

The importance placed on the value of an education has continued to the present time, as parents continue to look to send their children to the finest schools and encourage them to attain a college education. Consequently, Jews in our country continue to be high achievers. Although the Jewish people are still a small minority, we have produced an extraordinarily large number of Nobel Prize winners in many subject areas.

The current estimated world population is around six billion, while the Jewish world population is thirteen million, less than 1 percent of the entire world. It is therefore all the more remarkable that Jews and persons of half-Jewish ancestry have been awarded at least

158 Nobel Prizes, accounting for 22 percent of all such prizes awarded to individuals worldwide between 1901 and 2002. This adds up to Jews constituting 36 percent of all U.S. Nobel Prize winners. Such astounding statistics surely would continue to foster the reputation of Jewish culture and religion placing a high value on education.

Why do some people say that the Jews have killed Christian children and used their blood in a ritual to make matzah?

The term "Christ-killer" has been among the last words that thousands of Jews likely heard before they were murdered. It has been used by anti-Semitic people who continue to blame the Jews for the death of Jesus, an accusation based on a completely distorted, inaccurate, and misinformed reading of the New Testament. Meanwhile the "blood libel," meaning the accusation that the Jews murder non-Jews in a religious ritual and then drink their blood, originated in England in the twelfth century. Over the next seven centuries, it led to the murder of tens of thousands of Jews.

By the fourteenth century, the ritual murder charge had become associated with Passover. Jews were accused of mixing Christian blood into their matzah and wine. The Passover holiday then turned into a time of horror and terror for Jews because of their fear that anti-Semites would frame them by murdering a Christian child and then dumping the body in a Jewish house.

In 1840, Christian anti-Semites carried the blood libel to Damascus, where there the Jews were charged with murdering a monk. It was known as the "Damascus Affair," and Jewish communal leaders throughout the world organized a protest that was quite successful; most of the convicted Jewish victims were released.

The fact that so many Christians believed and spread the lie of the blood libels for so many centuries continues to astound me. Of course, the greatest irony of the term "Christ-killer" is that it was the Romans, not the Jews, who killed Jesus. One of the earliest references to Jesus occurs in the writings of the Roman historian Tacitus, who notes Jesus' name and the fact of his crucifixion by the Roman au-

thorities. At Vatican II in 1962, the Catholic Church officially ac-
quitted most of Jesus' contemporaries, and all subsequent Jews, of the
charge of killing Jesus. One can only hope the term Christ-killer and
the acts of blood libel will continue to decline, as they indeed have
since the Holocaust.

Why do Jews have a reputation for being tight with money?

During the period of the Middle Ages, Jews began to specialize in
banking and money lending. The banking profession was one of the
few open to Jews in an anti-Semitic society when many professions
were forbidden to them. For centuries, there had been no real need
for money; things not grown by a landowner on his own soil, and not
manufactured by serfs or slaves, were obtained by barter. Extra money
needed for building churches or castles or for waging wars used to be
borrowed, at some interest, from wealthy monasteries.

When European life became more settled in the Middle Ages,
human wants increased and merchants needed capital. Many Jews
lent the wealth they had accumulated during years of mercantile activity to princes or Christian merchants. Even some churches and
cathedrals were erected with money borrowed from Jews.

It so happened that about this time the Catholic Church began
to proclaim the theory that any interest, no matter how small, was
usury. It announced that a Christian dared not lend money to another Christian in the hope of gain. If he did so, he was guilty of a
great sin and deserved to be excommunicated.

William Shakespeare has been accused of anti-Semitism for his
creation of Shylock, the moneylender. Appearing in the play *Merchant
of Venice*, Shylock was a Jewish moneylender who insists that a non-
Jew, Antonio, repay his overdue loan in a pound of flesh drawn from
near his heart. Shylock is prevented by a legal trick from accomplish-
ing his goal, but the damage inflicted on the Jews by this occurrence
continues to this day. What has surprised many historians about this
character is that Shakespeare had never met or seen a Jew in his life,
since the Jews had been expelled from England in 1290, more than

350 years before his birth, and not readmitted until 1656, forty years after his death.

The image of Jews as a nation of money-lending Shylocks persisted through the Middle Ages into modern times. To this day, the illegal industry of high-interest loans is known as "shylocking."

In the nineteenth century, Charles Dickens fashioned another stereotypical Jewish villain called Fagin, who made his living training young boys to become pickpockets.

Is it true that Jews have big noses?

I don't have a particularly large nose. I know lots of other Jewish people with rather small noses, and I know others with bigger ones. The stereotyping of the Jew with the big nose is a racial slur that dates back many centuries. Anti-Semitic magazines often depicted Jews with beards and large noses.

In fact, some Jews from Eastern Europe and Russia do have a characteristic type of nose, which could be interpreted in a non-Jewish society as "big." Unfortunately, many Jews, especially teenage girls, buy into this kind of shameful and damaging self-image. Consequently, in the past many such individuals have gone to a plastic surgeon for a "nose job."

Recently, Gabriella Glaser wrote a book titled *The Nose: A Profile of Sex, Beauty and Survival.* In it she traces mankind's intrigue and obsession over the nose and writes about the "Jewish nose," which has been inseparable from the history of anti-Semitism, stereotyping, and the notion of the Jew as "the other." Citing anthropologist Robert Knox, who in 1850 described the Jewish nose as "a large, massive, club-shaped hook nose," Glaser cites the genesis of cosmetic surgery for nineteenth-century Berlin Jews.

The term "Jewish nose" continues to have currency, and Glaser notes a particular plastic surgeon who works in the affluent New York suburb of Great Neck who performs an average of two nose jobs a week, estimating that half of his clients are Jewish.

In these more enlightened times, though, I like to think that more and more Jewish women (one example being Barbara Streisand) are proud of their noses and would never think of trying to change them artificially to conform to some non-Jewish notion of beauty.

Why have so many people hated Jews throughout history?

Anti-Semite is the term that is used today to mean a person who hates Jews. Throughout history, anti-Semitism has been directed against Judaism and its values. It is caused by a variety of socioeconomic and cultural factors.

One theory is that Jews were hated in the medieval period because they were moneylenders. For centuries, the papacy and other powerful Christian institutions maintained that Jews were evil because they killed Christ. Some attribute anti-Semitism to the Jews being defiantly different from the majority society, isolated and keeping to themselves—primarily of course because they were forced to live in ghettos and denied privileges that most citizens enjoyed. Others have attributed hatred toward Jews because of their perceived wealth, which is largely mythical. Still another accounting for anti-Semitism is the one known as the scapegoat theory. Here, those who wish to mobilize the masses around a common hatred blame Jews for society's ills. Many people believe, for instance, that Hitler blamed the Jews for all of the problems Germany faced during that period in order to win elections in Germany.

In the nineteenth century, a major source of anti-Semitism in America was the negative image of the Jew prevalent in the popular culture. Americans were inundated with damaging stereotypes of immigrants' social and personality traits. For example, popular literature, dime novels, and the theater characterized the Jews as crude and greedy and as petty criminals.

In my own community today, there continue to be many anti-Semitic incidents. A few years ago, a student in our Hebrew school complained that some students of his school threw some pennies on the floor and then said: "Jew boy, why don't you pick them up?" This is a hate crime, and it cannot be overlooked.

Since September 11, 2001, Jews have been experiencing the worst anti-Semitism since the Holocaust and World War II. The violence includes countless synagogue bombings, desecration of Jewish buildings and dwellings, overt threats and violence, large political movements based on hatred of the Jews, and massive scapegoating of Jews for all the current problems the world faces in the Middle East and in the U.S. struggle against terrorism. All this blame has produced a new anti-Semitism that is more virulent than ever before.

Why do Jews have a reputation for being rich?

It is true that there are some very wealthy Jews in this country and around the world, but there are also very poor Jews as well. So the notion that all Jews are rich is another example of stereotyping the Jew.

If anything, Jewish tradition is known for its value of tzedakah, which I like to translate as righteous giving. The Torah legislated that Jews give away 10 percent of their earnings to the poor. Even a poor person is to find something that he or she can give away to another person. Therefore from Judaism's perspective, one who gives tzedakah is acting justly, whereas one who isn't is unjust. Jewish law views this lack of justice as not only mean-spirited but also illegal. Thus, throughout history, whenever Jewish communities were self-governing, Jews were assessed tzedakah just as everyone today is assessed taxes.

I always enjoyed reading about the highest level of tzedakah as proposed by the medieval Jewish philosopher Maimonides. He said that the top level of righteous giving is the person who finds work for another so that he or she will never have to beg from other people. He also wrote that this kind of righteous giving should be anonymous, invisible, and without personal gratification—in other words, selfless. I'd like to think that Jews who are doing it "right" have a reputation for being charitable people.

Why are Jews often associated with politically liberal causes?

Milton Himmelfarb, an American-Jewish intellectual who wrote for *Commentary* magazine, once said that American "Jews live like Episcopalians and vote like Puerto Ricans." Although the majority of Jews in the United State have gone from being poor twentieth-century immigrants to successful and fully integrated members of American society, they have remained overwhelmingly liberal in their politics. Known for almost always voting Democratic, Jews make up the one ethnic group the majority of whom consistently vote against their own personal economic interests. On social issues, too, the Jewish community has generally always stood behind liberal causes.

In his book *The Quest for Inclusion*, historian Marc Dollinger discusses the mythical Jewish affection for the downtrodden, the outsider, and the foreigner. Jews, he said, have also tended to favor liberal immigration policies, to preserve a particular image of the United States for themselves and all newcomers to the country. It was, after all, the Jewish poet Emma Lazarus, who wrote the now famous poem "The New Colossus" that hangs in the Statue of Liberty.

Chapter 21

❦ ❦

Jews and Christians

Was Jesus really Jewish?

Jesus was born of Jewish parents, Mary and Joseph, about the year 4 B.C.E. He seems to have had a number of brothers and sisters, and the Gospels mention the names of James, Joseph, Simon, and Judas. His childhood was spent in the typical surroundings of the poorer Jews who lived in Galilee, and undoubtedly he learned something about the Bible and rabbinic use of parables and stories. He spoke Aramaic, a Semitic language similar to Hebrew, which was used in Palestine during that time.

The Gospel of Luke reports that when Jesus was twelve, he astonished the sages at the Jerusalem Temple with his knowledge. Beyond this, the details of his first thirty years are practically unreported. However, many assume that he followed the customary pattern of Jewish life in northern Palestine, receiving the usual limited Jewish education, carrying out the various Jewish observances, and attending the synagogue.

In about his thirteenth year, Jesus met John the Baptist, a Jew who made his home in the desert regions of Palestine. John preached that the Messiah was coming. As preparation for the coming, John practiced baptism, or immersion in water, which was supposed to wash away the sins of all who submitted to it. Jesus was one of those baptized by John in the Jordan River, and he was profoundly affected by his experience. He thought deeply about it, and after intense self-searching, he came to believe that he was the Messiah, the one who would usher in the Kingdom of God.

The New Testament depiction of Jesus suggests that he was largely a law-abiding and highly nationalistic Jew, and a man with strong ethical concerns. Like many of Judaism's rabbis, he saw love of one's neighbor as religion's central demand. Though many Christians are under the impression that he opposed Judaism's emphasis on law, in actuality he strongly criticized those who advocated dropping it. "Do not imagine that I have come to abolish the Law [that is, the Torah] or the Prophets," he said to his early disciples. "I tell you solemnly, till heaven and earth disappear, not one dot, not one little stroke, shall disappear from the Law until its purpose is achieved." Jesus concluded his warning by saying, "Therefore, the man who infringes even the least of these commandments and teaches others to do the same will be considered the least in the kingdom of heaven" (Matthew 5:17–19).

Most statements attributed to Jesus in the New Testament conform to Jewish teachings. However, there are some exceptions. For example, in Matthew 9:6 we are told that "the Son of Man" (Jesus) forgives all sins. Judaism believes that only God can forgive sins committed against Him. Additionally, whereas Judaism believes that anyone can come to God, Jesus claimed that people could come to God only through him ("No one knows the Father [God] except the Son [Jesus], and anyone to whom the Son chooses to reveal Him"; Matthew 11:27).

Shortly before one particular Passover, Jesus made his way to Jerusalem. The city was crowded with thousands of Jewish pilgrims who had come to participate in the Passover observances of the Temple. Jesus himself went to the Temple and created a disturbance there by driving away the men who changed the people's money into the proper currency for the purchase of birds for sacrifices. His mission ended in failure, for by failing to denounce the Romans he antagonized the people whom he addressed. They expected a Messiah who would put an end to the injustices of Roman rule, while he insisted that the people should continue to submit to Roman authority and pay their taxes. Discouraged and disheartened, Jesus retired with his disciples to participate in the Seder, the Passover evening meal. This is what has come to be known as the "Last Supper," for Roman soldiers arrested Jesus shortly thereafter while his disciples fled in panic. He was later brought to Pontius Plate, the Roman governor, who heard the charges against him and condemned him to death as a revolutionary, self-styled "king of the Jews."

Such in brief is the life story of Jesus. Throughout, we cannot help but observe that, although somewhat of a mystic, Jesus was nonetheless a loyal Jew whose most intimate disciples and followers were also Jewish. His message that the Messiah was approaching was directed only to his fellow Jews, for whose welfare he was deeply concerned.

Who are the Jews for Jesus?

Among the Christian missionary groups whose volunteers consciously attempt to persuade Jews to accept that one can remain a Jew and believe in Jesus, is the group called Jews for Jesus. It is perhaps the best known and most public of the missionizers. This group was founded in 1973 by the Rev. Martin (Moishe) Rosen, a Jew who underwent conversion and was ordained a Baptist minister in 1956. In addition to its many programs, it spends more than $10 million annually for aggressive advertising, billboards, full-page newspaper ads, activities in transportation centers, college campuses, and in major immigrant communities.

There are more than six hundred Christian missions targeting the Jewish people. Most Hebrew-Christians hold the beliefs that are common to the Christian community:

- Every human is sinful and is separate from God.
- Jesus was the Messiah promised to the prophets, and he died for each individual's sins.
- The only way to become accepted by God is through confession of sins and acceptance of the belief that Jesus died for the individual. This requires belief in Jesus as the Messiah.

- Failure to find God's acceptance results in eternal separation from God and punishment in Hell.

It is disconcerting to realize that the conversion of the Jewish community has been and continues to be the focus and fulfillment of the spiritual needs of many people. For centuries, attempts have been made to foster the conversion of the Jewish people to Christianity. In the past, these efforts have resulted in the Crusades and other hostile acts that insisted on conversion at the pain of death in numerous European countries. The Jewish community has always resisted these attempts at forcible conversion. However, those seeking to convert Jews to Christianity have changed their tactics in recent decades. Rather than force Jews to learn to live as Christians, the Hebrew-Christian movement has created a religious setting proposing that Jews return to their Jewish identity while at the same time embracing Jesus.

A few years ago, a member of my own congregation was out of town and went to what he thought was a synagogue service on Shabbat. The synagogue called itself Shema Yisrael. He knew something was a bit strange, but he was not exactly sure what it was. All traditional Christian symbols were absent. There was no cross; the name of Jesus was not mentioned but the Hebrew equivalent, Yeshua, was. The congregational leader called himself a rabbi; kiddush over wine was chanted, the Kaddish recited and Shabbat candles lit. Later, he learned that he was in a Jews for Jesus temple.

Because of the success of the Jews for Jesus movement, many Jewish communities have become proactive and created counter-missionary movements. One of the largest is a group that calls itself Jews for Judaism, with offices in Baltimore, Los Angeles, New York, Toronto, South Africa, and Australia, as well as a network in Israel, Europe, and the former Soviet Union. It is the only full time counter-missionary resource in the world that works exclusively to monitor and combat deceptive Christian missionary efforts.

You might be surprised to know that it is estimated Christian missionaries approach four out of five Jews at some time in their lives. This missionary may be a professional or, more likely, a friend, neighbor, or colleague. Someone might come to your home, catch you on the street, or leave literature at your door. If someone starts talking about being a "messianic" or "completed" Jew or claims that a Jew can accept Jesus (or, as they sometimes call him Yeshua), without giving up Judaism, then you are speaking with a missionary.

Can someone believe in Jesus and still be Jewish?

Judaism cannot be detached from belief in or beliefs about God. Residing always at the very heart of our self-understanding as a people, and of all Jewish literature and culture, God permeates our language, our law, our conscience, and our lore.

All the major Jewish denominations affirm the critical importance of belief in an incorporeal God, but they do not specify all the particulars of that belief. However, belief in a Trinitarian God, or in Jesus as the Son of God, can never be consistent with Jewish tradition and history.

To Christians, Jesus is the Son of God and the Messiah. If one carefully reviews Jesus' attitude to Judaism, its laws, and its ways of life, it would be quite apparent that Jesus would not even qualify as a prophet, or a rabbi in the religious sense, let alone be the Son of God. In all-important respects, Jesus placed himself in opposition to the faith into which he was born. He also broke with a long and clearly established biblical tradition that no human being could ever be divine.

Since the halachic (Jewish legal) definition of a Jew is one born of a Jewish mother, a Jew who believes in Jesus would still technically qualify as being Jewish. However, such a Jew would be considered an apostate, a Jewish defector.

Recently in our own community, a Jews for Jesus messianic temple was formed. This Christian missionary group claims that Jews can observe Jewish holidays and religious forms and at the same time maintain an active belief in Jesus. Our executive board became aware of it and asked whether our synagogue would be willing to accept a Jew for Jesus as a member. On the basis of recommendations of the United Synagogue (our lay organization), our synagogue recently passed a resolution that is now part of our constitution:

Whereas: Temple Sholom respects the vast historic and theological differences between the Jewish and Christian faiths. Our organization recognizes that the movement going under the rubric of "Hebrew Christianity" and or "messianic Judaism" is, in fact, an attempt to blur the distinctions between the two religions with the aim of converting Jews to the Christian faith.

Whereas the mission or goal of Temple Sholom is to strengthen and promote Jewish continuity and community values, be it resolved that "Hebrew-Christianity" and/or "messianic Judaism" are not part of the Jewish community.

Essentially, this means that a member of Jews for Jesus, or any other Hebrew-Christian missionary movement, cannot become a member of our synagogue. This of course in no way alters our policy of warmly welcoming congregational family members who are not Jewish to be active participants in many aspects of Temple life.

Is it OK for Jews to sing Christmas carols in public school?

Growing up in Toronto, Canada, I was in the high school choir. Each winter, the choir would sing Christmas carols and the occasional Hanukkah song, and as a choir member I would sing them. Admittedly, I never paid much attention to the words of the Christmas songs. I enjoyed singing what was largely some pretty good music.

Now that I am older (and hopefully wiser), I have come to realize that requiring students to sing religious songs (especially ones that are filled with theological references) is inappropriate. The law of separation of church and state was created to keep observance of religion out of the public school system. A public secular school is not the place for religious songs, and many of the Christmas carols are just that. Students who are expected to sing them may well and rightfully feel uncomfortable; a better place for their performance would be in the various houses of worship for which the songs are representative.

Having said that, however, I add that if you don't mind singing Christmas carols and it is your choice to do so, there's certainly nothing wrong with participating on a musical and social level.

Is it true that Jews shouldn't go to church?

About twenty years ago, an Orthodox rabbi was the rabbi emeritus of my synagogue. His job included leading the morning worship service, teaching some adult education classes, and helping me out with life cycle events. I remember a student in our religious school asking him this same question: "Is it true that Jews shouldn't go to church?" He answered, "Yes, it is true." When asked why, he proceeded to tell them of his concern that they might see something that they really like, and come back again for more. He was also concerned that the kids would also pray in the name of Jesus, which of course is something forbidden in Jewish religion.

Years later, our synagogue was asked to have an ecumenical Holocaust service that would take place in a local United Methodist Church. The Orthodox rabbi was asked to participate, and to everyone's surprise not only did he say yes but he also led one of the readings while standing under a large cross! After reviewing the content of that service and having had time to reflect, he felt that to separate himself and the Jewish community from such an event, even though it was taking place in a church, was not what he now wanted to do.

Many Jews have attended church with Christian friends and neighbors, both for the regular Sunday services and for special ceremonies such as a confirmation ceremony for a friend or a funeral. They go to church, however, as visitors, not participants. We have many non-Jews visit us each week at our Temple on Shabbat morning as invited guests of a Bar Mitzvah or Bat Mitzvah. They are there as spectators and on occasion may have an opportunity to participate in a responsive reading that deals with a theme such as peace or truth, which is common to both Judaism and Christianity and therefore not in any way offensive to them. Remember also that should we kneel during services (even for the sake of conformity), or for that matter answer "amen" to prayers offered in the name of Jesus, we would contradict the tenets of Judaism, and our actions might be interpreted by some Christians as disrespectful, or even as subtle mockery.

Generally, I would recommend a benign and compassionate attitude toward the religious services of our Christian friends. There's nothing inherently wrong with visiting their services, with being respectful of their faith, and realizing how similar are many of the basic human yearnings, the universal spirituality that such rituals can represent. But it's also important to preserve our own identity, our integrity—and not appear to be joining in on the same level as those who are Christian participants.

Is it OK for a Jewish family to have a Christmas tree? Isn't Christmas an American holiday?

Today it is clear to me that the tree has become a secular symbol of the American commercial Christmas holiday and not of the birth of Jesus. So to a great extent, whether or not to have one depends on the character and judgment of each individual family. There are certainly Jewish families that feel they can have a tree in their home without subscribing to the Christian element of the holiday.

I remember that when I was a teenager some of my Jewish friends wanted their parents to buy and decorate what was then called a "Hanukkah bush." Essentially these bushes were marketed to Jews who were desirous of having some sort of tree analogous to that of the Christmas tree in their homes as well. Parents hoped that by purchasing these bushes their kids would not feel they were missing out on the fun of decorating a Christmas tree.

I now know, from the pleasure of being married and having two wonderful children, that one need not buy a Hanukkah bush to make Hanukkah feel like a true festival of lights. The success of any Jewish holiday is to become familiar with its rituals and observe them in a joyous manner. By making Hanukkah a fun-filled occasion, there is no need for any Jewish family to feel left out. Lighting a hanukkiah, playing dreidel and other games, eating latkes, and exchanging gifts and giving tzedakah certainly bring light into my home, and the homes of many others who celebrate Hanukkah with all its colorful ritual.

Why shouldn't Jews marry non-Jews?

Recall the discussion of this question at the beginning of Chapter Seven, "Marriage." As other religions do too, Judaism has always stressed the importance of marrying within the faith and preserving its heritage of culture and traditions. It has nothing to do with being prejudiced or feeling superior to other religions. Differences of religion have often been shown to constitute a serious obstacle to harmonious husband-wife relationships. Even if a mixed marriage endures, it often imposes a strain on the religious loyalties of one or both partners and causes difficult personal and family problems.

The earliest biblical story about the importance of marrying within the faith is related to Judaism's first patriarch, Abraham (Genesis 24). He sends his servant Eliezer to find a suitable wife for his son, Isaac, warning him with these words: "I will make you swear that you will not take a wife for my son from the daughters of the Canaanites among whom I dwell, but you will go to the land of my birth and get a wife for my son" (Genesis 24:3).

This is the first biblical reference on the subject of opposition to mixed marriage. Religion and family tradition are at stake, not ethnic or racial "purity."

Aside from the important consideration of marital harmony, traditional Judaism opposes Jews marrying non-Jews because it poses a threat to the future of the Jewish people, and to their faith, customs, and traditions. The Jewish people are and have always been a minority. Seeking to preserve their group identity, they find it crucial to resist the inroads of mixed marriage.

In our congregation, we have quite a number of mixed marriages. I have always worked diligently to make them feel comfortable in our synagogue, and in doing so many of the non-Jewish spouses have taken classes with me and even participated in our Jewish Family Matters programs. In several cases, the non-Jewish spouses had become so attracted to Judaism that they decided to convert to Judaism. Today they are among the most active participants in our programs, and leaders in the Jewish community too.

What should a Jew say when a Christian is trying to convert him or her?

There are many books on the market today written to help Jews confront and refute Christian missionaries. A popular one by Sam Levine is called *You Take Jesus, I'll Take God*. It presents ways of refuting the missionaries, who are experts in using and manipulating the Jewish Bible for their own agenda.

Although it's interesting to read such books and learn about the questions missionaries typically ask and the arguments they use, my advice to you is not to engage in conversation. Missionaries are very good at what they do, and they often have a better knowledge of the Jewish Bible than do Jews.

I personally have encountered several Christian missionaries during my rabbinic career. One missionary couple came to a Friday evening Shabbat service and secretly gave out missionizing tapes. When I learned what they had done, I made sure to contact them and tell them they were no longer welcome in our Temple.

Recently a so-called messianic "synagogue" was built not far from our community. We made certain to warn our congregants of its intentions, and now we are teaching our students in our Hebrew school and adult school all about the missionaries, to prepare them for a possible encounter.

Is it appropriate to consider Jesus to be a great rabbi?

Although the word *rabbi* means "my teacher," and although Jesus was known for his great teachings, Jews and Jewish tradition have never viewed Jesus as being a great rabbi.

It is true that some Jews believe Jesus was a great teacher and would have been given recognition in the tradition if some of his followers had not misinterpreted his teachings and made a messiah out of him. Joseph Klausner, in his book *Jesus of Nazareth*, expresses this view of the group: "Jesus is, for the Jewish nation, a great teacher of morality and an artist in parable. . . . If ever the day should come and

his ethical code be stripped of its wrappings or miracles and mysticism, the Book of the Ethics of Jesus will be one of the choicest trea-
sures in the literature of Israel for all time."

The Jewish tradition never overglorified any of its great person-
alities. They were represented as people possessing human weak-
nesses in addition to their nobler endowments. Generally speaking,
Jews believe that Jesus was a Jew, born of Jewish parents. He lived and
died as a Jew, and like many other sensitive Jews he was critical of the
formality of the Temple and of the immorality of his age. None of his
teachings was contrary to the great simplicities of essential Judaism,
but none was new to the Jewish tradition. Although he influenced a
small group of dedicated followers, he had no real impact on the
broad masses of Jewry.

What are the basic differences between Judaism and Christianity?

There are numerous differences between Judaism and Christianity.
Here they are in a nutshell:

- *God:* For Jews, God is one, invisible with no body or form. For
  Christians, God is three in one, called the Trinity—the Father, the
  Son, and the Holy Spirit. In Judaism, people pray directly to God,
  whereas in Christianity they pray to God through Jesus. There is
  also the possibility in Christianity of intercession through the Saints
  and the Virgin Mary. In Christianity, Jesus was sent by the Father
  of earth to teach religious truths and redeem humankind by his
  own death. For Jews, Jesus was simply a man and a Jew, who taught
  Jewish ideals and beliefs.
- *Sin:* In Judaism, people are born free of sin. In Christianity, people
  are born evil because of the original sin of Adam and Eve. Christians require the sacrament of baptism at birth, to be freed from the
  taint of original sin.
- *Symbols and images:* In Judaism, there are no images of Jewish
  heroes or teachers to be revered and worshipped. Christianity uses
  symbols to worship Jesus, Mary, and the Saints.

- *Forgiveness:* In Judaism, forgiveness is obtained through repentance, prayer, and making amends through a righteous life. God's love is given to all people. Christianity has the concept of grace, which essentially is God's free gift of His love and favor to people. Through faith in Jesus, a person accepts the gift of grace and is thus purified of sin and sanctified.
- *Communion:* Christians have the sacrament of Communion, the commemoration of the Last Supper in which Christians share in or partake of the bread and wine, as body and blood of Jesus. There is no equivalent ritual in Judaism.
- *Salvation:* For Jews, there is the belief that all people are given souls that are immortal. For Christians, people can only be saved from hell through their faith in the redeeming acts of Jesus and by participating in the Church.

Chapter 22

❦ ❧

Jews and Ritual

Why do I meet people who look religious but who are not very nice people?

It does seem hypocritical when a person professes to be religious but is not, as you say, a very nice person. You are quite right in being disturbed that your expectations of goodness of a religious person don't always turn out that way.

I remember reading a story of an Orthodox traditional Jew who owned a number of nursing homes and was caught in a cheating scandal that landed him in jail. My first thought was, How is it possible that an Orthodox Jew can cheat? Doesn't the Bible say "always be truthful and do not steal?" What was really quite amazing was the fact that this man then proceeded to ask for kosher food in jail.

The fact is that some people act out the superficial requirements of being religious—the rituals and cosmetic appearances—but they are not truly religious in their heart. They forget the moral and ethical tenets of Judaism and are not sincere in their actions.

Your question ought to be a constant reminder that when we follow the rituals of Judaism, we need to pay careful attention to their meaning and do them with proper intent and feeling. If your ritual acts become overly mechanical, you can easily fall into the trap of performing the right ritual but behaving inappropriately.

186

Why should I do all the Jewish rituals? Isn't it enough to be a good person?

I believe that God and Judaism demand of us to be good people. The rituals are intended to act as a kind of string around our finger, a reminder of the ethical intent of the ritual. That is why the Prophet Isaiah tells us that when we fast on a fast day, we must not only refrain from eating food but make the fasting a reminder of our obligation to help feed those who are hungry and do not have food.

The Prophets of the Bible assigned a clear priority to the ethical commandments over ritual. In the Book of Amos (5:21–22), it says, "I hate your festivals. I am not satisfied with your celebration of the holy days. Spare me the sound of your prayers." Reading this, you might think that Amos was against the ritual of prayer and holiday celebration. In fact, Amos was protesting the kind of practice of ritual that was only an end to itself. In championing the importance of ethics, he was not averse to ritual and ceremony. What he was condemning and chastising was adherence to the form of the ritual while violating the spirit and true intent behind it. This is why he complained that both he and God abhorred Israel's sacrifices and Sabbath observance when they were accompanied by flagrant violation of God's moral laws. In the eyes of Amos and the other prophets, the ritual had become rote and mechanical. It was ritual that was not leading to the ultimate goal, which was serving God and becoming a better person.

A colleague of mine, Rabbi David Wolpe, has said that Jewish ritual is the discipline of pause and focus. For example, the observance of the weekly Sabbath ritual and rest helps us pause and reflect upon the meaning of our lives and the role of God in the universe. Saying a blessing over bread helps us appreciate the fact that we have food to eat and that God is the source of our food. It may also help to arouse our awareness of others who do not have enough to eat and spur us to help the hungry.

The most important thing is to use ritual in a way that makes us better people.

Why are there so many commandments? Can't we just be good people?

It was once said by one of my teachers that the entire Bible may be understood as a positive response to the question Cain asked after murdering his brother Abel: "Am I my brother's keeper?" By doing the mitzvot, we are constantly reminded to be our brother's keeper. Whether it be helping disabled children, visiting the sick, feeding the hungry, or clothing the naked, know that what God wants of us all is to be actively involved in the betterment of our community and the world at large. Mitzvot give us constant reminders to do just that!

There are 613 mitzvot, commandments or religious obligations. Examples are the dietary laws, the laws of the Sabbath and holidays, wearing tallit and tefillin, praying every day, and so on. Many Jews wonder why we were given so many obligations and whether it's simply not enough to behave ethically and be a good person.

When asked to define an ethical person, people have often answered "Someone who does not hurt anybody." I believe that being an ethical person means more than just someone who does no harm to others. Rather, being an ethical person involves active pursuit of what is right and good. For example, it is not enough to merely refrain from hurting other human beings. One must intercede on their behalf, as the Bible tells us: "Do not stand idly by on the blood of your neighbor" (Leviticus 19:16).

Because being a good person consists of positive acts of goodness, Judaism has developed an extensive system of laws, which take the form of commandments. These mitzvot are intended to remind us of our obligation to be a force for good throughout the world, and a light unto the nations.

Even mitzvot that do not at first blush seem to have ethical import likely do, when understood more fully. Keeping kosher, for example, has often helped to train Jewish people in self-control. You can't have everything in the candy store if you keep kosher. When Jews go into a store, the mitzvah of feeding the hungry might well remind them to buy some extra food items and donate them to a food bank.

Chapter 23

❦ ❧

Israel

If Zionists believe that ancient Israel belongs to Jews, why don't they give America back to the Indians?

Indeed, ardent Zionists believe that God gave the Land of Israel to the Jewish people. The promise of land dates back to Abraham's time, when God told Abraham that he would be the father of a great nation on a land that God would show him. That land was none other than Israel, but over the centuries there were many invasions and other violent conflicts, and borders and boundaries changed.

A great deal of the current turmoil in the modern state of Israel is related to what exactly the boundaries are of the so-called Promised Land, and of course many anti-Israeli militants and terrorists don't believe that Israel has a right to exist altogether.

Regarding the Native American situation, the fact is that the white settlers and their government totally stole the Indians' land and then brutalized, cheated, murdered, and swindled the Indians for centuries. Therefore, the government of the United States has a terrible legacy of guilt for having stolen the land, but we're way beyond the point now where we could just give it back. Nor is that the priority of most Native Americans. Instead, they want justice, reparations, money that's owed to them, and appropriate settlement for countless claims, including some of the land that has been designated by old (largely broken) treaties as their own, sovereign land.

So, ultimately there's a big difference between the Jews of Israel (who have fought for more than fifty years to retain the land that was actually given back to them under the auspices of the Balfour declaration in 1917 and the UN resolutions of 1948) and the Native Americans (who are struggling for economic and cultural survival and not concerned with getting back the nation but are instead fighting for other forms of economic and social justice).

Why isn't the Temple being rebuilt?

There were two successive temples in Jerusalem, both on the same site. The first was begun in the reign of King Solomon and completed in seven and a half years. The Babylonians destroyed it in 586 B.C.E. The second temple was begun fifty years after the destruction of the first and was completed within twenty years (516 B.C.E.) by the exiles who returned to Judea.

The third temple, referred to as that of Herod the Great, was begun twenty years before the common era and was destroyed, after ninety years of existence, by Roman soldiers in the year 70 C.E.

The remains of the Temple have disappeared. Part of the wall enclosing Herod's temple is still standing in Jerusalem. It is known as the *Kotel Ha'ma'aravee*": the Western Wall, or the "Wailing Wall," a term used by gentiles; it has been regarded as sacred ever since the Talmudic period. It has served as a place of endless pilgrimage for Jews from all parts of the world; it was my first stop when visiting Israel for the first time in 1970.

The Temple has never been rebuilt because centuries ago Muslims built two mosques on the site of it. Periodically, various extremist Jewish groups have plotted to destroy the mosques of Al-Aksa and the Dome of the Rock, thus enabling the Temple to be rebuilt. Such an act would likely bring more terrorism in Israel, which is the last thing Israel needs with so many terrorist acts already occurring throughout the land.

Most modern Jews are in no hurry to see the Temple rebuilt, for they have no interest to returning to a time of sacrificing animals. Other Jews, especially some Orthodox Jews, pray for the building of a third Temple and continue to study the laws of sacrifice and prepare their kohanim for their leadership role, should their traditional function regarding sacrifices be reinstated.

Why are some fundamentalist Christians supportive of Israel?

Recently, a story on CBS's "60 Minutes" dealt with the large number of Christian fundamentalists and evangelists who are supporting Israel in pro-Israel American rallies. Although few Jews are traveling to Israel these days because of the threat of terrorism, many Christian fundamentalists continue to do so, and in large numbers.

Evangelical Christians are dedicated to the goal of converting Jews to Christianity. In the first half of the 1990s, there were approximately 200 Hebrew-Christian "synagogues," 469 Christian missions to the Jews, and 200,000 American and Canadian Jews who joined messianic groups.

This emphasis on converting the Jews has several reasons. Since Jesus was a Jew who Christians claimed was the Messiah, the messianic idea posited that a man at the end of days would usher in an era of world peace. The Jewish lack of acceptance of Jesus has always been a disturbing phenomenon for the Church. To evangelical Christians, the conversion of the Jews is directly linked to the credibility of the cross and the second coming of the Messiah.

Fundamentalist Christians are also consumed with eschatology, the Apocalypse, and what will happen at the end of days. Jewish scripture sees this as the time when nations will attack Israel over the status of Jerusalem. But the view of messianic days in Matthew 23:39 is where Jesus declares "I will not return until you [the Jews] say 'blessed be he who comes in the name of the Lord.'" This is interpreted by the Church to mean that Jesus can't come again to bring a truly messianic era on earth until all the Jews have been converted, including several million of them in Israel.

For evangelicals, the coming of the second millennium is when they believe Jesus will return. This makes it all the more imperative to prevent the Jews from holding up the show! You might remember from your history lessons that the year 1000 saw a similar fanatical desire to convert the Jews, and the Church interpreted the lack of a Second Coming of Jesus then to a Jewish obstinacy, thus visiting more atrocities on Jews as a result. Recently, one current evangelical group, called "Assemblies of God," actually created a program called Harvest Year 2000—the harvest to be the Jewish people.

The state of Israel has to be especially careful when it comes to visiting fundamentalist Christian groups to Israel. On the one hand, more than ever Israel needs the money that flows from tourism, especially since so few tourists are prepared to make visits. On the other hand, now that Israelis are beginning to realize the true reason for evangelical visits, they are ambivalent about their being there.

Israelis have a reputation for being harsh. Why is this?

It has been said that Israelis have a reputation for tending to be pushy and often irritable. I have visited Israel on numerous occasions and can remember instances when there was a long line of people waiting to get on a bus, and some Israelis tried to aggressively push themselves to the front. But I've also seen much the same thing happen in New York City when trying to get on a subway during rush hour.

Because Israel is surrounded by countries that are its archenemies, Israelis are, and must always be, on alert. Most Israelis are drafted into the army immediately upon completion of high school, and they continue to serve in the army as reservists until their midfifties. Although I am not a psychologist, I cannot help but think that the mind-set of an Israeli who must always be on the lookout for his or her survival would likely lead them to be increasingly tense and more aggressive.

Why are there certain places in Jerusalem where Jews are not supposed to walk?

Entering the area in Jerusalem called the Temple Mount is most problematic for Jews nowadays. This area (in Hebrew, *Har HaBayeet*) is a trapezoid-shaped, walled-in area in the southeastern corner of the Old City of Jerusalem. The four walls surrounding it were built around the summit of the eastern hill, identified as Mount Moriah, the traditional site of the sacrifice of Isaac and the known location of the two Temples.

Today, American Jewish tourists are advised from the U.S. Travel Bureaus to stay out of the area of the Temple Mount because of tension in the region. The Chief Rabbinate of Israel has also continued to bar entrance to certain sections of the Temple area.

Within the area of the Temple Mount, there are about one hundred structures, including the Dome of the Rock, a Moslem mosque. The site is also important for Christians, for according to their tradition Jesus was presented as a baby there.

The special status of the Temple Mount in Jewish law derives from its being the site of the Temple, which stood approximately at its center. There were differences in the degree of sanctity among the sections of the Temple Mount. Into the most holy section, only the high priest was permitted to enter, and then only once a year, on the Day of Atonement. Besides this, those who were ritually unclean were forbidden to enter the Temple, as well as the courts for the priest and of the Israelites. By rabbinic enactment, anyone ritually unclean was forbidden from entering any part of the Temple Mount.

After the destruction of the Temple, rabbinic authorities generally posited that the prohibitions against entry into the Temple Mount area ought to continue. A vehement controversy on the question of entry into the Temple area took place after the liberation of Jerusalem in 1967. It did not apply to the armed forces that captured and held the site, since their presence was regarded as a security necessity involving the principle of *piku'ach nefesh* (saving a life).

What does it mean when we say that the Holy Land is "holy"?

To Jews, Israel was, and always will be, the Holy Land and the Promised Land. The Hebrew Bible was born there, the prophets appeared there, and the great rabbis taught the word of God there.

The Torah tells us that God chose the people of Israel to be a holy people, commanding them to live a holy life in accordance with the law. The land where this life of holiness was to be lived was selected, promised, and given to the children of Israel by God, the Holy Blessed One.

In the past, Jews considered the land of Israel to be their homeland. Since the destruction of the Holy Land in the year 70 C.E., Jews all over the world have offered up daily prayers for the coming of the Messiah and the rebuilding of the land. These prayers were not motivated solely by patriotism but were a definitive acknowledgment of the position of Israel in their spiritual life.

Do Arabs have a legitimate right to claims on the same land as Jews do?

A common misconception is that the Romans forced the Jews into the Diaspora after the destruction of the Temple (70 A.D.) and then, eighteen hundred years later, suddenly returned to Palestine demanding the country back. In reality, the Jewish people have maintained ties to their historic homeland for almost four thousand years, on the basis of a national language and a distinct civilization.

The Jewish people base their claim to the land of Israel on several premises: they cite the biblical promise of the land to Abraham, the Jewish people settled and developed the land, the international community granted political sovereignty in Palestine to the Jewish people, and the territory was captured in defensive wars. Even after the destruction of the Second Temple in Jerusalem, Jewish life in Palestine continued and often flourished.

Many Palestinians have posited that Palestine has always been Arab country, and therefore the Arabs have a sovereign right to the land. The fact is that the Twelve Tribes of Israel formed the first constitutional monarchy in Palestine in about 1000 B.C., and King David made Jerusalem the capital. Jewish independence there lasted more than two hundred years, almost as long as Americans have enjoyed independence in the United States.

When Jews began to immigrate to Palestine in large numbers in 1882, fewer than 250,000 Arabs lived there; the majority of Jews have arrived in recent decades. Palestine was never an exclusively Arab country; no independent Arab or Palestinian state ever existed in Palestine. Palestine Arab nationalism is largely a post–World War I phenomenon that did not become a significant political movement until after the 1967 Six Day War and Israel's capture of the West Bank.

The Palestinian Arab refugee problem emerged as a tragic outcome of the war in 1948, and it has been growing ever since. The war and fighting today is over boundaries, terrorism, and the right of Israel to have defensible borders. The Israelis and the Arabs must find a way to agree on land ownership so that both can live peaceably and be able to protect their interests. Obviously, there have to be compromises; otherwise there will be no end to the fighting and war between the two.

Currently the Israeli leadership is willing to entertain the possibility of a Palestinian state but will not do so until terrorism desists. Hopefully, there will come a time when the peace process can begin anew.

Chapter 24

❦ ❧

Ritual Garments

Why do some Jews wear a yarmulke on their head?

Wearing a kippa is a custom, not a law. From a Talmudic statement (Shabbat 118b), it appears that the custom was for a man not to walk more than four steps without covering his head. Rav Huna was quoted as saying that he wore a head covering to indicate that the Divine Presence was above his head. The Torah did require the priests to wear a head covering while they were engaged in the Temple service. It was part of the sacred vestments they wore as a sign of respect and glory before God.

In the Western world, a person shows respect by taking off his hat. In Judaism, one shows respect by putting on a head covering, which symbolizes that there is a supreme force above the person.

The head covering worn by Jewish men (and some women too) is called a kippa, or yarmulke. It is usually made of cloth, and fancier ones can be made of leather as well. Orthodox men wear them almost all the time. Those in the Conservative movement who are more traditional may also choose to wear them all the time, or at least while eating or praying. More and more Reform Jews are choosing to cover their head while in synagogue, as Reform Judaism is beginning to return to a number of traditions that were formerly abolished, such as use of Hebrew in the worship service.

When I became a Bar Mitzvah in 1960, my custom was to wear a kippa only at times when I prayed or was eating and saying blessings over my food. Before going to college, I decided to try wearing a kippa at all times during the day. At first, it took a little getting used to, but over time it began to feel just right to me, always reminding me of who I was and that there was a God all around me.

Today, head coverings for men and women come in all colors and designs. It is even quite common to see sports logos on them, as well as cartoon characters. Although there are some who object to such designs, I personally have no problem with them. A few years ago the family of a Bar Mitzvah gave me a Toronto Blue Jays kippa as a gift (I grew up in Toronto, Canada). I told them I would wear it the next time the Blue Jays get into the World Series. I can hardly wait!

What are tefillin?

Tefillin are two small black leather boxes with straps attached to them. They are worn by adult male Jews, and some females too at weekday morning services, in conformance with the biblical command to "bind them for a sign upon your hand and for frontlets between your eyes" (Deuteronomy 6:8). Along with the tallit, they are the Jews' uniform of prayer.

The word *tefillin* is usually translated as "phylacteries," which means an amulet, suggesting that tefillin are some kind of protective charm. On the contrary, the word is derived from the Hebrew word for prayer, *tefillah.*

Inside the boxes of the tefillin are parchments (each with a reference to tefillin) with sections from the Torah, written by a scribe in the same way the Torah is written. The tefillin are a sign of faith and devotion. It is a Jew's way of binding oneself to God.

One of the most enjoyable parts of my day is early morning, when I get to attend the morning minyan and put on my tefillin, which I still have from the time when I became a Bar Mitzvah. Recently, I was moved when the president of our congregation, who also attends services, found his great grandfather's tefillin and put them on for the very first time. "Wearing them," he said, "made me feel not only closer to God, but to my great grandfather." It is no wonder, then, that some people call tefillin "the ties that bind."

What are the strings that hang down the bottom of the shirts of Orthodox boys and men?

The tallit, or Jewish prayer shawl, is worn as a reminder to perform mitzvot, religious obligations. Centuries ago, God commanded Moses to speak to the children of Israel and bid them to affix fringes to the corners of their overgarments. When they looked at them, they were instructed to remember all of God's commandments.

As styles changed, it became too cumbersome to wear overgarments all day long. In its place came a lightweight garment with four fringes attached to the corners; it could be draped over one's neck like a poncho. This garment came to be known as a *tallit katan*, a small tallit; it is often worn by traditional Jewish males, underneath their shirt or sweater.

Some Jews take the injunction in Numbers 15:39 literally. They assume that the words "and it shall be unto you for a fringe, that you may look upon it and remember all the commandments of God" mean that the four fringes must be visible at all times. The fringes, which are part of the undergarment, are purposely exposed because each fringe is said to represent the 613 commandments in the Torah.

Why do married Orthodox women wear wigs? Do they shave their head?

In the Bible, the sensuous hair of a woman is described as a mark of beauty. "You are beautiful my love . . . your hair is like a flock of goats, trailing down from Mount Gilead" (Song of Songs 4:1). Both in biblical times and Talmudic times, women covered their head as a sign of modesty. To expose a woman's hair was considered a disgrace. Toward the end of the eighteenth century, the *shaytl* (Yiddish for "wig") was introduced as a head covering. Today, only strictly Orthodox married women wear a head covering at all times. The reason generally given is so that they should not appear attractive to men. In some cases, Orthodox women shave their head or cut their hair very short before covering it with a wig.

Many Orthodox and Hasidic women today also wear a *shaytl*, but they use a kerchief (known as a *tichel*) as a head covering.

Who is supposed to wear a tallit, and when?

Rectangular in form, the tallit or prayer shawl is draped around one's shoulders during morning prayer; men and some women do so. The source of the law requiring the wearing of a tallit is the Bible. God spoke to Moses, who in turn was commanded to speak to the children of Israel, asking them to affix fringes to the corners of their garments. The fringes were to be a constant reminder of God's commandments.

The tallit is worn at all weekday morning services, except on Tisha B'Av, a fast day when the tallit is worn during the Mincha afternoon service only. It is also worn on the Sabbath and on Jewish holidays. The custom is for the leader of the service to wear a tallit whenever he or she is leading the congregation in prayer.

The tallit is worn only during the day because it is during the daytime that there is sufficient light for the fringes to be noticed. Only on the eve of Yom Kippur, at the Kol Nidre service, is a tallit worn at night, because of the added holiness of the occasion.

I've always taught my students that all commandments are meant to remind us of some important Jewish value, concept, or thought. In the case of the tallit fringes, they are like a string around our finger, reminding us of God's obligations.

If you should ever find yourself in a synagogue and see young men without a tallit, you can safely assume that they are not married (unless they happen to be non-Jewish visitors). In some Orthodox congregations, it is the custom for a young man not to wear a tallit until after his wedding day. If he happens to be called to the Torah for an *aliyah* or is asked to lead the service, he puts one on for the occasion.

Lately, I've seen a tallit that was very colorful, not just black and white or blue and white. Does a tallit need to be a certain color? What is the meaning of the colorful ones?

When I became a Bar Mitzvah in 1960, there were very few choices of tallitot to choose from. Most came in white, with black or blue stripes. Perhaps the manufacturers chose blue because it was traditionally understood as the color that was the reflection of God's throne. Blue was also a color of royalty.

There is no law that states that a tallit must be a certain color. Today, tallitot come in many sizes, colors, and designs. For my son's Bar Mitzvah, we were able to order a tallit that was made just for him, with a neckband that portrayed a view of the ancient city of Jerusalem. It also came with a matching tallit bag.

Cantors today often wear a prayer shawl whose neckband portrays musical notes with verses such as "Shiru L'Adonai shir chadash" (Sing to God a new song). As Jewish communities continue to encourage artisans to handcraft all kinds of ritual items and garments, the array of prayer shawl designs expands.

Is there significance to different kinds of kippot? Some are velvet, some knitted, some very big, and others small. What about the funny kippot (like those with cartoon characters on them)? It seems inappropriate to wear a kippah to the synagogue with a picture of Mickey Mouse on it.

In Jewish life, it is considered respectful for men to wear a head covering, conveying the sense that there is a Divine force above. Known in Hebrew as a kippa, or by its Yiddish name yarmulke, they are worn by Orthodox men most of the time, and by many other worshippers when in synagogue. Modern Orthodox men are apt to be seen wearing smaller, knitted kippot. When I was a youngster, most men wore the typical black yarmulke, which is still popular today.

Today, the selection of kippot has grown to enormous proportions. For those interested in a particular sports team, one can purchase a kippa with a favorite team's sports logo on it. Recently someone gave me as a gift a kippa with the Toronto Blue Jays baseball team logo on it. (I am Canadian born.)

For those who love Disney characters, there are kippot being designed today with the Disney logo on them, including the likes of Mickey Mouse and Donald Duck. They are usually purchased and worn by children, who are attracted to these characters. I admit I have never been offended or felt it was inappropriate to wear such a kippot. So long as there is nothing crude or lewd on them, I feel strongly that no one should be opposed to their creation. I also am in favor of having people feel the joy in worshipping, and wearing a kippa with which one is comfortable is likely to enhance the feeling of joy.

Chapter 25

❧ ❧

Holy Objects

❧ The Torah ❧

Why do we kiss the Torah in the synagogue? Isn't that idolatry?

Kissing is a universal sign of affection. It is an act of love and an expression of attachment between man and woman, parent and child. In Judaism, kissing is also the expression of one's feelings for the ritual objects and the religious duties associated with them.

Although there are no religious laws that require us to kiss a ritual or holy object, there is the force of custom that develops through the ages. For example, the neckband of a tallit is often kissed just before putting it on. I like to kiss my tefillin when taking them out of their bag and before replacing them.

I always kiss a mezuzah when I see it on a doorpost. I touch the mezuzah with my right hand and kiss the fingers that made contact with it. This is my way of embracing the words inside the mezuzah that remind me of my obligation to love God with all my heart.

The Torah, the holiest object in the sanctuary, is usually kissed when it passes by in the synagogue. Some touch the Torah mantle with their prayer book, others with their prayer shawl, and still others with the fingers. The Torah is also customarily kissed before one recites the blessings over it.

Many people in our congregation have the custom of kissing the prayer book or Bible before putting it away. A holy book is also kissed if it is accidentally dropped on the floor.

A student of mine once told me that he brought a non-Jewish friend to a Sabbath service at our Temple. It was the first time his friend had ever been in a synagogue. As the Torah was making its way around the synagogue in a processional, he saw all the people touching and kissing it, and he asked whether it was some sort of idol they were embracing. "No," the student answered. "The Torah is God's words and the way God wants us to live our lives. By kissing it, we are embracing it and showing God how much we love what He gave us!"

Is it true that if you drop a Torah you have to fast forty days?

There is in the Code of Jewish Law a statement that if a person drops a Torah scroll, he or she is obliged to fast. Some say the fast is to be for forty days. In addition, those who saw the Torah fall were also obliged to fast. Today, instead of declaring a fast, there is an alternate custom of making a tzedakah (contribution to a worthy cause).

The biggest risk of dropping a Torah is when a person is given the honor of *hagba*, the lifting of the Torah, and on Simchat Torah, when people are ecstatic and dancing wildly with the Torah high above their heads. I've never known anyone who saw a Torah fall, although there have been some close calls when those nearest saved the day. In our congregation, we always have a couple of people chosen as honor guard who stand very close to the person who is honored with lifting the Torah. That way, they are prepared in case it looks as if it's going to be dropped.

I once heard a person tell another (almost facetiously) that the trick in not having to worry if you drop a Torah is "to eat the night before."

Why do we dress a Torah?

For most of the worship service, the Torah scroll is in the Holy Ark, where it awaits being taken out for reading. It is generally adorned with a Torah mantle (*me'il* in Hebrew), and sometimes there is a silver breastplate, a crown (*keter*) or two silver small receptacles with bells (*rimonim*), and a silver pointer (*yad*) that is placed on the Torah handle. A sash (known as a *gartel* or a *wimple*) is used to bind the two sides of the Torah scroll together. It can be made of a variety of materials and colors. Sometimes, the swaddling clothes used at the circumcision of a boy are saved and fashioned into the sash used for the Torah that is read on his Bar Mitzvah. In our synagogue, we have a Bar and Bat Mitzvah retreat; we teach families how to make their own personalized sash, which is then used on the day of the Bar or Bat Mitzvah.

The purpose of the mantle is to both beautify and protect the Torah. According to the Talmud (Shabbat 133b), the Torah is to be copied by a talented scribe and wrapped in beautiful silk. Torah mantles come in a variety of colors and often have a notable biblical verse written on them or a picture of the Ten Commandments or the Lions of Judah. White mantles are used to cover all of the Torah scrolls on the High Holy Days of Rosh Hashanah and Yom Kippur.

The breastplate that often is placed on the Torah is made of silver and designed to imitate the breastplate worn by the High Priest, which was decorated with four rows consisting of a total of twelve precious stones engraved with the name of each of the twelve sons of Jacob.

Since the Torah is the holiest object in Jewish life, it is only natural to crown it with the symbol of sovereignty. The robe worn by the High Priest when he performed his priestly duties was decorated with bells. The vestment worn by the High Priest likely inspired the small bells that adorn the Torah crown.

I once read an article on Judaism and superstition that stated that evil spirits are warded off by the noise of bells, and this is why they traditionally adorn a Torah scroll. Another explanation I once heard related that even if one is visually impaired and cannot see the Torah, one can hear the sound of the bells and know that the Torah is being carried in a procession.

After the Torah has been dressed by the *gollel*, the custom is often to place a tender kiss on it before returning to one's seat. Kissing is a sign of endearment and showing one's love for the Torah.

After the Torah reading is completed, two persons are honored with the task of lifting up the Torah and rolling and dressing it. The person charged with the dressing is called the *gollel* (for a woman, the *gollelet*). After the two rolls of parchment on the Torah scroll are rolled together, the sash is placed around the parchment and the mantle is draped over the Torah scroll. The Torah is then ready to be returned to the Holy Ark.

Why is an open Torah scroll sometimes held up in the air by its poles in the synagogue?

After the Torah reading is completed, two people are honored with the task of lifting up the Torah by its handles and rolling and dressing it. The one who lifts up the Torah scroll performs the task of *hagbahah*. The one who rolls up the Torah scroll and dresses it by putting on the mantle performs the task called *gelilah*.

One of the highlights of the service for me is to watch a person lift the Torah. There is a correct technique to follow in doing this, and knowing the technique is especially helpful when the Torah scroll is heavy. The whole purpose of the lifting ritual is to enable the congregation to see the Torah script, so the custom has become for the lift to expose a minimum of three columns of script.

I once had a member of my congregation speak to me about how upset he was to have been given the honor of lifting the Torah. He preferred what he thought was the more prestigious honor of the *aliyah*, saying the Torah blessings. I was able to convince him otherwise when, the following week, I sent him the statement from the Talmud (Megillah 32a) that says the honor we call *hagbahah* embodies the spiritual reward of all of the other *aliyot* combined!

Is it true that if one single letter of a Torah scroll is written incorrectly or left out, the whole Torah is considered nonkosher?

According to halacha (Jewish law), a Torah scroll is written according to strict rules and traditions. Only a qualified scribe is able to write one, and it can take upwards of a year to complete it. As a general rule, a

Torah scroll in which there is even one error or that is in disrepair is considered *pasul*, not fit for use, unless and until it is repaired.

Sometimes an error is discovered before or during a Torah reading. I remember, a few years ago, the cantor was reading Torah and suddenly stopped and then paused. He had discovered a word in which one of the letters had faded so badly that it could not be read. Declaring the Torah as unfit, the Torah was immediately dressed and another Torah was removed and subsequently read from.

Today, it is common for a synagogue every few years to have all of the Torah scrolls checked by a qualified scribe for possible errors. This ensures that a Torah when read will not have to be replaced because it was found to be defective.

❧ Mezuzah ☙

What is a mezuzah, and what's inside it?

In our own synagogue, we have a wonderful gift shop. Recently, the gift shop lady related to me a story of a congregant who came into the shop to purchase a mezuzah for her home. She picked out a most beautiful one and was about to pay for it when the gift shop lady asked her, "Do you have a parchment for your mezuzah?" The buyer looked somewhat stunned and said, "I didn't know that anything had to go into it." The gift shop lady showed her the special mezuzah parchment and explained to her all of its words and history. When told that it was an additional forty dollars, the buyer said, "I'm going to pass on buying the parchment. Nobody is going to see it anyhow."

I'm thankful that this story is not representative of most of the people in our congregation. But the truth of the matter is that few people are aware of what goes into the mezuzah receptacle.

The word *mezuzah* literally means "doorpost," but it is normally taken to refer to the case that holds the parchment and is then affixed to the doorpost. On the parchment, which is handwritten by a scribe using a quill pen and ink, are the first two paragraphs of the prayer *Shema Yisrael* (Deuteronomy 6:4–9 and 11:13–31), which includes the commandment concerning the mezuzah. The parchment used comes from the skin of a kosher animal, usually a lamb or goat.

There are several words that appear on the backside of the parchment. One is *Shaddai*. In Talmudic times, it was believed that the mezuzah possessed protective powers and could ward off evil spirits. The Zohar, the Jewish book of mysticism, indicates that the acronym *Shaddai* is to appear in the mezuzah parchment because its three letters—*shin, daled, yud*—are a synonym for God, created from the first letters in the Hebrew phrase *shomer delatot Yisrael* (protectors of the doors of Israel).

In medieval times, mystics added three cryptogrammatic words to the bottom of the backside of the mezuzah, below the word *Shaddai*. These words, *kozu bemuchsaz kozu*, represent three real Hebrew words, *Adonai Elohenu Adonai*, meaning "The Lord our God is the Lord."

Substituting for each Hebrew letter in the phrase Adonai Elohenu Adonai the letter that follows it in the Hebrew alphabet, one arrives at *kozu bemuchsaz kozu*, believed by the mystics to have a secret magical meaning. Thus Adonai, which is spelled *yud, hay, vav, hay*, was spelled *kaf, vav, zayin, vav*, forming the word *kozu*. The same system of substituting one letter for another was employed to arrive at the next two words.

To protect the writing, it became customary to roll up the parchment and insert it in a metal or wooden container with a small opening on the side of the container, near the top. The word *Shaddai* was positioned so that it would be visible through the opening. Today, many modern mezuzah cases are elaborately designed in a variety of shapes and colors.

According to Jewish tradition, the mitzvah of the mezuzah includes affixing the receptacle to one's doorpost, with a kosher parchment handwritten by a scribe with the proper markings on the backside included. An unkosher mezuzah is one that was not properly written by a scribe (unscrupulous sellers have often photocopied them), or one in which a word or letter has been erased. To avoid having unkosher mezuzot, many Jews have their scrolls periodically checked by a scribe.

I like to kiss the mezuzah as I walk into my home. It serves as a kind of speed bump, slowing me down as I touch it, and constantly reminding me of my obligation to love God, with all my soul and heart.

Why do some people kiss a mezuzah?

In Jewish tradition, to kiss a holy object such as a mezuzah is a gesture of reverence and adoration. Just as a Torah scroll is often kissed as it is carried around the synagogue, so too many people follow the custom of touching the mezuzah with their fingertips and kissing it.

My philosophy teacher, Rabbi Neil Gillman, quoting one of his students, expressed a connection between speed bumps, which are built to slow cars down in a parking lot, and the mezuzah, which is a sort of speed bump. When a person enters or leaves a home and follows the custom of kissing the mezuzah, the person is allowed just enough time to slow down and be reminded that the home one is entering or leaving is a sanctified one in which the Divine is present.

Is it true that some people put up a mezuzah box without anything inside it? Is this OK?

A mezuzah without parchment is like a car without an engine. It simply won't work, and such a mezuzah has no sanctification attached to it. When one purchases a mezuzah from a reputable Judaic store, the seller is always sure to remind the buyer to purchase kosher parchment for the mezuzah. If the seller tells you that the mezuzah case comes with parchment inside, in my experience this is usually a sure sign that the parchment inside is a fake (perhaps a photocopied piece of paper).

The laws that apply to the writing of a Torah also apply to the writing of a mezuzah. A scribe, called a *sofer* in Hebrew, uses a quill from a goose or turkey and with indelible black ink writes the twenty-two lines from Deuteronomy (6:4–9) on parchment. The parchment in turn is rolled and inserted into the mezuzah container to protect the writing.

Should a mezuzah be on every door in your house? How about your work office? What about the cabin of a boat?

According to Jewish law, a mezuzah should be affixed to every room of one's home, except for a closet or bathroom. Only permanent buildings and rooms in which one eats or sleeps require a mezuzah. Thus, a structure such as a garage, even when attached to a home, does not require a mezuzah. One could put a mezuzah on one's office, but if it is in a building that is owned jointly by Jews and non-Jews there is no requirement to do so.

Regarding a boat, if a boat is a room in which one can sleep, the custom is often to affix a mezuzah to that room.

In a Jewish bookstore, I saw a mezuzah for a car. What's that about?

Some people view the mezuzah as a charm and good luck amulet. As with the Star of David and Chai charms, wearing a mezuzah can be viewed as an expression of pride in one's heritage.

There are Judaic shops that now sell mezuzot for cars. There is no requirement to affix a mezuzah to one's car. So-called car mezuzot do not come with kosher parchment and are often bought by people who want to feel more "protected" while driving. I often advise such people that they might try reciting the special Jewish traveler's prayer, which asks for God's protection when traveling. This is a much more traditional and authentic way of reminding ourselves of God's saving power while we travel.

Chapter 26

Anti-Semitic Documents and Statements

What are the Protocols of the Elders of Zion?

One of the most well-known anti-Semitic documents in history is the Protocols of the Elders of Zion. In the 1880s, a group of Russian exiles plotted to discredit the Bolsheviks and reestablish the czarist regime. They produced a document alleged to be the minutes (Protocols) of the "Elders of Zion," an international committee of prominent Jews—whose existence they invented. These elders were supposed to have met toward the end of the nineteenth century and devised schemes for the destruction of Christian civilization, so that Jews might seize complete control of the world.

Thousands of Jews have died because of this infamous forgery. In Russia itself, the Protocols were used to provoke hundreds of pogroms during the Russian civil war of 1918–1920, when the Jews were accused of having brought communism to Russia.

With remarkable rapidity, the Protocols spread to every part of the world. Even though the falsity of the document was clear from every page, hundreds of thousands of people took it seriously. In the United States, the most prominent proponent was Henry Ford, who for more than a year and a half in the early 1920s carried reports of the worldwide Jewish conspiracy in his weekly newspaper, the *Dearborn Independent*. In Germany, Hitler had these articles translated and widely disseminated. The late King Faisal of Saudi Arabia used to give copies of the Protocols to guests of his regime.

Today, there are still numerous forged documents in circulation spreading evil reports against the Jews that continue to be believed by thousands of people. Anti-Semitism continues to be a work in progress.

Why do some Arabs say that "Zionism is racism"? Was there really a UN resolution about this?

Although the United Nations played a vital role in bringing about the establishment of the state of Israel, it became a center of anti-Israel sentiment in the 1970s. At that time, its votes were generally decided by the twenty-three Arab states, the USSR and Soviet bloc, and a collection of Third World dictatorships. The voting of these three blocs almost always guaranteed passage of any resolution introduced by any one of them.

One issue that clearly united the Arab and Communist blocs was hatred of Israel and Zionism, the Jewish national movement that had brought the state into being. Politically, Zionism was a movement to reestablish the Jews as a people in the Land of Israel. Zionists believe that such a homeland will secure the welfare of Jews throughout the world and serve as a source of spiritual and cultural inspiration to the Jews of all lands.

The political efforts that led to creation of the new Jewish state began about ninety years ago. Since the middle of the nineteenth century, Jews of Eastern Europe living under the rigors of czarist tyranny saw in Palestine the only answer to the age-old problem of homelessness.

Beginning in the early 1970s, Arab delegates regularly tried to have Zionism denounced as "racist" in the official resolutions of all international conferences. (It is ironic that Israel is one of the only countries in the Middle East where citizens of every race live and enjoy equal rights.) Many of these Arabs would be happy to see the destruction and ultimate disappearance of the Israeli state.

On November 10, 1975, Resolution 3379, denouncing Zionism as "a form of racism," passed the UN General Assembly. Although the resolution had no concrete significance, since it is a nonbinding recommendation, its symbolic significance was considerable. This resolution essentially told Jews that they had no right to their own homeland. Although many U.S. senators and others denounced the resolution as obscene and vulgar, its passage lent encouragement to anti-Semites, who could now disguise their hatred for Jews under the rubric of Zionism.

Is it true that some famous people, like the poet Ezra Pound and the industrialist Henry Ford, were anti-Semitic?

Ezra Pound won international acclaim as a modern poet, having written more than forty volumes of poetry. In Italy, he became an admirer of Mussolini and adopted an increasingly pro-Fascist and anti-Semitic tone. It was not long before he became an advocate of Canadian C. H. Douglas's social credit doctrine, which blamed human misery on the financial manipulations of Jews. Pound's *Money Pamphlets*, which he composed in the 1950s, spoke repeatedly of the "Jewish poison"; back in 1939 he wrote an article for the Italian press entitled "The Jew, Disease Incarnate." Many of Pound's poems are also violently anti-Jewish.

During the 1920s, a most significant attack against Jews occurred. It focused not on religion or Jewish social climbing but on race and political subversion. The resurgent Ku Klux Klan activated the myths about Jews as Christ killers and racial polluters. Even more significant was the resurrection of the vicious slander of the Jews as conspiring to seize control of the nation.

This belief crystallized around automobile magnate Henry Ford. In May 1922, Ford's *Dearborn Independent* claimed that the press was owned, slanted, and muzzled by Jewish money. In addition, the newspaper posited that Jews were corrupting the labor movement with socialist ideas and that they were infecting youth with corruption and sin. Ford's ideas were most widespread and intense in the small-town, provincial culture of the South and West, where Jews were usually regarded as outsiders, especially if they were recent arrivals from the North or Europe. It is no coincidence, then, that one of the most brutal acts of violence against an American Jew occurred in Marietta, Georgia, when Leo Frank, convicted in a controversial trial of murdering a fourteen-year-old girl, was lynched by an anti-Semitic mob in the early morning hours of a day in August 1915. The hatred of Frank was permeated with racist perceptions of the Jew as foreigner and corrupter.

Chapter 27

❧ ❧

Sephardic and Ashkenazic Jews

What is the difference between Sephardic and Ashkenazic Jews?

The term *Ashkenazim* generally refers to Jews coming from Europe, while *Sephardim* generally refers to Jews coming from Spain, Portugal, or the Arab world. Sephardic communities today are found principally in Turkey, Greece, North Africa, Israel, England, Latin America, and the United States. Ironically, if one meets a Jew whose name is Ashkenazi, he is almost certainly a Sephardic Jew.

It has been estimated that worldwide some 80 percent of all Jews are Ashkenazim, and only 20 percent Sephardim. In Israel, however, more than half of the Jewish population is Sephardic.

One obvious difference between Sephardim and Ashkenazim is in pronunciation of Hebrew and the liturgy. The Sephardim claim that their pronunciation of Hebrew and their liturgy derived from the period of the Geonim, who led the great academies of Babylonia until the center of Jewish life shifted to Spain. The text of their prayer books is based on the siddur of the distinguished Babylonian Gaon, Amram.

The order of prayers, the customs, and the traditions of the Sephardic Jews are known as "Minhag Sepharad," as distinguished from "Minhag Ashkenaz." Examples of the Sephardic custom are:

- Naming a child after a living parent or grandparent, unlike the Ashkenazim, who name children only after the deceased

214

- Reciting the Kol Nidre prayer in the manner of a simple prayer; among the Ashkenazim, the cantor alone chants it aloud
- Sephardic Jews keeping the Torah in a hardened wooden case and reading it upright, while Ashkenazim keep their Torah scroll in a soft fabric cover and read it lying flat on a table
- At weddings, a Sephardic couple standing together wrapped in a tallit, whereas Ashkenazic couples stand separately
- Sephardic Jews calling the yearly anniversary of a loved one *anos*, while Ashkenazic Jews use the word *yahrzeit*

Like the Yiddish-speaking Ashkenazic Jews, Sephardic Jews speak a group language or vernacular known as Ladino. It is written in Hebrew characters and consists primarily of Castilian mixed with many Hebrew idioms and expressions. It is also studded with Turkish, Arabic, and Greek words.

One of my vivid memories of the Sephardim was a visit to the Italian Sephardic synagogue in Jerusalem. I heard the congregation sing songs of the coming of Shabbat with such heart and soul that the walls shook. It has been said that the Sephardim, especially those from the Middle East, are known to express extreme optimism and cheerfulness in their services.

Who are Oriental Jews?

Oriental Jewish communities are those that originated from various Moslem and Arabic-speaking countries, including Yemen, Iraq, Kurdistan (in northern Iraq), Persia (Iran), Afghanistan, and Cochin (in Southern India). All of these Oriental Jews have established communities throughout Israel, having fled there in the 1950s thanks to discrimination and national oppression in their home communities. Today, more than 50 percent of all Jews living in Israel are Oriental.

Each of these Oriental Jewish groups has its own original customs and traditions. One of the wildest I've heard relates to the Kurdistan Jews, who on the last day of Hanukkah each year make a doll that is nicknamed Hanukkah. The doll is dressed to look like King Antiochus, and they throw it into a fire to burn on the eighth day of Hanukkah.

Chapter 28

❦ ❧

Language

What's the difference between Hebrew and Yiddish?

Hebrew belongs to the Canaanite branch of Semitic languages. It is known as *leshon ha-kodesh*, the holy tongue, because God gave us the Torah in Hebrew. Hebrew was spoken in Palestine before the Israelite conquest. It was the language of the children of Israel who sojourned in Egypt, who were enslaved there, and who were led forth by Moses. The Hebrew Bible, called the Tanach, is written in Hebrew.

Hebrew gradually ceased being a spoken language after 70 C.E., when the Jews were driven from the land of Israel by the Romans and scattered throughout the world. It continued to remain alive, however, and was used constantly in many ways. It was the language of prayer, study, reading the Torah, and correspondence. Above all, it was used as the language of a tremendously rich literature of law, theology, philosophy, science, medicine, astronomy, poetry, grammar, and other fields of human knowledge.

With the rise of Jewish nationalism in the late nineteenth century, Hebrew returned to being a spoken language. A man by the name of Eliezer ben Yehudah was the chief figure in the revival of Hebrew as a spoken language. He published a modern dictionary of the Hebrew language, compiling in it thousands of new words. When he began the project, there was not even a real word for "dictionary" in Hebrew. He took as his base the Hebrew word *millah* (word) and created from it *millon*, the word for dictionary. Today, it is taken for granted that Hebrew is Israel's official language.

A little over a century ago, however, no one used Hebrew as a language of daily communication. Eastern European Jews generally spoke Yiddish, a Jewish language based largely on German and Hebrew. The word for Jew in Yiddish is *Yid*, which is why people who are speaking Yiddish will sometimes say they are speaking "Jewish." This usage however, is incorrect, for the language's correct name is Yiddish.

Four main components entered into the formation of Yiddish: Hebrew, Loez (a combination of Old French and Old Italian), German, and Slavic. Of these, medieval German was the most important; about 85 percent of the vocabulary and the basic Yiddish grammatical structure is German. Yiddish uses Hebrew characters.

As a rule, Jews only spoke Yiddish in societies where they did not have equal rights. Whereas Polish and Russian Jews spoke Yiddish, the overwhelming majority of Jews in nineteenth-century France and Germany spoke French and German. In the 1920s, Yiddish newspapers published in New York sold more than two hundred thousand copies daily.

Because Yiddish is such a colorful language, some of its more evocative words have entered into the vocabulary of non-Jews. Recently in our synagogue a teacher in a Jewish Day School came to present a siddur (prayer book) to one of my Bat Mitzvah students. In her remarks, she talked about the good manners and righteousness of the student, using the well-known Yiddish word *menschlachkeit*. Other well-known Yiddish words that have made it into the English vocabulary include *mazal tov* (congratulations), *maven* (expert), and *kibitz* (to joke), just to name a few.

Hasidic Jews continue to use Yiddish exclusively in their daily language, believing that use of Hebrew is appropriate only in holy acts such as prayer. In 1978, Isaac Bashevis Singer, a Yiddish writer who won the Nobel Prize for literature, predicted the demise of Yiddish. Even he must have been surprised when he saw with his own eyes the return of Yiddish to the college campus.

Today, there are many colleges and universities that are teaching the Yiddish language, as well as a proliferation of Yiddish book clubs and speaking groups. I myself enrolled in Yiddish class in college, so I could understand all the things that my grandmother would say to my parents in Yiddish when they didn't want me to understand.

Why do some people say Shabbat and some say Shabbos? Also potato kugel and potato kigel? Can you explain why we pronounce the same words differently in so many cases?

All countries have dialects and variations in the pronunciation of words. For instance, I grew up in Toronto, Canada. Whereas most Americans pronounce the city of my birth *Toronto*, in the city itself Canadians pronounce it *Torana*.

One of the most obvious differences between Sephardic Jews (from Spain, Portugal, and North Africa) and Ashkenazic Jews (from Germany and Eastern Europe) is in the pronunciation of their Hebrew. They have different customs, traditions, and pronunciations. With regard to the words *Shabbat* and *Shabbos*, the pronunciation here has also to do with their dialects.

In the Ashkenazic dialect, the word for the Sabbath is *Shabbos*, because the Hebrew letter *tav* without a dot in it is pronounced as an *s*. In the Sephardic dialect, which is used today in spoken Hebrew in the state of Israel, the word for Sabbath is *Shabbat*. Because of the *t* and *s* variation, you might also hear someone call a girl who has become a Jewish woman either a Bas Mitzvah or a Bat Mitzvah depending on the dialect. Many Orthodox yeshivas teach the Ashkenazic dialect to its students, whereas students in the other branches of Judaism are more likely to learn Sephardic Hebrew, because it's the spoken Hebrew of modern Israel.

There are also other variations in Jewish or Yiddish words, depending on where a person was born in Eastern Europe. This would be the cause of the variation in the potato pudding being called *kugel* or *kigel*, depending on whether a person was from Poland, Russia, or some other Eastern European country.

The good news here is that most people who use one form of a word in spoken language have little trouble being understood by a person using another dialect.

Chapter 29

❦ ❦

Jews and Cults

Is it true that there are a lot of Jews in cults?

A brilliant Ivy League college undergrad writes his parents a short, cryptic note informing them that he has found new life with the Children of God. They never see their child again. We had such a case in our own congregation with the Moonie missionary group.

The world is full of young Jews in search of everything but Judaism, and often their searching can take some strange twists and turns. It has been reported in many publications that 10–12 percent of converts to Rev. Moon's Unification Church are Jewish. Hundreds of Jewish youths have joined Jews for Jesus groups. Many others have become Children of God, members of the Hare Krishna sect, followers of the Divine Light Mission, or "Scientologists." A large proportion of them come from stable, middle-class Jewish families and have had several years of Jewish education.

Adolescence in society has been recognized as a time of searching for an identity and adult goals. Rebellion against parental values is part of the search. The point of searching and rebelling often leaves the youths open to suggestion. The result is that a young person can be highly vulnerable to the warm yet casual invitation to join a cult recruiter for dinner with friends. Surrounded with love, the naïve youth finds it difficult to resist the subtle messages to joining in fighting the ills of society.

Cults offer instant friendship and communion, a sense of belonging. They are experts in love-bombing techniques, and to those hungering for truth and meaning in a complex world, a cult offers simple answers.

In our own synagogue high school, we offer a course each year on missionary and cult movements. The course is intended as an overview of the Hebrew-Christian missionary movements, their tactics, and an overview of countermissionary tactics. By educating our students on who these groups are and the inherent dangers in them, we have succeeded in keeping our group of kids out of harm's reach.

Isn't it a cult when Hasidim do whatever their rebbe says?

Some people have noticed similarities between the leader of a cult and the rebbe, the spiritual leader of the Hasidim. Each has a charismatic central authority, and its members are beholden to the leader for all kinds of practical advice.

However, in a cult there is blind obedience to the leader, and all assets belong to the cult. In addition, a cult requires its members to break their family ties. The new community becomes a substitute family. In addition, a cult views itself as the only true religion, and anyone who disagrees with the group is viewed as an agent of the devil.

There is still personal autonomy among the members of any Hasidic group, although their spiritual and religious customs tend to be similar to one another. The family in a Hasidic sect is not required to give its earnings to the rebbe. Certainly, members of any Hasidic group are allowed to think for themselves, although the rebbe is generally the final authority.

Chapter 30

❧ ❧

Kabbalah

Some people say that we shouldn't study kabbalah, and others seem to be teaching it. What is kabbalah, and should we be studying it or not?

The term *kabbalah* derives from the Hebrew word "tradition" or "receiving." Kabbalah designates the mystic teachings of Judaism, originally handed down from generation to generation. The mystical philosophy of the kabbalah is hidden and unintelligible to those who have not been properly prepared and instructed in its secret wisdom.

The subjects treated by the kabbalah concern the essence of God, the origin of the universe, the creation of man, the destiny of man and the universe, and the significance of the sacred Torah.

Kabbalah took hundreds of years to develop into a mature mystical teaching. Its origins can be traced to the inner life of the Essenes, a mystic brotherhood of about four thousand people who flourished in the time of the Second Temple. They were ascetics who preferred silence, wore white clothes, and ate and prayed together.

First handed down orally to a chosen few and then committed to writing, the mystical interpretation of the Torah is principally embodied in the work known as the Zohar (brightness), which made its appearance for the first time in thirteenth-century Spain.

The rabbis in Talmudic times regarded the mystical study of God as important yet very dangerous. A famous talmudic story tells of four rabbis—Azzai, Ben Zoma, Elisha ben Abuyah, and Akiva—who would meet and study mysticism. Azzai, the Talmud records, looked and went mad, and Ben Zoma died. Elisha ben Abuyah became a heretic and left Judaism. Only Akiva survived the experience, beginning it and ending it in peace. As a result of these legends during the Middle Ages, the rabbis wanted the study of kabbalah to be limited to people of mature years and character.

Because kabbalistic ideas are subtle and their interpretations often too daring for the average person, it is important to get a good grounding in the Bible and Jewish philosophy before engaging in the study of Jewish mysticism.

Why are some non-Jewish celebrities studying kabbalah?

Next to one of the star-studded parties after the annual Academy awards, a good place to run into Hollywood celebrities may be at the Kabbalah Learning Center in Los Angeles. Kabbalah, the mystical Jewish tradition, has in recent years been attracting a growing number of stars in search of spiritual fulfillment and insights into the relationship between God and humans.

Perhaps the most popular seeker is Madonna, who is said to have studied during her pregnancy in order to seek advice as to the best day on which to deliver her child. Strangely enough, having been told that Rosh Hodesh was the most preferred of days on which to have a child, Madonna gave birth to her daughter Lourdes on the new Jewish month. Having grown up Catholic, it is reported that Madonna has said that nothing affected her as much as her kabbalah lessons.

Kabbalah centers continue to attract celebrities, both Jewish and non-Jewish. Reputed disciples included singers Courtney Love and Barbra Streisand; and actors Elizabeth Taylor, Diane Ladd, Jeff Goldblum, and Roseanne Barr.

Where do I go if I want to study kabbalah?

Kabbalah study began in earnest in the Middle Ages, when it was passed on to Jewish men over forty who were deemed to have the maturity and biblical knowledge to handle mysticism's great power. Today, kabbalah centers are emerging throughout the United States and around the world, teaching a hybrid version of kabbalah with no restriction on age, gender, or religion.

It has been reported that Jews and non-Jews alike, to the tune of 3.9 million, have gravitated to the kabbalah centers. The largest of the new kabbalah groups is the Kabbalah Learning Center, which claims ten thousand students in eight countries. Some rabbis are known to be critical of some of these centers, claiming that they are nothing but New Age imitations of kabbalah.

Rabbi Phillip Berg, preeminent leader of the Kabbalah Center, opened his first facility in the United States in 1969. Over the next three decades, Berg and his followers launched worldwide centers in France, Israel, Canada, South America, Mexico, and Japan. The Kabbalah Center of Los Angeles, the organization's U.S. headquarters, is currently located in Beverly Hills.

Another popular center for studying Jewish mysticism is the retreat center Elat Chayyim, located in Accord, New York, in the Catskill Mountains. This organization, described as a Jewish spiritual retreat center, has assembled a team of teachers who offer a variety of topics, including Jewish mysticism, Jewish healing, Jewish meditation, and even Jewish yoga.

Finally, most universities and colleges throughout the United States and Canada have Jewish studies program where one can study kabbalah. We even offer it in our teenage Hebrew high school program, where it has perennially been one of our most popular electives!

Chapter 31

❧ ❧

Classic
Jewish Books

What is the Talmud?

The Talmud is the major source for the rabbinic interpretation of the law. The Mishnah, which is part of the Talmud (sometimes called the Oral Law), sought to explain the laws as set forth in the Torah. It consists of the teachings of the *tanaaim*, scholars and sages who lived prior to 220 C.E.

Judah HaNasi and his associates sifted through, evaluated, and edited a large number of legal opinions that had been expressed over the centuries in the learning academies. The product of their work was the Mishnah, a six-volume collection of legal opinions. It deals with topics from Jewish holidays and observing them to issues of what one does when one's ox wounds another's animal.

The Mishnah could neither encompass all the situations in any person's life nor cover new situations that were constantly developing. New situations and ambiguities in the text of the Mishnah often led to a discussion among the rabbis, and soon new rulings and decisions began to appear. Numerous life experiences, cases presented to the rabbis, and questions asked of them combined to expand and elaborate the teachings of the Mishnah. These later teachings were set down in the Gemara, which was completed around 500 C.E. For the most part, these scholars lived in Babylonia, where the greatest academies were situated. The Mishnah and the Gemara together make up the

Talmud, the major compendium of discussions on Jewish law held by the rabbis, and the record of their decisions. The Talmud also contains Jewish folklore, sayings, and stories.

A second Talmud, the Palestinian or Jerusalem Talmud, was also composed. This one consists of all the discussions that took place among the scholars in the learning academies in Palestine. The Palestinian Talmud has always enjoyed a lesser status than the Babylonian Talmud because its academies were not equal in stature to those of Babylonia.

Because the Talmud is written in a mixture of Aramaic and Hebrew, it has remained inaccessible to the Jewish public. An incredible scholar by the name of Rabbi Adin Steinsaltz has changed all of that. Within the next decade, he hopes to complete his modern commentary on the entire Talmud. In 1989, Random House began publishing his volumes of commentary, and it is likely that more than one million copies have been sold.

What is the Mishnah?

In addition to the written laws of the Torah, there developed over the centuries oral interpretations of these written laws that were essential to understanding the Torah. For example, the Torah did not go into detail concerning observance of the Sabbath. What did it mean when it said that one should not work on the Sabbath? What is the definition of work?

These and many other questions are answered in the work called the Mishnah, compiled and edited by Judah the Prince and his colleagues at the beginning of the third century.

The Mishnah is divided into six sections or Orders, called *Sedarim*: (1) "Seeds," dealing with agricultural laws; (2) "Festivals," relating to the Sabbath and holidays; (3) "Women," including laws of marriage and divorce; (4) "Damages," which includes laws of inheritance, lost property, and usury; (5) "Holy Things," relating to laws of sacrifice and the Temple service; and (6) "Purities," laws pertaining to ritual cleanliness.

One of the Mishnah's sixty-three tractates contains no laws at all. It is one of my favorites, called *Pirke Avot* (Ethics of the Fathers)—

the "Bartlett's of the rabbis," in which their most famous sayings are recorded. "If I am not for myself, who will be for me?" is one of the most memorable quotations in the book.

What is the Midrash?

The Hebrew term *midrash* means "investigation" and signifies study and interpretation. The purpose of midrashic writing is to explain the biblical text from ethical and devotional points of view. It is a way to explain internal difficulties in the text and draw out meaning relevant to religious and cultural life.

Today, midrash often refers to the famous compilation known as *Midrash Rabbah*, a collection of rabbinic comments on the Torah, as well as the Five Megillot.

Midrash continues to be created. For example, a group called Avodah came to our synagogue to perform what is known as Dance Midrash. A group of dancers creatively interpret various portions of the Bible through a variety of dance movements. Another new kind of midrash is called handmade midrash. It was designed by Jo Milgrom and described in her book *Handmade Midrash: Workshops in Visual Theology*.

For example, in attempting to understand the story of the binding of Isaac, participants are asked to tear forms out of sheets of colored construction paper without using scissors. In this case, the instructions are to represent Abraham, Isaac, the ram, the altar, and Divine Presence, gluing them in a relationship to a background sheet of paper. This process draws on the imagination of participants, allowing them to relate to a biblical passage with forms and shapes. After completing their artistic task, the participant is asked to describe what she or he sees in the work done.

What is the Zohar?

The Zohar (Book of Splendor) is a rabbinic commentary on the five books of Moses. It is the fundamental work of the mystic teachings of Judaism. Rich with deep religious inspiration, and containing many mystical interpretations of the Torah that have been in existence for centuries, the Zohar has served ever since its first appearance as the starting point for every kabbalistic discussion of Judaism.

The Zohar first became known about the middle of the thirteenth century as the work of Simeon ben Yochai, who had lived (during the second century) for thirteen years in hiding from the Roman persecutors after the unsuccessful Bar Kochba revolt. Hidden in a cave, Rabbi Simeon and his son, Elazar, are said to have been visited on frequent occasions by Elijah, who instructed them in the esoteric teachings of the Torah, which form a large portion of the subject matter of the Zohar.

According to the Zohar, everything in the Torah has threefold significance: the outward, the inner, and the innermost, this last the most important and the most to be desired. The highest goal of the religious person is to penetrate into the innermost purpose of the precepts and practices.

After the Bible and the Talmud, the Zohar is said to have exercised the deepest influence on Judaism.

What is the Megillah?

The word *megillah* means scroll. There are five biblical books known as the "Chamesh Megillot" (Five Scrolls). These five books are recited in the synagogue, as part of the liturgy, on special occasions: Song of Songs, on Passover; Ruth, on Shavuot; Lamentations, on the Fast of the Ninth of Av, commemorating the destruction of the Jerusalem Temples; Ecclesiastes, on Sukkot; and Esther, on the festival of Purim.

Because Purim is such a fun and lively holiday, it is likely that Jews would have the most familiarity with the book known as the Scroll of Esther, with its hero and heroine Mordecai and Queen Esther.

What is a siddur?

No religion in the world can be thoroughly understood if its normal daily worship of God is left out of account, for here is where the real pulse-beat of genuine religion is to be felt. This applies particularly to Judaism as reflected in the siddur, the prayer book, which is the most popular book in Jewish life.

If any single volume can tell us what it means to be a Jew, it is the daily prayer book, embodying the visions and aspirations of many generations. Interwoven throughout the texture of the prayers are many meaningful passages from the Bible, the Talmud, and the Zohar.

One of the compilers of the first systematic prayer book was Rav Saadia Gaon, who in the ninth century wrote in his introduction, "I have decided to assemble in this book the authoritative prayers, hymns and benedictions, in their original form as they existed before the exile and after."

Today each branch of Judaism has its own siddur, with its own translation and commentary. What is amazing to me is that although there are many differences and variations in the translation, each prayer book by and large contains similar prayers that appear in the same order as the others. This was a comforting fact when I attended the Italian synagogue in Jerusalem and had no difficulty finding or following along in their prayer book.

What is a machzor?

Because there are so many prayers that are distinctive to Rosh Hashanah and Yom Kippur, a special prayer book known as a *machzor* is used on these holidays. One of the most famous prayers in it is the one called Unetaneh Tokef, which addresses the fundamental theme of life and death. "On Rosh Hashanah," the prayer reads, "it is written, and on Yom Kippur it is sealed, how many shall leave this world, and how many shall be born into it, who shall live and who shall die. . . . But penitence, prayer and good deeds can annul the severity of the decree."

As in the siddur, there are passages from the Bible, Mishnah, Talmud, and Zohar that are interwoven into the machzor. Many other special poems, called *piyyutim*, are also found in the machzor, to give expression to the intense emotions and aspirations of the Jewish people.

What is a Chumash?

The Chumash is the Hebrew word for the five books of Moses: Genesis, Exodus, Leviticus, Numbers, and Deuteronomy. These names are descriptive of the contents of the books. Genesis (origin) begins with the story of creation. Exodus (going out) tells of the going out of the Israelites from Egypt. Leviticus (pertaining to the Levites) contains laws, which relate to the priests, members of the tribe of Levi. Numbers derives its name from the census of the Israelites in the desert. Deuteronomy (repetition of the law) contains a restatement of the laws of Moses.

The Chumash is divided into fifty-four Torah sections, read as part of the Sabbath morning services consecutively. Each week is identified with its current section and bears its name.

According to tradition, sometime around 1220 B.C.E. God dictated the five books of Moses, shortly after the Exodus from Egypt.

What is the Tanach?

The Tanach is an acronym for the three categories of books that make up the Hebrew Bible: Torah, Nevi'im (Prophets), and Ketuvim (Writings). Christians commonly refer to the Tanach as the Old Testament.

There are a total of thirty-nine books in the Tanach. The first five are the five books of Moses. The second category of biblical books is the Nevi'im, twenty-one books that trace Jewish history from the time of the death of Moses to the period after the Babylonians destroyed the First Temple (586 B.C.E.). The early books of the Nevi'im are the books of Joshua, Judges, Samuel I and II, and I and II Kings. These books are sometimes called the Early Prophets.

The Later Prophets are Isaiah, Jeremiah, Ezekiel, and the twelve Minor Prophets (Hosea, Joel, Amos, Obadiah, Jonah, Micah, Nachum, Habakkuk, Zephaniah, Haggai, Zechariah, and Malachi).

The final books of the Tanach are known as *Ketuvim.* They are the books of Psalms, Proverbs, Job, Song of Songs, Ruth, Lamentations, Ecclesiastes, Esther, Daniel, Ezra, Nehemiah, and I and II Chronicles.

The Tanach has been the most influential book in human history. Both Judaism and Christianity consider it one of its major religious texts.

What is Tehillim?

Tehillim refers to the Book of Psalms, the poems that have been on the lips of more people throughout the centuries than any other written compositions. They represent the highest product of the religious poetry of all nations.

There are 150 Psalms in all, with Jewish tradition ascribing them to the tenth century King David. The keynote of the Psalms is simplicity of heart, faith in God, and good conduct. In the Psalms, we find the human heart in all its moods and emotions—in penitence, danger, desolation, and triumph.

Many of the Psalms were used during the Temple services in Jerusalem. The Book of Psalms is also the backbone of the Hebrew prayer book.

Religious Jews regard recitation of Psalms as one of the ways of beseeching God's mercy. When in Israel in the early 1980s, I had a chance to visit the holy city of Hebron. There, at Rachel's tomb, were a bunch of women gathered around the tomb reciting a variety of Psalms. Our guide told us that the tomb of Rachel was a gathering place for women who were having trouble becoming pregnant, and that by reciting Psalms they thought God might intercede on their behalf and help them have a child.

Chapter 32

✿ ✿

Jewish Renewal

What is Jewish renewal?

The term Jewish renewal refers to organizations of those who are dedicated to reclaiming the Jewish people's sacred purpose of partnership with the Divine in the inseparable tasks of healing the world. Jewish renewal groups seek to bring creativity, relevance, joy, and an all-embracing awareness to spiritual practice as a path to healing one's body and mind.

The current phenomenon of Jewish renewal traces its roots to the Havurah movement, feminism, and other late twentieth-century phenomena, but primarily to the work of Rabbis Shlomo Carlebach and Zalman Schachter-Shalomi. Both of these charismatic rabbis were trained in the Lubavitch Hasidic movement and later left it to found their own institutions and plant the seeds of renewal worldwide. The Aleph: Alliance for Jewish Renewal organization is the outgrowth of B'nai Or Religious Fellowship, founded by Reb Zalman in 1962.

Many of the Jewish renewal groups put their emphasis on direct spiritual experience and kabbalistic teaching. They are known for their creative liturgy and often use meditation, dance, and chant. There is a large worldwide network of Jewish renewal communities.

For an extensive history of Jewish renewal, you may wish to read *Godwrestling, Round 2,* a chronicle of the movement by Arthur Waskow.

Is Jewish renewal a movement like Conservative, Orthodox, and Reform?

No, Jewish renewal is not considered a movement in Judaism like the Reform, Conservative, Orthodox, and Reconstructionist ones. To be a legitimate movement, there must be certain components within its infrastructure. For example, each movement has its own school in which it trains future leaders and rabbis. The Jewish renewal movement does not have a rabbinical school.

Jewish renewal is truly nondenominational (sometimes referred to as trans- or postdenominational) Judaism. It honors the important and unique role of each denomination, but it does not seek to become a denomination itself. Because of its emphasis on direct spiritual experience and mystical teachings, Jewish renewal is sometimes referred to as Neo-Hasidic or Four Worlds Judaism (a reference to the "four worlds" of Jewish mysticism).

Is it true that Jewish renewal is "new-age" Judaism?

No, Jewish renewal is not "new-age" Judaism, although it is often referred to as that. Jewish renewal uses age-old techniques (meditation, dance, chant) that have been present in Judaism throughout the ages. Because these techniques have been lost for so long thanks to assimilation, many contemporary Jews simply are unaware of them. This is one reason so many spiritually sensitive Jews have sought spiritual expression in other faith traditions, such as Buddhism.

Resources

Artson, B. S. *It's a Mitzvah! Step-by-Step to Jewish Living.* Springfield,
   N.J.: Behrman House and Rabbinical Assembly, 1995.

Donin, H. H. *To Be a Jew.* New York: Basic Books, 2001.

Hammer, R. *Entering Jewish Prayer.* New York: Schocken, 1994.

Isaacs, R., and Olitzky, K. *The How-to Handbook for Jewish Living* (3 vols.).
   Hoboken, N.J.: Ktav, 2003.

Jacob, L. *What Does Judaism Say About . . . ?* Jerusalem: Keter, 1973.

Kertzer, M. *What Is a Jew?* New York: Collier, 1993.

Kolatch, A. *The Jewish Home Advisor.* New York: Jonathan David, 1990.

Robinson, G. *Essential Judaism: A Complete Guide to Beliefs, Customs,
   and Rituals.* New York: Pocket Books, 2000.

Rosenthal, G. *The Many Faces of Judaism.* New York: Behrman House,
   1978.

Rossel, S. *Israel: Covenant People, Covenant Land.* New York: UAHC,
   1985.

Scharfstein, S. *Chronicle of Jewish History.* Hoboken, N.J.: Ktav, 1997.

Strassfeld, M. *The Jewish Holidays: A Guide and Commentary.* New York:
   Harper and Row, 1985.

Telushkin, J. *Jewish Literacy.* New York: Morrow, 1991.

Books by Ron Isaacs
I have authored a series of books on major topics in Jewish life. These books make up a good library of basic information about Judaism and Jewish living. Here is a list of them.

Ascending Jacob's Ladder: Jewish Views of Angels, Demons, and Evil Spirits. Northvale, N.J.: Jason Aronson, 1998.

The Bible: Where Do You Find It and What Does It Say? Northvale, N.J.: Jason Aronson, 2000.

Close Encounters: Jewish Views About God. Northvale, N.J.: Jason Aronson, 1996.

Critical Jewish Issues: A Book for Teenagers. Hoboken, N.J.: Ktav, 1996.

Every Person's Guide to Death and Dying in the Jewish Tradition. Northvale, N.J.: Jason Aronson, 1999.

Every Person's Guide to Hanukkah. Northvale, N.J.: Jason Aronson, 2000.

Every Person's Guide to the High Holy Days. Northvale, N.J.: Jason Aronson, 1999.

Every Person's Guide to Jewish Philosophy and Philosophers. Northvale, N.J.: Jason Aronson, 1999.

Every Person's Guide to Jewish Prayer. Northvale, N.J.: Jason Aronson, 1997.

Every Person's Guide to Jewish Sexuality. Northvale, N.J.: Jason Aronson, 2000.

Every Person's Guide to Passover. Northvale, N.J.: Jason Aronson, 2000.

Every Person's Guide to Purim. Northvale, N.J.: Jason Aronson, 2000.

Every Person's Guide to Shabbat. Northvale, N.J.: Jason Aronson, 1998.

Every Person's Guide to Shavuot. Northvale, N.J.: Jason Aronson, 1998.

Every Person's Guide to Sukkot, Shemini Atzeret, and Simchat Torah. Northvale, N.J.: Jason Aronson, 2000.

Rites of Passage: A Guide to the Jewish Life Cycle. Hoboken, N.J.: Ktav, 1992.

The Author

Rabbi Ron Isaacs is the spiritual leader of Temple Sholom in Bridgewater, New Jersey. Ordained at the Jewish Theological Seminary of America, he received his doctorate in instructional technology from Columbia University Teacher's College.

A prolific author, his many books include the well-known *Every Person's Guide* series and *Ascending Jacob's Ladder: Jewish Views of Angels, Spirits and Evil Demons*. Rabbi Isaacs was a founding member of the acclaimed Hebrew folk rock group Arbaah Kolote and served as host of Central New Jersey's popular radio program "The Jewish American Hour." Rabbi Isaacs's Website, rabbiron.com, is constantly visited by his many students.

Known as "the teaching rabbi," he is currently adjunct lecturer of professional and pastoral skills at the Jewish Theological Seminary's Rabbinical School. He has also chaired the Rabbinical Assembly's publication committee, where he currently serves as a member. For more than a decade he and his wife, Leora Isaacs, have designed and coordinated the adult learning experience called Shabbat Plus at Camp Ramah in the Poconos.

Index